WHEN HOME IS A PHOTOGRAPH

Blackness *and* Belonging *in the World*

I0445952

LEIGH RAIFORD

Duke University Press   *Durham and London*   2026

Printed in the United States of America on acid-free paper ∞
Project Editor: Livia Tenzer
Designed by Courtney Leigh Richardson
Typeset in Garamond Premier Pro and Field Gothic by Copperline Books

Library of Congress Cataloging-in-Publication Data
Names: Raiford, Leigh author
Title: When home is a photograph : blackness and belonging in the world / Leigh Raiford.
Other titles: Blackness and belonging in the world | Visual arts of Africa and its diasporas
Description: Durham : Duke University Press, 2026. | Series: The visual arts of Africa and its diasporas | Includes bibliographical references and index.
Identifiers: LCCN 2025028030 (print)
LCCN 2025028031 (ebook)
ISBN 9781478033318 paperback
ISBN 9781478029861 hardcover
ISBN 9781478062066 ebook
ISBN 9781478094623 ebook other
Subjects: LCSH: African American photographers | Photographers, Black—United States | Photography—Social aspects—United States | Photography—Political aspects—United States | Photography, Artistic—Themes, motives | Aesthetics, Black
Classification: LCC TR681.B52 R354 2026 (print) |
LCC TR681.B52 (ebook) | DDC 770.92—dc23/eng/20251128
LC record available at https://lccn.loc.gov/2025028030
LC ebook record available at https://lccn.loc.gov/2025028031

Dedication page: The author and her father at City College, Harlem, New York, ca. 1985. Photograph by Dwight and Joshua Raiford. Collection of the author.

Cover art: Sadie Barnette, *Family Tree II*, 2022. Thirty-four inkjet prints, spray paint, collage, and rhinestones on paper, and a holographic vinyl couch, 195 × 204 × 34 in. (495.3 × 518.2 × 86.4 cm). Whitney Museum of American Art, New York; purchase with funds from the Director's Discretionary Fund, Bill Gautreaux, the Lumpkin-Boccuzzi Family Collection, and the Jackson Family Trust, 2023.45a-ii. © Sadie Barnette. Photograph by Ron Amstutz, courtesy of the Whitney Museum of American Art.

This book is freely available in an open access edition thanks to the generous support of the University of California Libraries.

WHEN
HOME
IS
A
PHOTOGRAPH

THE VISUAL ARTS OF AFRICA AND ITS DIASPORAS
A Series Edited by Kellie Jones and Steven Nelson

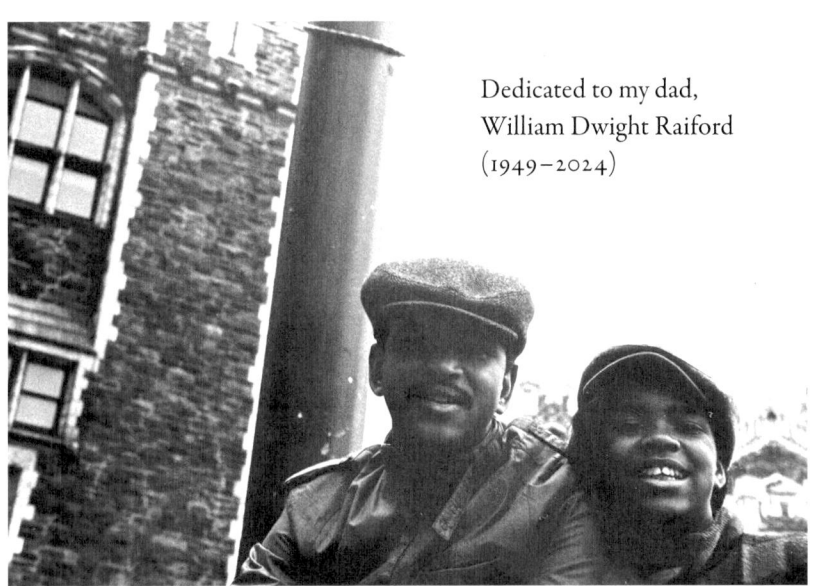

Dedicated to my dad,
William Dwight Raiford
(1949–2024)

Contents

When I Think of Home ... (acknowledgments)

With enormous gratitude to the people, places, institutions, ancestors, nonhumans, and other entities that have made this book possible.

510

Alexa Fenton • Aracely Funes • Berkeley Art Museum and Pacific Film Archive • Berkeley Art Studios • The Black Aesthetic Collective (Jamal Batts, Leila Weefur, nan collymore, Ra Malika Imhotep, Zoé Samudzi) • The Black Studies Collaboratory • Brandi Summers • Christina Zanfagna and Duncan Allard • Donald Moore • East Bay Regional Parks • Jacob Hanson • Jake Kosek • Lauren Kroiz • Lava Thomas • Lez'li Waller • Mildred Howard • Ms. Daphne Muse • Museum of the African Diaspora • Nadia Ellis • Sadie Barnette • UC Berkeley Department of African American and African American Studies aka the 6th Floor, especially Ula Taylor, Darieck Scott, Nikki Jones, Sandy Richmond, Maria Heredia, Barbara Montano, Tianna S. Paschel, and my students

The Citizenry of Photography

Aperture Foundation • Ariella Aïsha Azoulay • Bonaventure Soh Bejeng Ndikung • Christopher Roberts • Dawoud Bey • Deborah Willis • Delphine Sims • Emilie Boone • Erica Deeman • Gordon Parks Foundation (Michal Raz-Russo and Peter Kuhnhardt) • Hrag Vartanian (*Hyperallergic*) • Laura Wexler • LaToya Ruby Frazier • Kellie Jones • Kobena Mercer • Natalia Brizuela • Oluremi Onabanjo • Patricia Hayes and the Center for the Humanities, University of the Western Cape • Sarah Elizabeth Lewis • Shawn Michelle Smith • Stanley Wolokau-Wananbwa • Steven Nelson • Susan Meiselas • Teju Cole • Theo Eshetu • Tina Campt • Toronto Photography Seminar (Thy Phu and Elspeth Brown) • Wendel White • Wendy Ewald

Thinking Places / Feeling People

Adam and Lorraine Weinberg • Adriana Green • Autumn Womack • Black One Shot (Lisa Uddin and Michael Gillespie) • Cheryl Finley • Courtney Baker • Daphne Brooks • Essence Harden • Heidi Julavits • Heike Raphael-Hernandez • Ianna Hawkins Owen • Institute for Cultural Inquiry (Berlin) • Jasmine Elizabeth Johnson • Johannes Von Moltke and Kerstin Brandt • Josh Begley • Joshua Tree National Park • Juana María Rodriguez • Julia Bryan-Wilson • Koyo Kouoh • Larne Abse-Gogarty • Lia Bascomb • Matthew Frye Jacobson • Michael J. Myers II • Nijah Cunningham • Samantha Schnee • Sam Levi Jones • Siddhartha Mitter • Stevie Wonder • Torkwase Dyson • Toyin Ojih Odutola • Yosemite National Park

Keepers of the Past / Securers of the Future

American Academy in Berlin • American Council of Learned Societies • Andrew W. Mellon Foundation • Beinecke Rare Book and Manuscript Library • Duke University Press (Ken Wissoker and Kate Mullen) • Fulbright Program • Jessica Silverman Gallery • John Stephens • Joju Cleaver • Kathleen Neal Cleaver • The Metropolitan Museum of Art Digital Images • Paul Lee • Rodger Birt • Sean Kelly Gallery • Sierra King • Stephanie Alvarado • Susan Robeson (Robeson Family Trust) • UC Berkeley Division of Social Sciences • UC Consortium of Black Studies in California • Volkswagen Foundation

Always Home

Alison Perry • Andrea Woloschuk • Kyla Kupferstein Torres • Yavette Holts • Dwight Raiford • Iris Raiford • Josh Raiford • Maceo Raiford Cohen • Maya Raiford Cohen • Michael Mark Cohen • Rosa Barks

1968: THE BALLOT OR THE BULLET

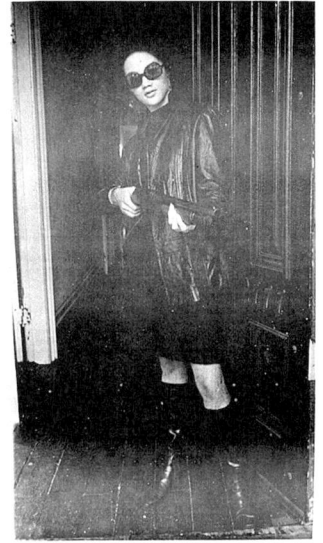

KATHLEEN CLEAVER

COMMUNICATION SECT.,   18th ASSEMBLY DISTRICT
BLACK PANTHER PARTY   S.F. PEACE & FREEDOM PARTY

SHOOT YOUR SHOT

INTRODUCTION

WHEN HOME IS

A PHOTOGRAPH

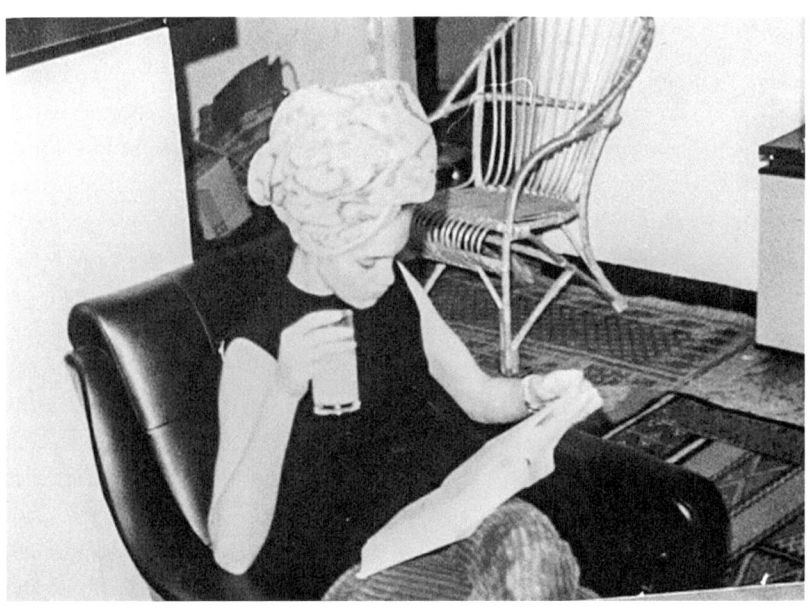

FIGURE I.I. "1968: The Ballot or the Bullet; Shoot Your Shot." Campaign poster, 1968. *Black Panther*, September 28, 1968.

FIGURE I.2. "Pointe Pescate [Pescade], Nov. 1969." From Kathleen Cleaver family photo album. Photograph of album by John Stephens. Courtesy and © Kathleen Neal Cleaver Archive.

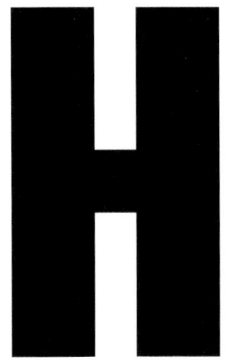

Here are two photographs of Kathleen Neal Cleaver at home (figures 1.1 and 1.2). One is famous, while the other is faded and forgotten. Both are true.

In the first photograph, Kathleen wields a heavy-gauge pump-action shotgun as she stands guard at the entrance to the San Francisco apartment she shared with her husband, Eldridge Cleaver. Kathleen, Black Panther Party (BPP) communications secretary, had purchased the gun immediately after Oakland police shot through the plate glass windows of BPP headquarters in violent, drunken retaliation for the reduced verdict of voluntary manslaughter against Party leader Huey P. Newton for the death of Oakland police officer John Frey. Kathleen and Eldridge had already endured months of FBI and police surveillance since moving into the grey Victorian house on Pine Street, and the attack on the Party headquarters only confirmed for them the need to protect themselves and their home. As a convicted felon on parole now facing his own trial for his part in a shootout with police, Eldridge could not be seen with guns or have any registered in his name. Thus, Eldridge, Kathleen, BPP chairman Bobby Seale, and Stew Albert, a white Berkeley activist, crafted a publicity event to circulate the story and image of Kathleen arming herself to protect her home. Image and text would offer a message of inspiration to the Panther rank-and-file membership and issue a warning to Panther detractors and self-declared enemies. To produce an attention-grabbing cover story, the Cleavers enlisted writers Marvin Garson and Albert, who both wrote for Bay Area radical newspapers, and Alan Copeland, a white photographer who would later form Photon West agency with another frequent BPP photographer, Stephen

Shames. While the articles are buried in the archives, the photographs have become iconic. Kathleen, "as usual . . . wearing a short black skirt, a black turtleneck sweater, a leather jacket and high black boots," knew immediately that the photographs were "striking" and "had hundreds printed up for a campaign poster."[1] The photograph is loud, amplified by its transformation into a campaign poster and underscored by Malcolm X's ultimatum, "The Ballot or the Bullet." The photograph is unapologetic and polemic; sensational, sexy, resistant. It's the origin of a thousand Blaxploitation fantasies and a million neo–Black Nationalist dreams, highly reproduced, widely circulated, and occasionally imitated. It is at once fierce and fearsome but also funny, by which I mean so iconic as to have occluded some of its iconoclasm. It has become almost a caricature.

I have lived with this image for so long, wondered over it, sometimes fashioned myself after it, and also refused it. I have written about it and with it.[2] It is an image nestled deep in my visual repertoire and optical unconscious. And yet I never gave a lot of thought to what lay through the black portal of the door, or what exactly—materially, not just abstractly—Kathleen was protecting so fiercely.

The second photograph was made a year later and six thousand miles away in Algiers. Here, Kathleen is seated in a black chair, holding reading material with one hand and a beverage in the other. She wears a casual sleeveless top and rust-colored pants that might be corduroy or striped. Her gaze is averted from the camera and its unknown photographer (unknown to us yet likely very familiar to Kathleen). Instead, her attention is focused on the book in her lap. A towel is wrapped around her head suggesting she's just washed her hair (in my imagination she's deep conditioning), tending to the afro that was so central to her public image. A source of pride, a marker of militancy, the afro, as sister radical Angela Y. Davis noted in the charged anti–Black Power moment, also served as "a historical pretext for something akin to a reign of terror for countless young black women" surveilled and harassed by law enforcement for wearing their hair natural and large.[3] Yet, here, in this intimate photograph the afro is unseen, protected, and Kathleen's alone. This color snapshot is affixed to a page of a family album where beneath the photograph Kathleen has written "Point Pescate [Pointe Pescade] Nov. 1969." The date indicates that this is the first home she and Eldridge have shared since the house on Pine Street, since Eldridge fled almost certain imprisonment and possible execution in the United States for exile in Cuba and then Algeria in November 1968, since Kathleen joined him in Algeria in June 1969, and since the birth of their first child, Maceo, a month after.

This photograph is as quiet as the first is loud. Quiet in the way scholar Kevin Quashie invokes that word: not silent (or silenced) but inward-facing, "selffull," suggesting surrender.[4] This photograph is intimate and meditative. It is full of breath and air and a stillness that is not immobile, a calm that suggests the capacity to receive. Like the towel wrapped carefully around her hair, the photograph outlines Kathleen's interiority, acknowledging its presence while withholding its substance. At twenty-four years old, Kathleen had become comfortable with the "popping of flashbulbs and press of crowds," as she writes in her memoir. "It felt unsettling, becoming known to thousands of people, but it was exciting to have our message broadcast so widely."[5] She had honed her talking points, learned her angles, developed her personal style, and grown confident in her capacity to lead a movement. Here, though, inside her home, she is indifferent to the photographer (and by extension indifferent to us) but fully present to herself. Perhaps above all this is an image of an icon of the Black radical tradition at rest. Whatever Kathleen is protecting so fiercely in this photograph is hers and hers alone.

It was only after I first visited Kathleen's home at her invitation to begin work organizing her personal photography archive, and encountered the Pointe Pescade snapshot, that I began to understand the ways these two photographs, when taken together and when situated within her vast and varied collection, are fundamentally revealing of Kathleen's lifelong engagement with photography. In three years of working with Cleaver in her home while leading a team organizing and cataloging her archive, I would come to learn that photographs are central to her self-making and sense of belonging. For Kathleen—the keeper of her family's archives spanning more than a century and a half and the collector of photographs of herself across the many geographies of her life— photographs function as a tool to situate herself in place and time, and in her own narrative. Although the organizing work of our team was generally confined to Kathleen's upstairs office, photographs, far more than any other visual medium, decorate and warm every room. There is no space in her home from which one cannot see or touch a framed photograph. Kathleen's relation to and practice of photography reminded me of Deborah Willis's evergreen assertion that photographs of all kinds regardless of genre are central to Black storytelling, and it underscored bell hooks's insight that interior home walls of photographs "announced our visual complexity."[6]

Although I first approached them as opposites, I soon came to recognize the two images of Kathleen at home as mutually informative. The Pine Street poster alerts us to photography's role in amplifying public performances of Black resistance, while the Pointe Pescade snapshot offers an image of "the sovereignty of quiet," the domain of self beyond the demands of an external gaze. But more than counterweights, what might each of these photographs reveal about the other? How, for example, is the campaign poster "an exquisite balance of what is public and what is intimate," following Quashie's generative reading of the iconic image of Tommie Smith and John Carlos with fists raised on the medal podium at the Mexico 1968 Olympics?[7] How might my isolated reading of the poster's boldness fail to hold space for the "vulnerability and interiority" I chose to identify so clearly in the Pointe Pescade snapshot?

What if, instead, we read these two photographs side by side as if they were a stereograph, the popular nineteenth-century visual technology that mimicked binocular vision to produce an illusion of depth? To achieve this effect, the same sight—whether a landscape, an event, an individual sitter, or a comedic scene—is photographed once and then again. When paired side by side and looked at through the special device of the stereograph (or by crossing one's eyes) the two images become magnified and present a wider field of view and an opportunity to perceive detail. Approaching the two photographs of Kathleen at home in this way enables us to witness the depth of Kathleen's living: image(d) events not as counter to each other or as consecutive or causal (i.e., protest, then rest, then protest again), as if there is a linear singularity to Black life. Rather, viewed together in this manner they indicate a fullness to living that photography promises but can never deliver.

Finally, working to grasp these two photographs of Kathleen at home in their breadth and abundance alerted me to the limits of my own sight, which is also a way of saying the limits of our ability to imagine Black belonging in the world. And yet it was allowing myself the patience to wonder about the unseen in these images—beyond the apartment door, under the head wrap—that began to suggest another way of engaging photography. Tina Campt avers that beyond looking at images, to listen to images "is to perceive their quiet frequencies of possibility—the possibility to inhabit a future as unbounded black subjects."[8] Following Campt and Cleaver and all of us who seek a home in photography, I ask, What do we have to unlodge, unlearn, or undo in order to reimagine photography's relationship to Black life?

This book is about how Black people use photography to make home in the world. I focus on a handful of well-known Black American activists and artists who traveled the world for study, for work, or for movement building, sometimes for pleasure and sometimes because their lives and the lives of their loved ones depended on it. As for many of us, their personal sense of self and their political platforms were elaborated through these encounters with the world. And like most of us, they made and collected photographs at every stage. *When Home Is a Photograph: Blackness and Belonging in the World* considers the everyday image-making practices and habits that this group of Black Americans, each committed to improving the conditions of Black lives globally, have engaged in order to imagine, identify, create, fabulate, inhabit, leave, defend, and, sometimes, destroy "home."

Home can variously reference a physical location, a material possession, or an imagined geography. It can be a site of shelter and comfort where we are encouraged to be our best and truest selves. For Black Americans, home has at turns been offered and withheld, forcibly imposed and violently dispossessed. There is no shortage of historical examples in which Black Americans have built home only to have it devalued or destroyed under racial capitalism: the separation of enslaved Black families under slavery in the South, carried out while laws that prevented free Black persons from owning property proliferated throughout the country including its expanding territories; the burning of thriving Black towns like those in Tulsa, Oklahoma, or Rosewood, Florida, by white "neighbors" in the Jim Crow era; housing made contingent on conformity to middle-class sexual and gender mores dictated and imposed by Progressive-era reformers and the modern welfare state, while restrictive racial covenants and "predatory inclusion" forced substandard homeownership in underserved neighborhoods on the aspiring Black middle class; the destruction of Black and brown neighborhoods through "urban renewal" in the mid- to late twentieth century, followed by the displacement of Black and brown residents through processes of gentrification at the turn of the twenty-first century.[9]

Home can also be a place of violence and uncertainty, ground zero of our most enduring traumas. Scholar Keeanga-Yamahtta Taylor has emphasized the difference between *housing*, the commodity of real estate, and *home*, a place of belonging. Yet in a country that understands property ownership as a right and the route to personal happiness and national stability, this distinction gets elided. Taylor's devastating *Race for Profit* demonstrates how the federal government in alignment with an explicitly racist real estate industry exploited African Americans' need for housing and desire for home to extract wealth and extend the reach of racial capitalism into the post–civil rights era. Yet, as Taylor reminds us, even when those houses were not ours, were dilapidated and substandard, were temporary and transitional, Black homes could be "sources of connection, places of communion, and sites of refuge."[10]

Similarly, Christina Sharpe describes in her books *Ordinary Notes* and *In the Wake: On Blackness and Being* how throughout her working-class childhood, her mother taught her that "beauty is a method" by managing to find and make "beauty everyday" in the series of childhood homes they moved through, never quite settled and always at the edge of precariousness.[11] Further back in the twentieth century, bell hooks extolled "homeplace as a site of resistance" against the terrors of white supremacy in the Jim Crow south.[12] For Black folks in the United States, from those brought forcibly in 1565 to those arriving full of hope next week, there is really no place, no time in this country's history that we have been allowed to be settled, to be free, to be safe, to claim home. It is no wonder that "home" has emerged as an elusive object of desire of the natally alienated.[13]

And yet Black Americans still make home wherever, whenever, and however possible.

Persistently, Black people have looked beyond (which does not always mean outside) national borders to claim home and seek belonging—that is, recognition, efficacy, meaningful community.[14] Diaspora might be defined as the twin readings of Blackness *in* the world and Blackness *and* the world. *Diaspora* is one word that Black people have invoked to mean a desire for elsewhere, for not this and something more. It has been used to mean almost home, not home but nearly there. For those who consider themselves members of a diaspora or who are hailed as diasporic subjects, their experience is generally marked by dispersal from an original homeland and marginalized status in their new locations; it involves making and maintaining affective ties to imagined homelands, even a hope for eventual return; and it often depends on forging a group consciousness and solidarity that at once creates and depends on a continued relationship to, and identity with, the place of "origin." In these ways, *home*, however contentious a term, becomes a key mode for understanding diaspora, even and especially for people who have never met, never shared a location, and who may share little beyond chosen identification. Thus, at its heart, "Black diaspora" wrestles with the idea of home, simultaneously enacting an embrace of home and an acknowledgment of its absence. It embodies a tension between familiarity and unbelonging, and figures attachment in deferral and deferred elsewhere. In its concern with the past, its reckoning with the present, and its insistence on the future, diaspora becomes marked by inhabiting multiple temporalities: the prelapsarian, the daily grind, the fantasy of eventual return, the time of Justice. To the list of what home encompasses—location, possession, geography—we might also add a distinct temporality outside the flow/time regulated by the accumulationist demands of racial capitalism and the epistemes of Western modernity.

Home is not an uncomplicated concept. But then, neither is photography. In traditional histories of the field, "photography" variously references the technological equipment (the camera and its offspring); the people who wield the equipment to make photographs; the modes of distribution, circulation, and consumption of photographs; the relationships generated by photographs; the constantly expanding set of audiences, spectators, and witnesses; and of course the photograph itself. Rather than any single aspect, photography encompasses all of these. The "event of photography," Ariella Aïsha Azoulay tells us, is "an infinite series of encounters" that defies linear sequentiality and is never over.[15] Photography names a mode of engaging the world, a set of habits of image making that can never be singular but at its heart is collaborative, that is, a relationship between two or more actors and thus a collaboration that is sometimes imposed, sometimes coerced, sometimes given freely. The photograph, then—the knowledge that the photograph produces—is never settled, never fixed. Photography is a persistent way of people trying to know themselves and the world. And the photograph is only one outcome of that engagement.

Long have we (scholars, critics, artists, activists) understood and described photography and the visual more broadly as a site of violence, "a scene of negative instruction."[16] And, in doing so, we have thus framed Black and other subaltern groups' engagement with the medium as "oppositional," redemptive, recuperative.[17] We have held a tentative, if sometimes apologetic, place for pleasure (especially for ambiguous, ambivalent modes of visuality); even visualizing joy becomes an act of resistance.

When Home Is a Photograph argues that, yes, the photograph is a site of violence. And, yes, it is a site of resistance. But/and so too is photography an invitation to refusal. "To look is an act of choice," John Berger states foundationally.[18] And photography offers a series of choices about where we choose to focus our gaze, where we choose to linger, to stop, with what and with whom we choose to sit. It is about attention. Which is to say, photography is also about refusal. That is, I choose to look here and not there. This might be a refusal to accede to a colonial gaze that demands our concentration and energy, denies our knowledge and twists our visions, a gaze that forces us to consume our deaths on autoplay and expects us to whittle our dreams down to what can fit into the tiniest of boxes and the most banal of diversity, equity, and inclusion statements (where they may still exist). Photography can also be an opportunity to give our attention to the spaces, practices, and visual vocabularies with which Black people see otherwise, sometimes as armor against this world and sometimes as a portal to other worlds entirely.

But/and so too is photography a space of practice and experimentation. That is to say, photography as a practice never performs a single function and in a sense is not bound to a single ontology. It is a document, it is performance, it is surveillance, it is violence; it is speculative and fabulation, it is aspiration, it is comfort. The photograph achieves or is employed for a range of different kinds of work.

Photography is a practice that emerged within and alongside racial capital-ism, that is, the historical coemergence of white supremacy and capitalist ex-ploitation.[19] We might date the medium's origins to 1839, the year that scholars often designate as the "birth of photography." Or we might follow Azoulay's invitation to imagine photography's birth date as 1492, concomitant with the emergence of a structure of seeing made possible by imperialist aims that ad-vanced a world-building enterprise imposed through land dispossession and the transatlantic slave trade. As a recording mechanism imbued with scientific authority, photography has been made to codify racial sight across political, social, and cultural realms. Photography thus has been elaborated with and de-fined against Blackness.[20]

Photographs further organize meaning through the specific forms they take and the generic conventions they implement. Photographic genres, a cho-reography of forms, contexts, and cultural desires, are ways of staging different encounters within the event of photography, affixing meaning and asserting that connotation as above all others. Portraiture, ethnographic photography, family snapshots, and landscape photography—the genres I consider in this book—each engender different expectations, enable different revelations about the self in the world to come into focus. The portrait is an agreed-on fiction that purports to represent the individual but instead produces the individual as a "visualizable fact."[21] Similarly, ethnographic photography claims to "record" difference but, through a repertoire of angles and dress (and undress), widens the distance between viewing subject and visual object. Family photography "documents" kinship through its conscription into a "familial gaze" that pro-jects culturally mythologized notions of family. Through perspective, landscape photography "captures" the natural world as topographic, mappable, explorable, and exploitable. But if we have learned anything from the work of Christopher Pinney, Marianne Hirsch, Shawn Michelle Smith, Coco Fusco, Rosalind Krauss, Martin Berger, and W. J. T. Mitchell, alongside Azoulay, Berger and many, many others, these forms of photography are made to enact and produce that which they are claimed to document and apprehend.[22] Thus, through these genres of photography, the camera as apparatus mediates—shapes, regulates, interpolates, and interpellates—complex encounters between differently positioned dias-poric subjects and between Black people and the world.

Indeed, the question of "genre" is fraught terrain, and I am generally skeptical of any rigid proclamations of structure or hubristic impositions of form. This is a skepticism rooted in my training in Black studies, a field which demonstrates that Blackness is always already a modifier that alerts us to the limits of any categories when "universally" applied. Blackness is "anagrammatical," in Christina Sharpe's generative language. That is, Blackness as lack or excess, as "signifying property plus," reorganizes, if not fully changes, the meaning of what are perceived to be stable categories.[23] In such applications we come to recognize how many such categories—male, female, human—and so too the mediums of their expression—the novel, the painting, the photograph—are defined in opposition to Blackness. In order to fully express itself, Blackness emerges as necessarily peripatetic and interdisciplinary if not undisciplined.

Photography has functioned as such an analytical frame, classifying and confining Black people to "prevailing racial scripts," hemmed us into boxes "woven out of thousands of stories, anecdotes, details."[24] From scientific objects to criminal suspects, video vixens to gangbangers, unloving welfare queens to unlovable Black mothers' sons slain by the ever longer arm of the state, Black camerawork has often sought "a truer word" (Spillers), it has "insist[ed] Black life into the wake" (Sharpe), attempted to "think black life otherwise" (Hartman).[25] To do so, it has worked to carve a space for photography beyond (which does not always mean outside) Eurocentric and anti-Black practices, a way to imagine or experience Black life beyond or outside the "algorithmic logics" that foretell black premature death, that seek to fix—that is, both cement and resolve—the "problem" of Black humanity.

So, to the list of what photography encompasses, we might also add physical location and an imagined geography, photography as a "black sense of place":[26] the places from where Black folks make photography, the places where photography takes us, and what photography can tell us about the place of Blackness.

When Is Home a Photograph, and How Can a Photograph Become a Home?

This book attends to the ways Black artists and activists engaged photography as a mode of emplacing themselves in an anti-Black world. These Black habits of photography, as I now understand them, are not simply (or solely) about a "comforting" self-image but about the ways photography serves as a pedagogical tool for learning oneself in a world where Blackness is often foreclosed as a finite answer rather than an unbound series of questions. "Black habits" mobilize the photograph as a site where the terms of belonging can be worked out, where values can be iterated and practiced, whether of the Black collective asserting home in the world, Black kin longing for home in one another, or the Black individual seeking home in their own skin.

Such a sense of homeplace and belonging is certainly found in the photographic practices of Frederick Douglass and Sojourner Truth, formerly enslaved abolitionists who created images of themselves in the nineteenth century to visualize self-possession. The photograph, here the photographic portrait of the formerly enslaved, emerges as a place where one can represent oneself, a place where one can be fully in control of one's faculties, one's body, one's direction in life. Consciously leaving a record of themselves for the future, Douglass, Truth, and many others also mobilized photography to project a material trace of the present into a future that did not yet exist.

As a material object—and here I consider any image as material that can be held in your hand or held in the phone in your hand—the photograph offers a document one can turn and return to. And thus we can also think of the ways the photograph functions as a "diasporic resource." Photographs are the bit of home that dislocated peoples carry with them when they could carry little else with them.[27] The photograph functions as a home that necessarily has to always be in motion, as respite and retreat that necessarily has to be mobile. Likewise, photographs have housed the performance of self-making that dislocated photographed persons send "home" to visualize new belonging(s). In these ways we might think of the photograph as its own shelter-in-place: the place where we can find cover in the midst of migration, transformation, and catastrophe.[28]

"Home" has long been a setting for Black cultural production that understood the domestic sphere as a battleground over citizenship, belonging, and Black bodily integrity. Here I am indebted to an earlier generation of Black feminist scholars including Hazel Carby, Ann duCille, and Claudia Tate who theorized the domestic as sites where nineteenth-century Black women writers "offered [their] recently emancipated [readership] an occasion for [imagining] and exercising political self-definition in fiction at a time when the civil rights of African Americans were constitutionally sanctioned but socially prohibited."[29] Likewise, I draw from the subsequent generation of theorists, Quashie among them, along with Elizabeth Alexander, who offers the language of "the black interior" to highlight the intimate relationship between the home and self, and self as home.[30] So too am I inspired by Saidiya Hartman, who in *Wayward Lives, Beautiful Experiments* reminds us that the post–Civil War dichotomy of gendered public and private spheres rooted in anti-Black constructions never held for Black life, and that Black folks have long engaged in a process of making such concepts as gender, family, home, and freedom resonate in ways outside or beyond the confines of racial enclosure.[31] The photographic event plays an important role in Hartman's book: the seeming intractability of pornographic images and mugshots that appear unwilling to unfix their subjects, as well as portraits, snapshots, and mugshots again that offer the possibility to imagine a different outcome and to stage another encounter. And a next generation of Black feminist and queer of color critique, including Marlon Bailey, Jafari Allen, and Savannah Shange, demonstrates how queer Black communities (and the queerness of Black communities) have troubled the very notion of home even as they have forged new modes of kinship and insisted on homeplace.[32]

Home, then, is always more than home. I am interested not merely in how the Black subjects considered in this book are utilizing photography to emplace themselves in the world but how the choice to use photography is itself a way to mediate one's relationship to the world and to reimagine the world itself. Using photography to comprehend one's place in the world—photographing toward understanding—makes sense given that photography also names and makes manifest a relation of the body as a vessel for sight to the physical world as mediated by the apparatus. What, then, might these Black habits of photography reveal about new modes of making and seeing photography, and making and seeing Black life?

"Between me and the other world there is ever an unasked question.... How does it feel to be a problem?" wrote W. E. B. Du Bois at the very opening of *The Souls of Black Folk*.[33] Photography has long been deployed and conscripted to come up with an answer, to address the relationship between Blackness and the world. And if *The Souls of Black Folk* has taught us anything—besides the fact that the question is itself a problem—it is that to answer the question of what is the texture of Black life, we must first exceed the disciplinary and generic tools that we have been handed.

Like my first book, *Imprisoned in a Luminous Glare: Photography and the African American Freedom Struggle*, *When Home Is a Photograph* offers an opportunity to consider photography as practiced by figures of the Black (and specifically Black American) radical tradition. Across the longer arc of my research, I have come to recognize that the photographic archives of Black activists, intellectuals, and organizations provide a critical yet understudied resource for illuminating the fraught history and politics of Black representation, as well as the role of photography in conceptualizing Black freedom in both the personal and public arenas. My first book was especially concerned with photography as a social movement strategy for antilynching activists, SNCC (Student Nonviolent Coordinating Committee) organizers, and Black Panther Party militants, a necessary tool in an ongoing battle for justice that takes place in the visual field, as well as in courtrooms and classrooms, in the streets, and increasingly in public memory. Photography as a conscious weapon. In this book, I consider photography in its more intimate context, equally as fraught and political, but imbued with more complex personal motivations. More specifically, I am interested in the way quotidian photographs—quiet images of family, of the domestic, of the everyday and unspectacular—give shape to our understanding and visualization of Black life, even for those who are the most recognizable, most vocal, and most resistant figures in our political culture.

In each of four chapters, I consider the employment of a distinct, though interrelated, mode of photography by key Black intellectuals over the past century. I begin with photographic portraiture through the collaboration of famed Harlem, New York, studio photographer James Van Der Zee and Pan-African leader Marcus Garvey, who as head of the Universal Negro Improvement Association (UNIA), hired Van Der Zee to document the organization's activities in the summer of 1924. This collaboration reveals the importance that Garvey and the UNIA placed on photography to both document and confer consistency and legitimacy on Garvey and the movement in the midst of organizational tumult. Through Van Der Zee, Garvey and the UNIA employed photographic portraiture to mobilize racial feeling and to assert a vision of a masculinist Black modernity rooted in an imagined Africa and routed through the authority of the camera and the promises of portraiture. Certainly, in the interwar period, both Black portraiture and Pan-Africanism were projects engaged in a kind of corrective work, redeeming derogatory images of Black people and committed to Black self-possession. To manifest the "double consciousness" of photography, that is the "twoness" of self and other that W. E. B. Du Bois described as endemic to the condition of Black modern subjects, I develop the hermeneutic of "reading stereoscopically," drawing on the nineteenth-century photographic technology that mimicked binocular vision to produce an illusion of depth. This analytic reveals the ways photography has worked to articulate—to join up and express—African diaspora.

Chapters 2 and 3 move from formal portraiture to family photography, from masculinist visions of power and belonging to domestic images of home, as practiced by Black women activists and mothers. Chapter 2 turns to ethnographic, family, and travel photography as made by author, activist, and anthropologist Eslanda Goode Robeson in the 1930s and 1940s. In 1936, Goode Robeson, perhaps best known as the wife of celebrated singer, actor, and activist Paul Robeson, set off on a three-month tour of southern Africa, as part of her field study toward completion of an advanced degree in anthropology at the London School of Economics. Also a political mission to see firsthand an Africa in the early stages of anticolonial struggle, the trip quickly became a family vacation when she chose to bring her then-eight-year-old son, Paul Jr. In 1945 Robeson published her travel diary and photographs as the memoir *African Journey*, which featured her son prominently. Chapter 2 considers Robeson's vision of Africa and asks what forms of diasporic identification and belonging might have been nurtured through the presence of Paul Jr. as a photographic subject. Robeson's photographs in *African Journey* draw on, and blur, the line between ethnographic photography and family snapshots; a desire to note the familiar unknowingly slips into recording the familial. If anthropological photography finds pleasure in difference, family snapshots locate joy in sameness, in the filial and the familiar. In this chapter, I examine how, in Robeson's deft hands, anthropological field image and family and tourist snapshots collide and collude to produce a distinct photographic archive of an African continent on the verge of decolonization not merely as "homeland" but as "homeplace."

Chapter 3 continues the exploration of family photography through close examination of a family photography album made by Kathleen Neal Cleaver of her family's time living in exile in Algeria and France, 1969–72. The Algiers album, in which the Pointe Pescade snapshot lives, is one particularly rich artifact in Cleaver's personal photography collection, and the chapter draws on my three years of working with Cleaver in her home leading a team organizing and cataloging this archive (acquired by Emory University's Rose Library in spring 2020). While this photography collection broadly and the family album specifically have great political and historical significance, enriching our knowledge about the Black Panther Party, the work of Black internationalism in the era of Black Power, and gender politics in the context of Black revolutionary struggles, it is perhaps best understood as a family archive. Thus, I read the Algiers album as a Black woman–authored text that offers an affective and personal history of a movement that has been conveyed primarily as historical document. Its form as a family album forces us to reckon with the messiness of movement and cannot deny the failures and disappointments of family relations—whether a difficult marriage, a growing community of exiles, family as a metaphor for nationalism, or as a map of intergenerational kinship ties. This chapter addresses the role of photography, archives, and curatorial practice in the making of the Black radical tradition and Black feminist futures.

By the time you've read this introduction and the chapters themselves, my hope is that this book will have offered you a sense of some of these Black habits of photography—of love and kinship, of failure and possibility that photography can explore, express, and produce. What I cannot promise, however, is a conclusion that provides definitive proclamations about home and belonging and photography. Since March 2020, what is "belonging" in a system set on killing us, and what is "home" in a world literally on fire? If photography is an apparatus for world-making, what can it actually achieve in the face of disinformation, deepfakes, and unfolding and ongoing catastrophe? And isn't "definitive" just hubris in an unending marathon of uncertainty? By way of conclusion, I turn instead to the photographic (plus) projects of two contemporary artists, Dawoud Bey and Sadie Barnette, who deploy photography to engage a set of questions about Black life, belonging, and photography itself. Dawoud Bey's crepuscular 2018 landscape photography series, *Night Coming Tenderly, Black*, revisits locations of the Underground Railroad and renders the experience of fugitives from slavery by embracing the limits of sight. Sadie Barnette's installation *Family Tree* (2021) explodes the notion of the family photograph and asks us to expand our notion of to whom, to what, to which time, and to which realm we belong.

Bey and Barnette's projects demonstrate that while photography proves a useful tool for learning oneself and can function as a "home" for notions of self, community, belonging, and futurity, the investment in specific genres rooted in Enlightenment conceptions of apprehending the world and visualizing the human proves unsatisfactory. Taken alongside the other practitioners in *When Home Is a Photograph*, we see that the engagement with these genres has always been anagrammatical, inadequate if not inimical to the task of envisioning Black life in its complexity, and we therefore demand new modes of making and seeing photography.

This book doesn't ask, What if Black people invented photography? exactly, because the answer is that we already have and we do every day.[34] Rather, it asks, What forms, what habits of photography have Black Americans invented in their practices of the medium that attend to the violence of anti-Blackness but are neither captive to that violence nor beholden to anti-Blackness's rules, rationale, or systems of order? I want to imagine a different life-place for photography, one that honors the myriad ways Black folks practice photography. I want to consider that the work of "decolonizing the camera"[35] is what Black folks (and others) do every time they bend the camera outside of the imperialist colonialist logics of consumption, enclosure, and dispossession, documenting possibility and coaxing potential lurking in each photograph.

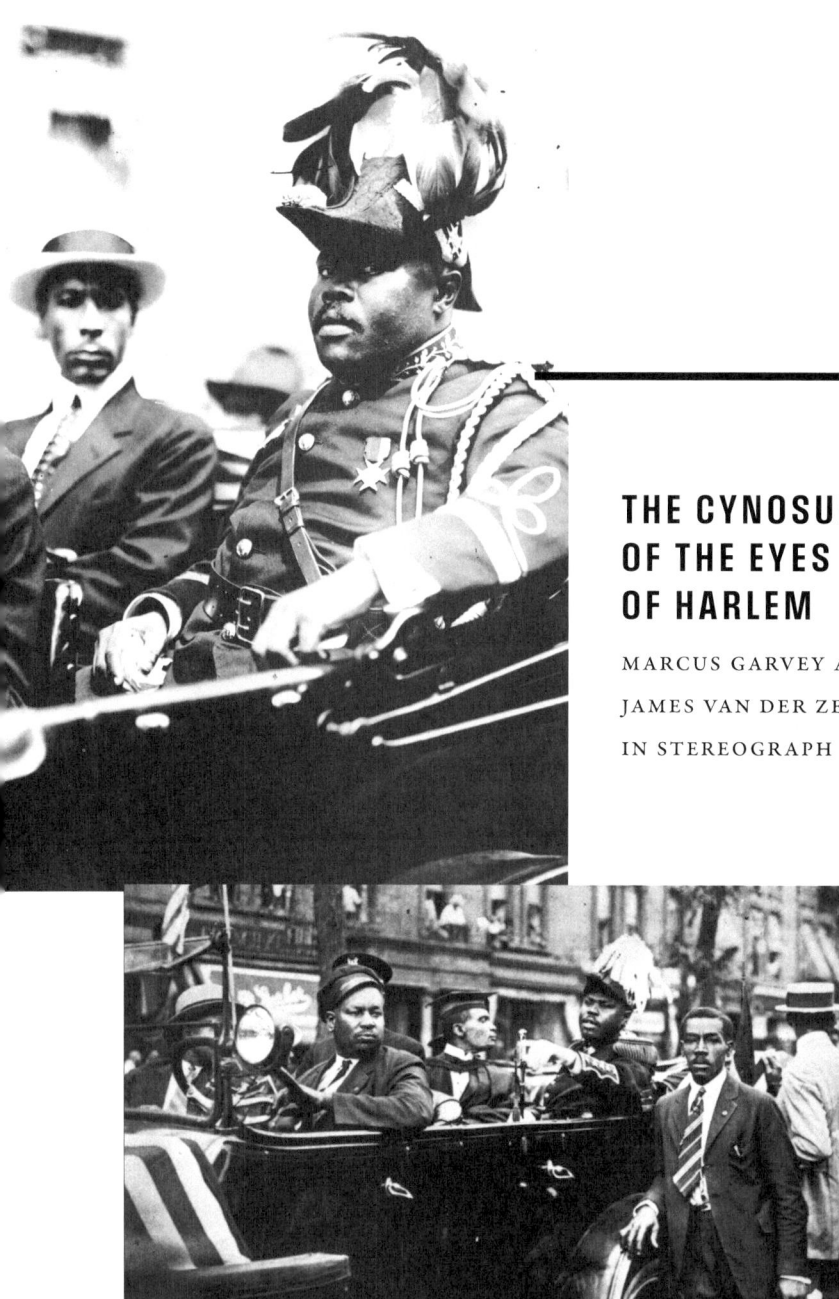

1

THE CYNOSURE OF THE EYES OF HARLEM

MARCUS GARVEY AND
JAMES VAN DER ZEE
IN STEREOGRAPH

FIGURE 1.1. *Marcus Garvey, New York City*, 1922. Photographer unknown. © Pacific and Atlantic Photographs.

FIGURE 1.2. James Van Der Zee, *Marcus Garvey in a UNIA Parade, New York*, 1924, printed later. Gelatin silver print, image: 6 ⅞ × 10 1/16 in. (17.5 × 25.5 cm); sheet: 10 × 12 in. (25.4 × 30.5 cm). James Van Der Zee Archive, The Metropolitan Museum of Art, Gift of Donna Van Der Zee, 2021 (2021.446.1.45). © James Van Der Zee Archive, The Metropolitan Museum of Art. Image source: Art Resource, NY.

There are two photographs of Marcus Garvey that, though made almost exactly two years apart and by different photographers, are near copies of each other. They were taken during the grand inaugural parades of the third and the fourth International Convention of the Negro Peoples of the World, August 1922 and August 1924, respectively. The first image (figure 1.1) was snapped by an unknown photographer and initially appeared in the *New York Daily News* on August 2, 1922; likely, the photographer was a white male who made his way uptown to capture the curiosity of the "Negro Moses" and his Back to Africa movement. The second photograph (figure 1.2) was made by Harlem photographer James Van Der Zee as part of his Universal Negro Improvement Association (UNIA) commission to document the organization's activities, members, and leader in the summer of 1924. Van Der Zee's Guaranteed Photo Studio had achieved a reputation among Harlemites for producing beautiful, technically excellent photographs. Moreover, the studio was conveniently located at 109 West 135th Street, next door to a branch of the New York Public Library (now the Schomburg Center for Research in Black Culture) and just on the other side of Lenox Avenue from UNIA headquarters, at 56 West 135th Street. Both images, though made by different photographers for distinct purposes, portray Garvey as supreme commander of his organization and at the center of the thousands-strong parades along Harlem's Seventh Avenue.

Stereograph 1: Garvey 1922 and Garvey 1924

In each image, Garvey appears in the back seat of a convertible, his corpulent figure pressed into an elaborate military jacket and his head adorned with a plumed admiral cap, variations on World War I field marshal uniforms.[1] Garvey is resplendent in formal military attire and is chauffeured in a black touring car polished to such a high shine, we can make out reflections of the fender and the street opposite. In each image, as well, Garvey is photographed from nearly the same vantage point. The photographers have placed themselves on the driver's side of the vehicle, just ahead of Garvey, most likely to stay a few steps ahead of the processional. The bricks and windows of Harlem's buildings form an urban backdrop, while similarly, though perhaps not as extravagantly, well-dressed Black men surround Garvey and confirm this masculine enterprise. In both images, the body of the car cuts a slight angle across the photograph's frame, emphasizing Garvey's privileged distance as passenger; he reviews the scene of the parade as the photographers review him. Yet, in concealing Garvey's lower half, the car bifurcates the images both two- and three-dimensionally, curtailing any imagined intimacy with the provisional president of Africa, as Garvey titled himself. Separately, each photograph shows us a Black leader central yet aloof.

These two photographs are so strikingly similar that a viewer might mistake them as documenting a single moment (and for longer than she'd like to admit, this viewer did conflate the two photographs). Yet, when we place them side by side, we become aware of the distinctions between them, both subtle and substantial: the slight variation in costume; the wider frame of the second image, which reveals the changes in personnel allowed close access to Garvey; the varied direction of Garvey's gaze. We are led to ask, Why "replicate" the earlier photograph, and what are the significances of the differences? What work does visual repetition and juxtaposition perform in the elaboration of Garvey's complex and often self-contradictory platform? These two images rhyme yet together produce a complex verse that demands a closer consideration of the role of photography, specifically portraiture, in the UNIA, as well as a revised lens through which to contemplate these images.

Taken together, these images open a space in which to explore the photographic practices of diaspora. I borrow this phrase from Brent Hayes Edwards's important book *The Practice of Diaspora* in order to interrogate how photography has been used to produce transnational Black communities and identities. Or, to paraphrase Paul Gilroy, "What forms of belonging have been nurtured by visual cultures?"[2] First, through an examination of two iconic photographs of Pan-African leader Marcus Garvey, I reveal the importance that Garvey and the UNIA placed on photography to both document and confer consistency and legitimacy to Garvey and the movement in the midst of organizational tumult. The organization broadly, and Garvey especially, used photography to mobilize racial feeling and to assert a vision of Black modernity. Second, I consider the collaboration between Harlem studio photographer James Van Der Zee and Garvey, who through the UNIA, hired Van Der Zee to document its activities in the summer of 1924.

More capaciously, these pairings encourage us to think about the relationship between photography, diaspora, and home. Certainly in the interwar period, Black portraiture and Pan-Africanism were both projects engaged in a kind of corrective work. Pan-Africanism emerged as a political endeavor that envisioned and enacted a transnational set of communities against, outside, and ultimately beyond the catastrophic conditions of Black peoples enacted by racial capitalism, New World slavery, imperialism, and colonialism. When Garveyites read the UNIA newspaper, *The Negro World*, or passed an entire Sunday listening to speeches at Liberty Hall and its various outposts, they understood themselves as belonging to an international community, greater and stronger than the national homes that subjugated, marginalized, and belittled them.

As a site of cultural contestation, portraiture was similarly concerned with renovating Black images. In photography's first century, the photographic portrait served as a key visual mode through which African diasporic peoples might counter an onslaught of derogatory depictions. Portraiture at once imaged interiority, self-possession, and an idealized self, visions of personhood that daily life in a white world—from London to Los Angeles, Paris to Philadelphia—denied them. When Harlem's Black residents entered James Van Der Zee's Guaranteed Photo Studio to carefully craft beautiful images of self, they flouted the fixity of Black stereotypes and left, if only temporarily, the seemingly already written tragic denouement of Black life at the studio door.

Portraiture and diaspora are linked, then, in their efforts to counter the abjection of Black peoples and assert Black subjectivity.[3] We might think of them as paired tools that helped early-twentieth-century Black peoples to "emplace themselves" visually in the world and enact transnational connections, belonging, and subjectivity.[4] Photographic practices of diaspora reveal that Black people were not simply specters that haunted (or spectacles that populated) our received narratives of modernism, but were contemporary interlocutors and therefore active architects of modernity and its visual practices.[5] In Garvey's uses of photography and in his relationship to Van Der Zee, we see the necessary use of the visual to at once conceal catastrophe, hold it at bay, and produce a vision of stability and possibility.

We might consider each of these pairings—the photographs, the men, and indeed photography and diaspora—as stereographs. Like the popular nineteenth-century photographic form the stereograph, two similar but slightly different images give the viewer the impression of depth as well as closeness when placed side by side and looked at through the proper device, the stereoscope. By juxtaposing first these two iconic images and then these two iconic race men—Garvey and Van Der Zee—and reading them "stereoscopically," I explore broadly the ways photography has worked to articulate—to join up and express—African diaspora. And in the unevenness of the relationship between Garvey and Van Der Zee, I interrogate the limits of the camera as a "prosthetic device."

The stereograph and the stereoscope offer a provocative frame for thinking about photographic practices of diaspora, and here I am merely venturing what such a hermeneutic might be and might do. The stereograph came into popularity in the 1840s with the birth of photography and, like the medium itself, was quickly put to a range of uses. Most significantly, stereographs were employed as informational tools, educating viewers about distant lands, exotic animals, or other cultures. The stereograph mimics binocular vision, whereby the brain processes the sight from each eye into a three-dimensional picture; the same sight—of the Pyramids at Giza, Northern Plains Indians, markets in Hong Kong, Civil War dead—is photographed once and then again from a few inches along a lateral axis (or shot with two cameras simultaneously, or with specially designed stereograph cameras using multiple lenses). When paired side by side, the two images become magnified and present a wider field of view and an opportunity to perceive detail. Through the stereoscope, the images produce a sense of proximity and veracity. Or, as sound studies scholar Tsitsi Jaji describes the phenomenon, the stereo "creates the impression of being surrounded by the contours of a voluminous, extensive, three-dimensional body."[6] Especially alluring to European and American viewers who had never encountered a "real" Indian or an "authentic African," who might never make the expensive and arduous journey to newly acquired US possessions in the South Pacific, or who would never find themselves on an actual battlefield, the stereograph heightened visual senses, creating a virtual experience of genuine presence. As physician, inventor, and photography enthusiast Oliver Wendell Holmes Sr. averred, "By means of these two different views of an object, the mind, as it were, feels rooted . . . and gets an idea of its solidity."[7]

In juxtaposition, the 1922 and 1924 photographs make tangible the visionary —though, in practice, ill executed and even chimerical—aims of the UNIA: the unification of the 400 million Negroes of the world for the purposes of self-determination. They create an aspect of sameness in order to obscure the political realities that separated the two. But more than simple comparative analysis, I want to employ the stereograph as a means to recognize what Kobena Mercer has referred to as an "antinomial rhythm," in which contradiction and divergence "yield new insights" into the "material complexities of black life under worldly conditions of diaspora."[8] These two photographs, and the two men who respectively occupy and fabricate the photographic frame, are engaged in an ongoing process of image making that at once imagines sameness, performs solidity, and dances with precarity.

Garvey founded the UNIA in his native Jamaica in 1914. The organization was the culmination of four years of traveling through Central America, the Caribbean, and Europe, observing and writing about the common subjugated position of Black peoples living within imperialism and industrial capitalism. Garvey, along with his first wife, Amy Ashwood, brought the UNIA to the United States in 1916. There, in the vibrant diversity of Harlem, working-class and dark-skinned Black audiences especially—migrants from the southern United States, immigrants from the West Indies—found inspiration and empowerment in what Garvey identified as the UNIA's "program of uniting all the Negro peoples of the world into one great body to establish a country and government absolutely their own."[9] This program built local Black businesses, produced and circulated its own weekly newspaper, *The Negro World*, corresponded with world leaders, and above all, was not interested in bargain or compromise. At the centerpiece of Garvey's UNIA was the ambitious Black Star Line, a fleet of ships that would carry commercial cargo and transport Africa's scattered children back home (figure 1.3).

The hypocrisies of World War I served to swell the UNIA's ranks. These included the failure of the Treaty of Versailles, a reinvigorated colonialism in Africa and in the United States, and the continued refusal to extend constitutional rights to returning Black soldiers, as well as the rise of lynchings and racial pogroms. In the United States especially, the outbreak of World War I had raised Black expectations of inclusive citizenship. But instead the war impressed on African Americans the violent limits of US democracy and engendered a decidedly military (as well as militant) brand of New Negro consciousness. Many who joined the UNIA, including a significant number of World War I veterans, agreed with Garvey that efforts against lynching and for political equality in the United States by the National Association for the Advancement of Colored People (NAACP) and other organizations were futile if not outright laughable. Instead they saw a redeemed—that is, reclaimed, reconstituted, and recompensed— African continent as a more realistic promised land. While wildly impractical, Garvey's expansive vision provided hope and dignity, possibility and promise.

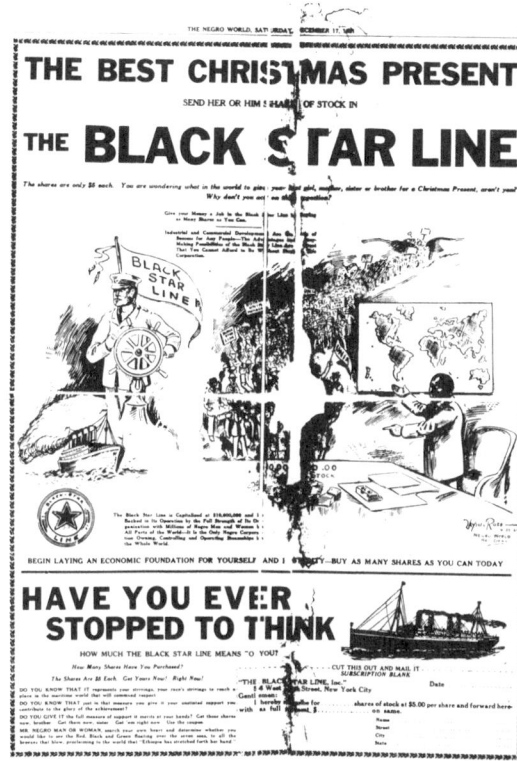

FIGURE 1.3. Advertisement for shares of stock in the Black Star Line, *Negro World*, December 17, 1921. Marcus Garvey and UNIA Papers Project, James S. Coleman African Studies Center, UCLA.

He stirred up and nurtured feelings of Black pride, a fluttering, fragile entity in the dark days of Jim Crow and global colonialism. As one historian commented, "Garvey sold Africa to the Negro and the Negro to himself."[10]

By the inaugural parade of the August 1924 convention, the UNIA boasted a worldwide membership of six million, organized by nearly fourteen hundred separate branches in more than thirty countries throughout the Western Hemisphere and the African continent.[11] This growth was aided by the circulation of *The Negro World*, published in both English and Spanish. The two photographs reveal Garvey at the center of the UNIA. In the words of a *Negro World* article in August 1922, "As never before, the Hon. Marcus Garvey was the cynosure of the eyes of the entire Harlem public today."[12] The photographs present Garvey as the nucleus of a Pan-African political movement and as the embodiment of diasporic feeling and possibility.

A sense of palpability, and not just possibility, was crucial for the UNIA and integral to the work of photography for the organization. Despite the UNIA's expansiveness, the organization's material and business ventures flailed between

1922 and 1924 due to mismanagement and corruption on the part of a number of trusted officials. Most notably, financial mishandling, inexperience in industry, and too lofty goals led to the demise of the Black Star Line.[13] The organizers' inexperience was exploited and exacerbated by the Bureau of Investigation's targeting of Garvey as a "foreign radical" during the Palmer Raids (1919–21).[14] A young J. Edgar Hoover was appointed Attorney General A. Mitchell Palmer's assistant, marking the beginning of Hoover's relentless career-long pursuit of radical social movements. Through the Bureau's surveillance and infiltration tactics (including the hire of its first Black agent, referred to as "800," for just this work), Garvey was ultimately convicted in 1923 and imprisoned in 1925 on the charge of defrauding investors through the US Mail.[15] Most of the alleged victims, however—Black working-class people from Oakland, California, to Colón, Panama—maintained their faith in both the Black Star Line and its director-general. Amid the difficulties faced by the organization, the two photographs together offer an image of the depth of Garvey's command and the closeness of his vision to becoming reality.

Stereographs provide an illusion of three dimensionality via a subtle shift in space. These two images of Garvey produce depth by way of a shift in time—a lateral move of two years rather than two inches. Indeed, if we read these photographs through the stereoscope, they image the consistency of the movement and its leader. Despite the uncertain grounds and precarious futures of both Garvey and the UNIA (being surveilled and even infiltrated by the Bureau of Investigation); despite vociferous critiques and campaigns by other Black leaders, including a "Garvey Must Go" drive waged by A. Philip Randolph and Chandler Owen, editors of the Black socialist publication *The Messenger*; despite financial crises; and despite Garvey's own fierce obduracy—despite all these challenges, the 1922 and 1924 photographs suggest organizational terra firma.[16]

In their gesture to the pomp and power of imperial nation-states, the photographs document the movement's celebration of national spectacle with parades, processions, and military drills that borrowed from royal national pageants. The images also represent a ritual of ceremony, a tradition developed over two years whose symbols—flags, elaborate titles, patriotic hymns, and fetishized order and procedure—were firmly rooted in the modern mapping of the nation, which ironically must outline and confer its own eternal and divine right.[17] The showy display of these parades invoked both the modernity of the nation-state and the splendor of an imagined African past. As one *Negro World* writer reported regarding the court reception of the 1921 Convention of the Negro Peoples of the World, the convention where Garvey debuted his military costume,

"It was a ceremonial that may correctly be regarded as a revival of ancient glory, pomp and splendor of Ethiopia in the days of the Queen of Sheba, centuries long ago, of her greatness and world supremacy, comparable to similar state functions held in the ceremonial courts of England, Germany, Italy, France and the United States."[18] For Garvey and the UNIA, this event, and its attention to pageantry, was neither "an empty display of grandeur" nor "any slavish imitation of the social standards of other races." Rather, the spectacle was meant to mark the emergence of a new nation—in Garvey's own words, "a manifestation of the tremendous possibilities within the black people of the world for their future development along industrial, economic, political and social lines."[19] In its planning and execution, the court reception performed Black modern nationhood for both its citizens and its skeptics.

Photography at once documented such splendor and confirmed modernity. Reproduced in the *Negro World* weekly newspaper, photographs further offered that sense of simultaneity and inclusion intrinsic to the modern nation, here Garvey's Black empire. As Walter Benjamin suggested, the camera as a tool of mass movements also offered an opportunity for "cognitive and perceptual transformation."[20] "If one considers," wrote Benjamin in the second version of his "Work of Art" essay, "the dangerous tensions which technology and its consequences have engendered in the masses at large—tendencies which at critical stages take on a psychotic character—one has also to recognize that this same technologization has created the possibility of psychic immunization against such mass psychoses."[21] The camera, which for Black people and other subalterns had often been a technology of violence wielded against them—in the names of Jim Crow, colonialism, racial science, pornography, state surveillance, and "progress"—also became a tool for reimagining the individual and collective Black body.

Of course, Benjamin also warned us of the dangers of such new technologies in the representation of political life, the aestheticization of politics, which in Benjamin's estimation was a signal component of fascism. Such imagery enabled the masses to see themselves ("mass movements are more clearly apprehended by the camera than by the eye") and thereby contributed to a militarized mass while foregrounding such visual representation as a stand-in for true political expression and social transformation.[22] Certainly, the collusion of Van Der Zee's camera with Garvey's mass movement potentially lent itself to such aestheticism. Indeed, Garvey once famously declared, "We were the first Fascists. We had disciplined men, women and children in training for the liberation of Africa. The black masses saw that in this extreme nationalism lay their only hope and readily supported it."[23]

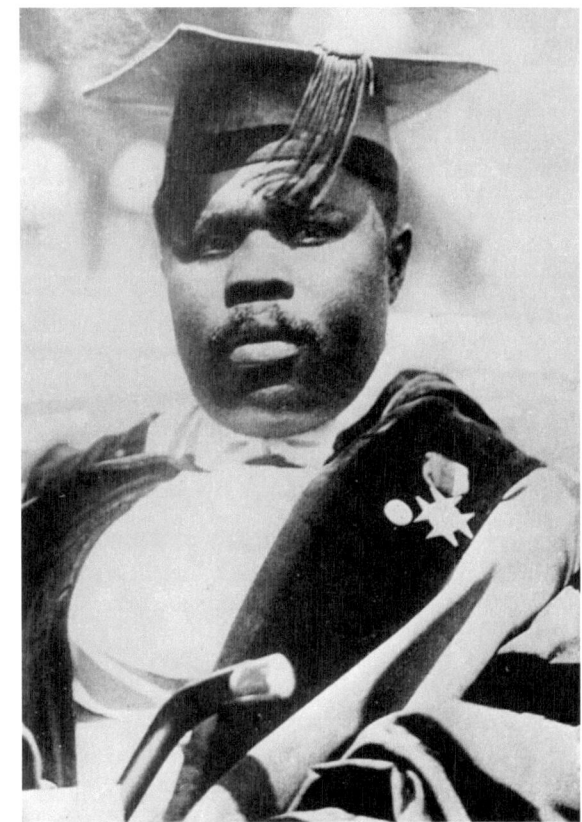

FIGURE 1.4. *Marcus Garvey, Eminent Scholar*. Schomburg Center for Research in Black Culture, Photographs and Prints Division, The New York Public Library. New York Public Library Digital Collections. https://digital collections.nypl.org /items/8e0981a2-4adf -a10a-e040-e00a180 63089.

The choice of military costume suggests this aestheticism as well. Such self-fashioning was an evolving practice, for in the opening parades of the 1920 and 1921 conventions, Garvey donned flowing crimson professorial robes, with three velvet bands on their wide sleeves, patterned after the raiment of a doctor of civil law (figure 1.4). Garvey possessed no university degrees; an autodidact, he attended church school in his native St. Ann's Bay, Jamaica, until the age of fourteen, when money for further education dried up. Garvey would later sit in on law classes at Birkbeck College in London.[24] The robes were meant to indicate official erudition and present Garvey as a man of letters. But the transition to military attire signaled Garvey as commander in chief, capable of mobilizing martial forces in assertion and defense of a Black nation. As Garvey proclaimed in a January 20, 1924, speech at UNIA's Liberty Hall in Harlem, "We are going to make our contribution through the building up of one of the greatest nations and empires in the world."[25] In another 1924 speech he declared, "The ideal of nationhood . . . [is] the highest ideal among peoples at the present time."[26] Such

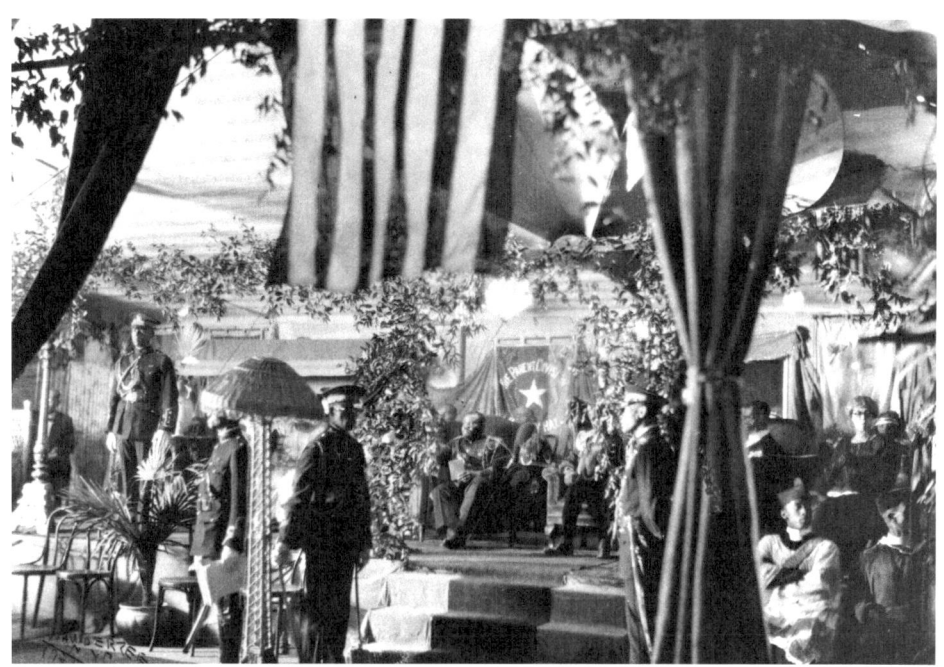

FIGURE 1.5. James Van Der Zee, *Marcus Garvey at Liberty Hall, UNIA Headquarters, 120 West 138th Street, New York*, 1924, printed later. Gelatin silver print, approx. 8 × 10 in. James Van Der Zee Archive, The Metropolitan Museum of Art, Gift of Donna Van Der Zee, 2021 (2021.446.1.149). © James Van Der Zee Archive, The Metropolitan Museum of Art. Image source: Art Resource, NY.

language and self-fashioning also recalls the renderings of Toussaint L'Ouverture, another Afro-Caribbean man in uniform. Adorned with medals, epaulettes, and polished buttons, seated in the semiprotected interior of an expensive automobile proceeding up a major thoroughfare in New York City, Garvey in these photographs embodies the performance and presentation of the Black empire his organization strove for: its wealth, its militarism, its modernity, and its masculine pomp and circumstance.[27] We must, then, consider the field marshal's uniform as assertion of military might, as display for Black peoples of their own possibility, as indication of an atavistic desire for autocratic power but one that imagines—creates in this case, not entirely fictionalizes—an ancient precolonial, prelapsarian African glory (figure 1.5).

The two images which open this chapter (figures 1.1 and 1.2) suggest the need to evoke a tradition of Black militancy and self-possession when history had imaged Black peoples as persistently disempowered and dominated. Such "restaging" also functions to imbue the UNIA and Garvey with a sense of order and stability in the face of uncertainty and impending catastrophe; for, by the time of the second photograph, Garvey had been convicted of mail fraud and was facing incarceration and eventual deportation. Further, hiring the services of a local and popular African American photographer, Van Der Zee, not only fell in line with the UNIA's support for Black entrepreneurship but also ensured that the UNIA would retain access to Van Der Zee's archive of negatives and would continue to possess the photographs themselves and the image of the movement as a whole.[28] The photograph with Garvey at the organization's literal and metaphoric center would provide the necessary link to the movement. His charisma and command remained steadfast. The repetition of images to be circulated primarily through *The Negro World* and UNIA ephemera—signed photographic postcards, framed portraits suitable for home display, even medallions bearing Garvey's photographic image—would create sentiments of pride useful in transforming a scattered diaspora into a Black empire. We can thus see how photography becomes a necessary tool for the "practice of diaspora."[29]

Stereograph 2: Garvey and Van Der Zee

Now that I've identified a photographic practice of diaspora through an interrogation of two specific images and the political uses to which they were put, what happens if we juxtapose Garvey and his photographer James Van Der Zee (figures 1.6 and 1.7)? Two dark-skinned Black men, these two contemporaries inhabited the same vibrant Harlem. Born a year earlier than Garvey, Van Der Zee opened his Guaranteed Photo Studio in 1916, the same year Garvey brought the UNIA to New York City and the United States. Each was a New Negro at the height of his representational powers in the 1920s, and each was committed in his chosen vocation to renovating Black self-perception. If Marcus Garvey sold the Negro to himself, figuratively speaking, such an enterprise was Van Der Zee's job, ten hours a day, six days a week. The studio portrait, that form of projecting idealized visions of his mostly Black clientele, was Van Der Zee's specialty, his bread and butter. Van Der Zee's portraits image exactly the self-possession and stability that Garvey hoped the photographer would bring to his summerlong commission with the UNIA. These two men, placed side by side, would seem to form a stereograph, making tangible New Negro consciousness.

And yet, when we look more closely at the two figures juxtaposed, we begin to see differences in background and aesthetics, leading to what would seem to be a persistent misrecognition between them.

While Garvey settled in New York City after years of peripatetic wandering, Van Der Zee's journeys were far more circumscribed. Born in Lenox, Massachusetts, in 1886, not far from the Great Barrington birthplace of Garvey's political rival W. E. B. Du Bois, Van Der Zee lived a comfortable life afforded by his family. His parents, grandparents, and aunts and uncles lived in neighboring houses. They earned stable wages working variously as a sexton of the local church, as bakers, while serving white residents and weekenders in the nearby hotels and restaurants. They supplemented their incomes by growing their own food and keeping a few domestic animals. Besides Lenox, Van Der Zee would call only two other cities home in his lifetime: Hampton, Virginia, where he lived in 1908 with his first wife, Kate, and their daughter, Rachel, and where he enrolled in music classes at the all-Black Whittier School; and New York City, where he settled permanently in 1911.[30] While Black citizens of every social class and political stripe and from nearly every point on the globe passed through Van Der Zee's studio or sat before his camera, Van Der Zee himself rarely ventured beyond Harlem. But he relished the diversity and sought to make each person unique even as the work of a studio portraitist could be quite repetitive: "I posed everybody according to their type and personality and therefore almost every picture was different."[31] For Garvey, Harlem was but one location in the Negro world. For Van Der Zee, Harlem *was* the world.

These different positionalities, the different locations from which Garvey's and Van Der Zee's gazes found each other, become more apparent when we closely consider the photographs that emerged from Van Der Zee's commission. Although they are important documents of one of the most significant Black social movements of the twentieth century, when placed in the larger body of Van Der Zee's work, the images appear less crisp, a bit harried and off-center. If we return to the first stereograph of Garvey in the touring car (figures 1.1 and 1.2), Van Der Zee's wider frame allows for multiple subjects to come into view, undermining the intimacy and force of the first portrait. Even more, all the subjects look in different directions, giving a feeling of chaos, and suggesting an individualism that potentially reads as disunity.

Some of this disorder is no doubt a product of shooting outdoors, photographing parades and processionals in motion and under time pressure, amid the rumble and accented noise of international Black crowds. Such energy and excitement is palpable, but it also threatens to swallow the images or to unravel the confident frames for which Van Der Zee was known. Van Der Zee was working outside the familiarity of the studio he had occupied for eight years, with its known lighting, its favored props, and the standard backdrops he himself had painted "with the collaboration of fellow Harlem photographer Eddie Elcha."[32] The studio provided calm, structure, and above all, control. And control allowed for creativity: the time, space, and ingenuity to touch up photographs, to remove signs of bad health, to add symbols of wealth and prosperity, to hand-color

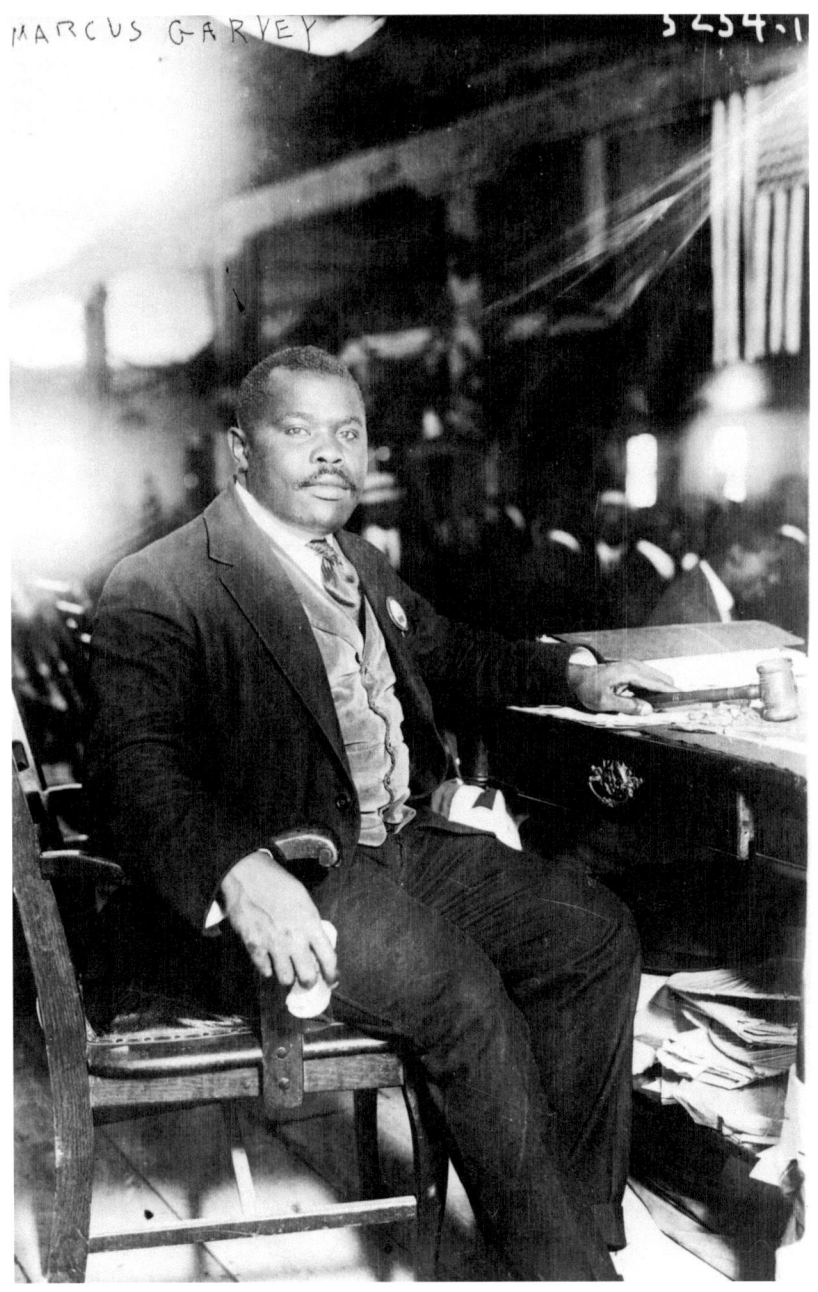

FIGURE 1.6. *Marcus Garvey, 1887–1940*, August 5, 1924. Bain Collection, Prints and Photographs Division, Library of Congress, Washington, DC. https://www.loc.gov /item/2003653533/.

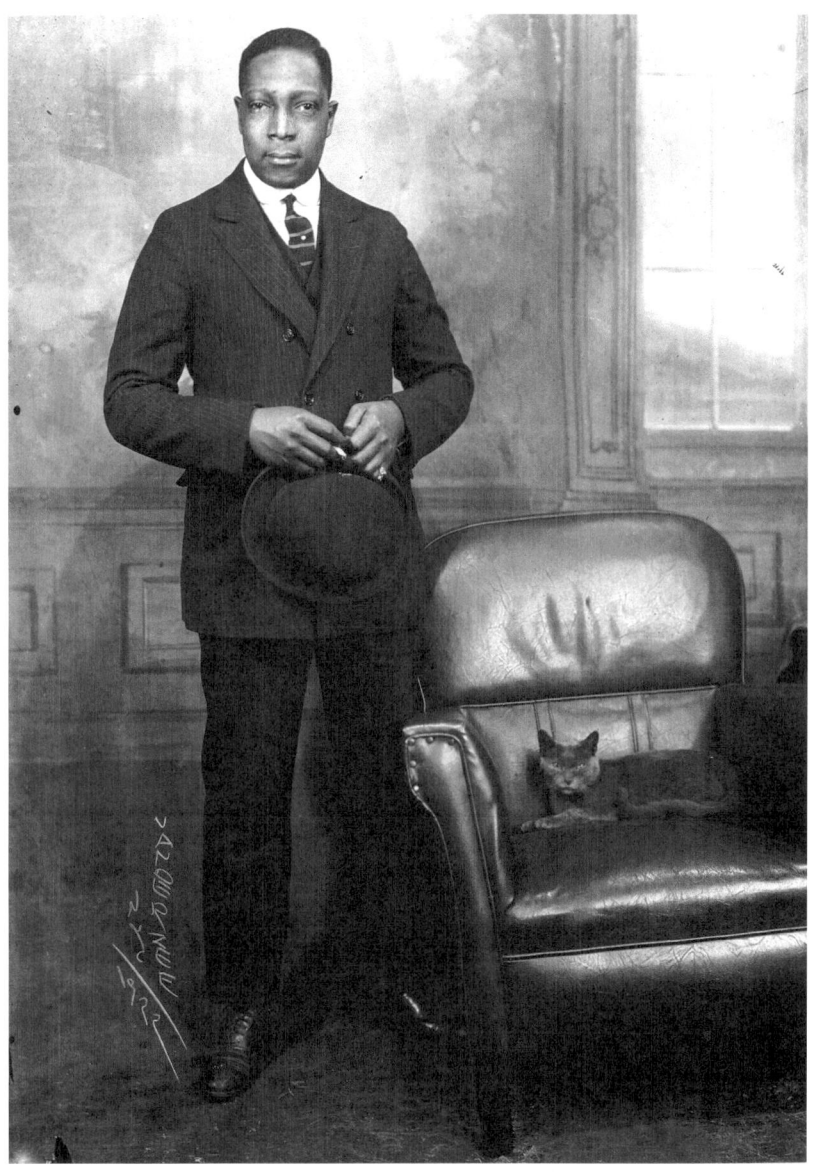

FIGURE 1.7. James Van Der Zee, *Self-Portrait*, 1922. © James Van Der Zee Archive, The Metropolitan Museum of Art. Image source: Art Resource, NY.

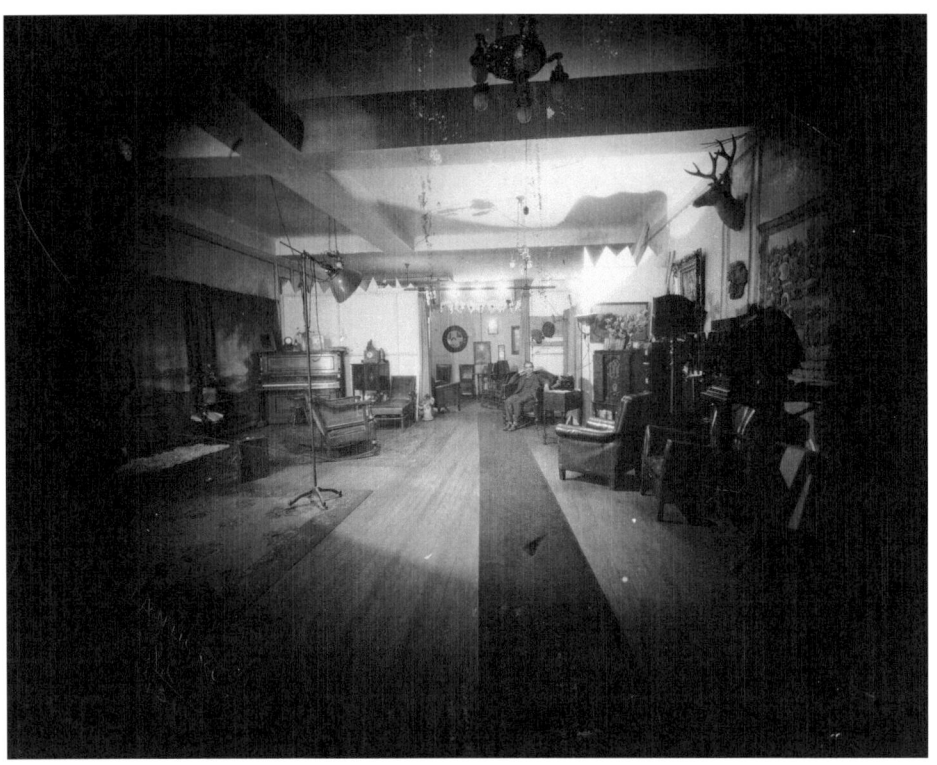

FIGURE 1.8. James Van Der Zee, *G. G. G. Photo Studio Interior with Man Seated in Chair, 2065 Seventh Avenue, New York*, 1931. Gelatin silver print, image: 7 × 8 ¾ in. (17.8 × 22.3 cm); sheet: 7 × 8 ¾ in. (17.8 × 22.3 cm). James Van Der Zee Archive, The Metropolitan Museum of Art, Purchase, Louis V. Bell, Harris Brisbane Dick, Fletcher, and Rogers Funds and Joseph Pulitzer Bequest, Alfred Stieglitz Society Gifts, Twentieth-Century Photography Fund, Ann Tenenbaum and Thomas H. Lee Gift, Joyce F. Menschel Fund, and Ford Foundation Gift, 2021 (2021.443.4). © James Van Der Zee Archive, The Metropolitan Museum of Art. Image source: Art Resource, NY.

prints with oils or watercolors, to create composite images.[33] Control in the studio made it possible for Van Der Zee's clients to leave the stressful conditions of Black life at the studio door. Control enabled Van Der Zee and his sitters to craft personalized images, to inscribe his subjects as individuals, and make them the cynosures of their own Harlem publics (figures 1.8 and 1.9).

It was exactly this control that eluded Van Der Zee out on the street. Some of his outdoor photographs are striking for their precision and stillness—those images of the drill exercises of the African Legion and Women's Brigade para-

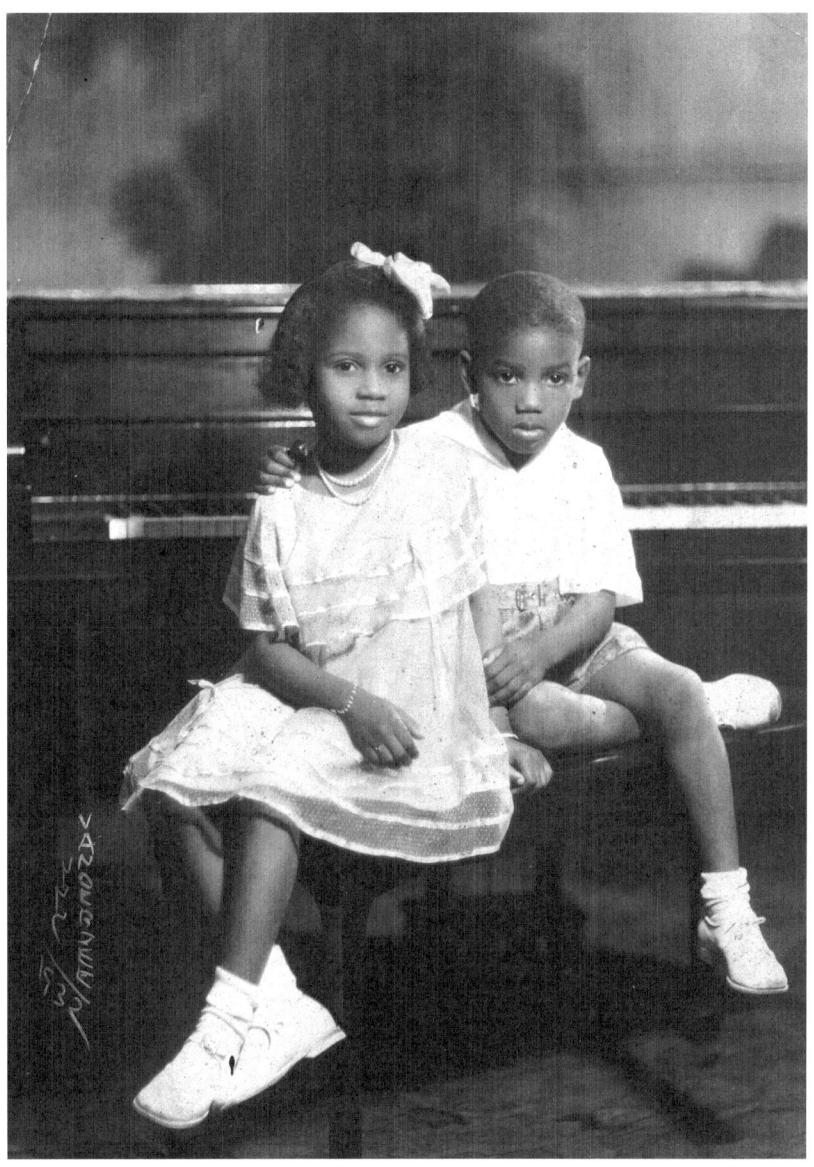

FIGURE 1.9. James Van Der Zee, *Children at Piano*, 1932. Gelatin silver print, sheet: 7 × 5 in. (17.8 × 12.7 cm). James Van Der Zee Archive, The Metropolitan Museum of Art; Purchase, Louis V. Bell, Harris Brisbane Dick, Fletcher, and Rogers Funds and Joseph Pulitzer Bequest, Alfred Stieglitz Society Gifts, Twentieth-Century Photography Fund, Ann Tenenbaum and Thomas H. Lee Gift, Joyce F. Menschel Fund, and Ford Foundation Gift, 2021 (2021.443.267). © James Van Der Zee Archive, The Metropolitan Museum of Art. Image source: Art Resource, NY.

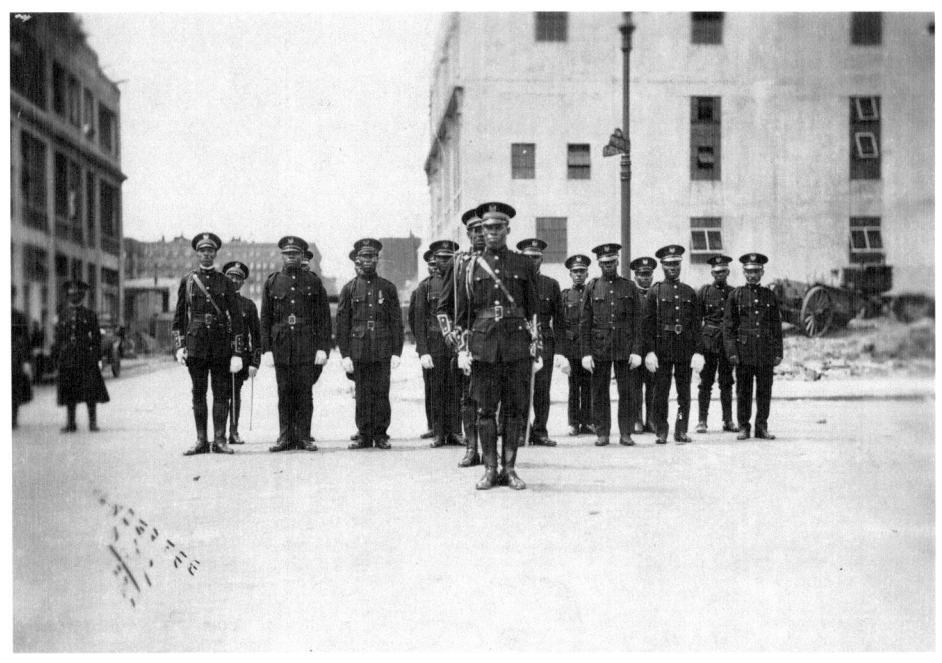

FIGURE 1.10. James Van Der Zee, *African Legion Militia in Formation, Marcus Garvey's UNIA, Fifth Avenue and 138th Street, New York*, 1924. Gelatin silver print, image: 4 ½ × 6 ½ in. (11.4 × 16.5 cm); sheet: 4 ¹⁵⁄₁₆ × 6 ¹¹⁄₁₆ in. (12.5 × 17 cm). James Van Der Zee Archive, The Metropolitan Museum of Art; Purchase, Louis V. Bell, Harris Brisbane Dick, Fletcher, and Rogers Funds and Joseph Pulitzer Bequest, Alfred Stieglitz Society Gifts, Twentieth-Century Photography Fund, Ann Tenenbaum and Thomas H. Lee Gift, Joyce F. Menschel Fund, and Ford Foundation Gift, 2021 (2021.443.42). © James Van Der Zee Archive, The Metropolitan Museum of Art. Image source: Art Resource, NY.

military units, for example (figures 1.10 and 1.11). They reveal the discipline and regimentation of both the movement and the photographer. But for most of Van Der Zee's exterior images, however, it would seem the movement moved too fast for Van Der Zee to capture. And indeed, it was such drama, energy, and movement that the UNIA capitalized on in its lively reproductions of Van Der Zee's photography in the *Negro World*, dynamism that afforded the paper's editors to craft movement "narrative[s] of abundance, excitement and pride."[34]

Garvey, too, sought control. But as the UNIA grew in a host of directions and locations, such control would prove elusive for him as well. Neither could Garvey fully command the attention of Van Der Zee. In a photograph made in late summer 1924, Garvey and UNIA supreme deputy George O. Marke flank Paris-based Dahomean lawyer and journalist Kojo Tovalou Houénou (figure

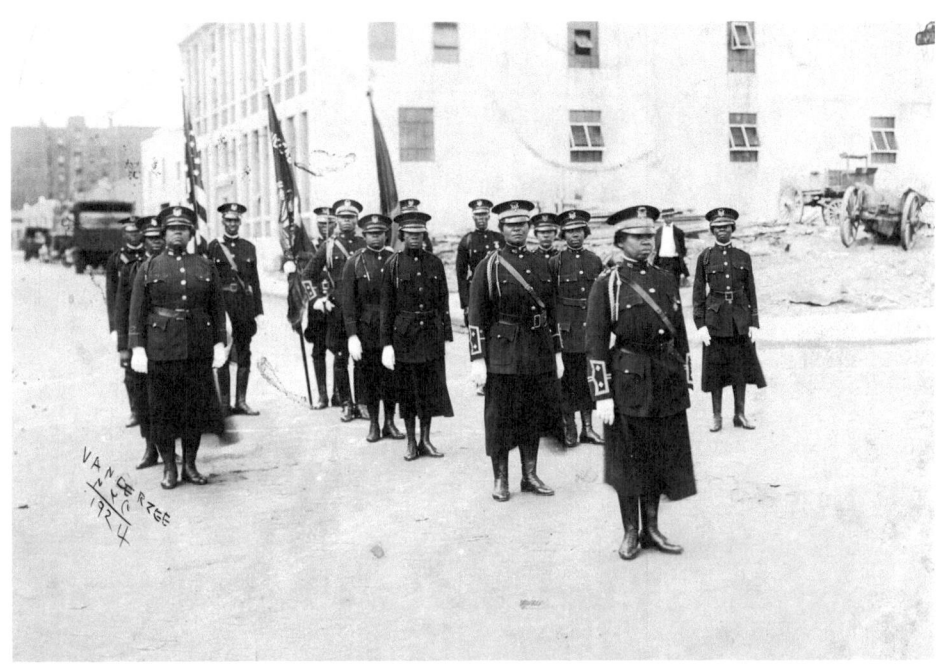

FIGURE 1.11. James Van Der Zee, *African Legion Militia in Formation, Marcus Garvey's UNIA, Fifth Avenue and 138th Street, New York*, 1924. Gelatin silver print, image: 4 ½ × 6 ½ in. (11.5 × 16.5 cm); sheet: 5 × 7 in. (12.7 × 17.8 cm). James Van Der Zee Archive, The Metropolitan Museum of Art; Purchase, Louis V. Bell, Harris Brisbane Dick, Fletcher, and Rogers Funds and Joseph Pulitzer Bequest, Alfred Stieglitz Society Gifts, Twentieth-Century Photography Fund, Ann Tenenbaum and Thomas H. Lee Gift, Joyce F. Menschel Fund, and Ford Foundation Gift, 2021 (2021.443.43). © James Van Der Zee Archive, The Metropolitan Museum of Art. Image source: Art Resource, NY.

1.12). Tovalou Houénou's title of "Prince" perhaps referred as much to his cosmopolitanness, his striking carriage, and what art historian Richard Powell describes as his "dandified elegance" as to his royal lineage.[35] In New York City to publicize the Black Francophone journal *Les Continents* and "to extend its black internationalist connections," Tovalou Houénou was a featured speaker at the UNIA convention, addressing the gathering in French. In Van Der Zee's framing, it is clearly Tovalou Houénou, in his dazzling white summer suit, who is our focal point. Van Der Zee has attempted to effect a studio on what appears to be a rooftop. Tovalou Houénou is framed by one window in the background while another window edges the left frame like the trompe l'oeil backdrops at the Guaranteed Studio. While appearing businesslike, though perhaps a bit rumpled, in their three-piece suits, Marke and Garvey do not stir Van Der Zee's eye

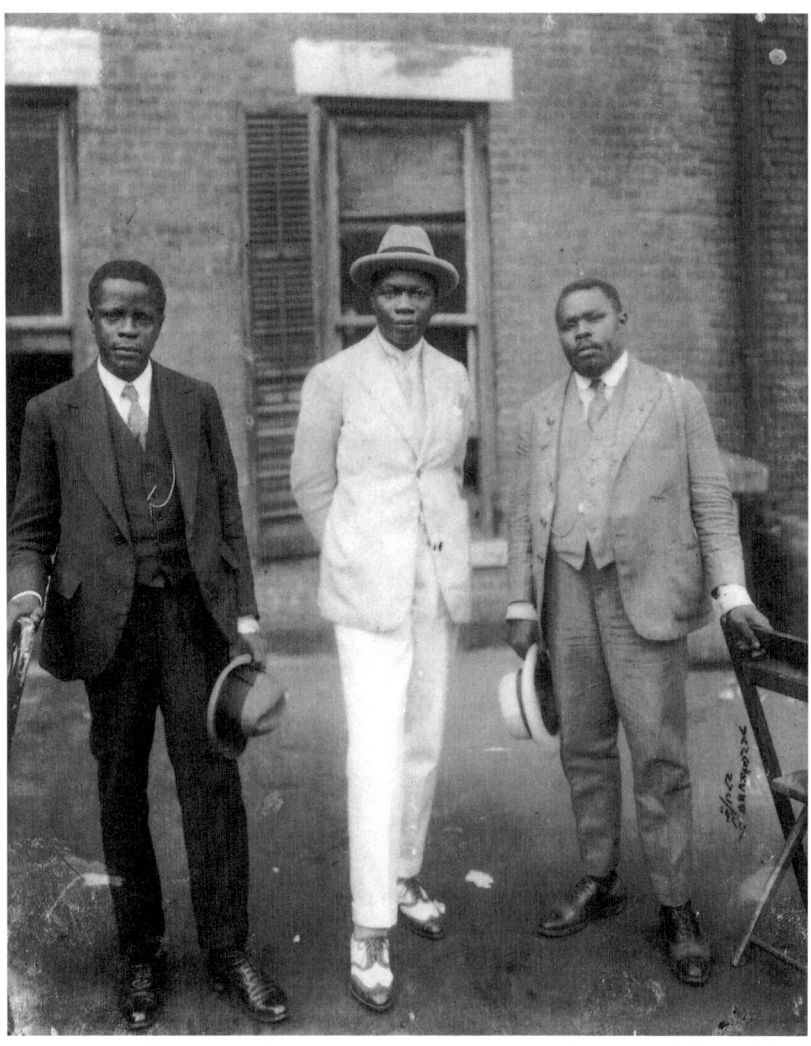

FIGURE 1.12. James Van Der Zee, *Marcus Garvey with George O. Marke and Prince Kojo Tovalou-Houénou*, 1924. Gelatin silver print, image/sheet: 12.8 × 18.1 cm (5 ¹⁄₁₆ × 7 ¹⁄₈ in.). National Gallery of Art, Avalon Fund (2019.127.6). © James Van Der Zee Archive, The Metropolitan Museum of Art. Image source: Art Resource, NY.

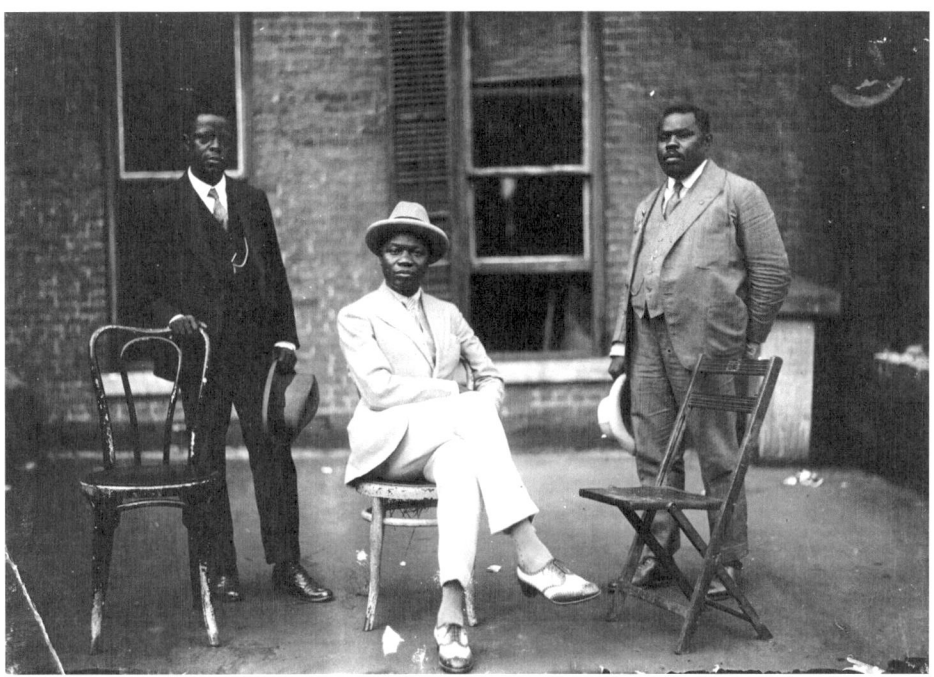

FIGURE 1.13. James Van Der Zee, *Marcus Garvey Standing with George O. Marke and Prince Kojo Tovalou-Houénou*, 1924. Gelatin silver print, image: 17 × 21.5 cm (6 ¹¹⁄₁₆ × 8 ⁷⁄₁₆ in.); matted: 40.6 × 50.8 cm (16 × 20 in.). The Cleveland Museum of Art, The Jane B. Tripp Charitable Lead Annuity Trust (1999.54). © James Van Der Zee Archive, The Metropolitan Museum of Art. Image source: Art Resource, NY.

as does the "six foot, well-formed, straight as birch" prince.[36] The photographer has placed the UNIA officials so as to create symmetry for his centerpiece: Marke and Garvey hold their hats in their inside hands while their hands farthest from Tovalou Houénou rest on the back of folding chairs. In another photograph from this session, Tovalou Houénou sits in partial profile accentuating his long lines, his legs crossed and hands folded to one side between knees and hip, while the other men stand in wait (figure 1.13). They are placed as visual asides. To add insult to injury, Van Der Zee misspelled Garvey's name in the etching on the print, forgetting the *e* in "Garvey."[37] One can imagine that for a man who so ostentatiously fashioned his own public image and then guarded it anxiously, these photographs (not to mention the mislabeling) would have been no mere slight for Garvey. For Van Der Zee the portraitist, however, diaspora calls in the figure of Tovalou Houénou, smooth, graceful, and comfortable before the camera. Tovalou Houénou responded in kind by requesting fifteen hundred copies of one of Van Der Zee's luminous portraits of the prince.[38]

Garvey used neither of these images, at least not in the forms Van Der Zee staged and printed them. Garvey chose instead to crop himself out into a stand-alone portrait that he then had reproduced as a signed image for sale to supporters (figure 1.14).[39] In addition, Garvey selected another photograph of his visit with Tovalou Houénou for publication on the front page of *The Negro World*.[40] In this image, the prince is still in the center, but both he and Marke direct their attention to a seated Garvey, who gesticulates as he addresses the two men. Almost hieratic, this photograph is less visually arresting than others from the session. In the pages of *The Negro World*, however, Garvey remains supreme commander.

There seems to be mutual misrecognition here. Van Der Zee refuses to see Garvey as Garvey wishes to be seen. And Garvey refuses to acknowledge Van Der Zee's aesthetic choices. To borrow from performance theorist Tavia Nyong'o, diaspora never looks back from the place from which we see it.[41] Yet photography functions as a mechanism through which each might stage his own needs and interests. Here, looking stereoscopically tells of the gap between Garvey and Van Der Zee, of a collaboration tinged with ambivalences and ambiguities.

In Van Der Zee's commission, we might also see the efforts of a photographer to widen his own horizons. Van Der Zee encountered difficulties not only with form, moving from the studio to the street, but also with subject matter. Indeed, how *does* one photograph diaspora? What does it mean to photograph—document, picture, frame—a condition, a process, an analytic? How does one photograph movements? Throughout this broad and indeed uneven archive, we see Van Der Zee struggling with relations of scale, constantly widening and tightening his frame and then widening it again, moving away from a tight focus on the charismatic leader to images of Garvey in the midst of the movement and to the faces of membership. The realities of diaspora, on the street at least, seem to have unnerved Van Der Zee and also stretched him as an artist. These struggles that Van Der Zee encountered in giving face and form to both a mass movement and to racial feeling are challenges inherent to the project of visualizing diaspora generally, a project in which chaos threatens to overwhelm connection. But such struggles also suggest that what articulations of diaspora that do emerge will be informative for their dissonances as well as their harmonies.

With these two pairings, I experiment with the stereograph and the stereoscope as hermeneutics for mapping photographic practices of diaspora. As a binocular

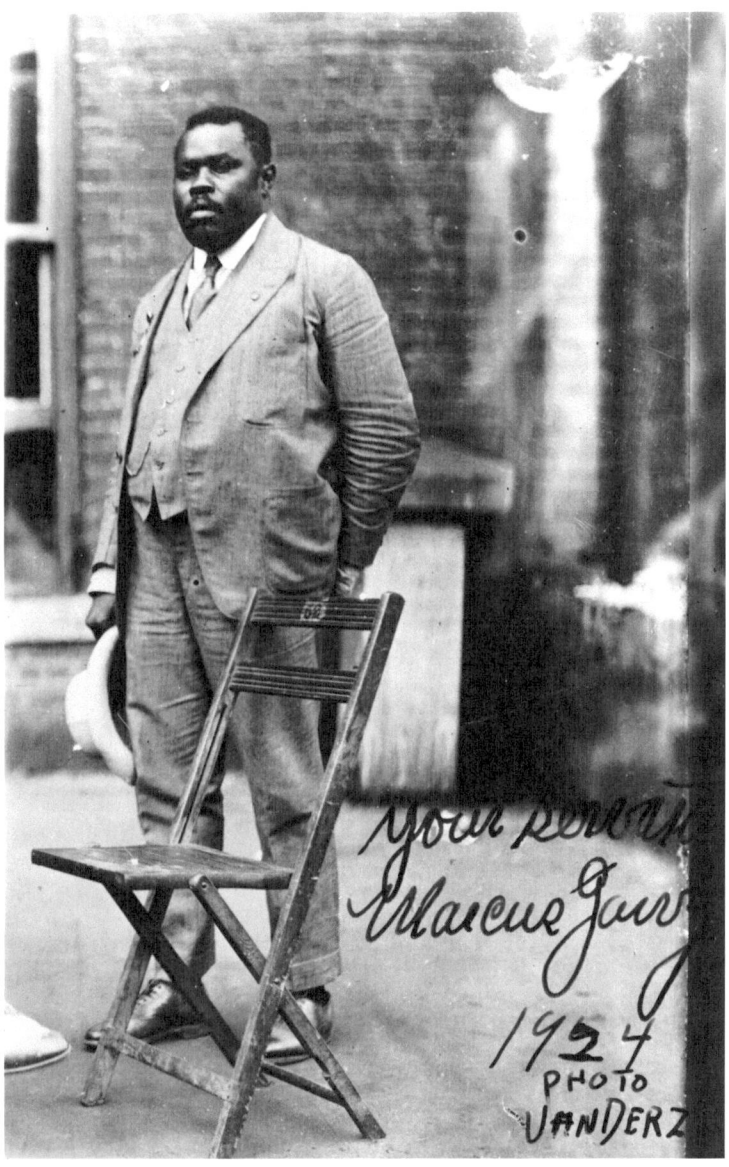

FIGURE 1.14. James Van Der Zee, *Marcus Garvey*, 1924. Gelatin silver print, image: 6 ½ × 4 ¼ in. (16.5 × 10.8 cm); sheet: 7 ¼ × 4 ¾ in. (18.4 × 12.1 cm). James Van Der Zee Archive, The Metropolitan Museum of Art; Purchase, Louis V. Bell, Harris Brisbane Dick, Fletcher, and Rogers Funds and Joseph Pulitzer Bequest, Alfred Stieglitz Society Gifts, Twentieth-Century Photography Fund, Ann Tenenbaum and Thomas H. Lee Gift, Joyce F. Menschel Fund, and Ford Foundation Gift, 2021. © James Van Der Zee Archive, The Metropolitan Museum of Art. Image source: Art Resource, NY.

mode of seeing, the stereograph evokes the "twoness" often described as endemic to the condition of Black modern subjects. The stereograph, composed of two parts that together bring into play further layers of depth and detail, reminds us that the articulation of diaspora necessarily involves at least two interlocutors. Through their back-and-forth exchange, new meanings about transnational Black subjectivity emerge, and modes of identification and belonging are nego-tiated. The stereograph then impels us to consider what Mercer has variously described as the "dialogic" and the "call and response" in diaspora visual cul-ture.[42] We become attentive to the "relational within aesthetic experience," the intersubjective exchange in which viewer and object, sitter and photographer consider each other.[43] Such exchange translates and elaborates meaning—as the stereograph creates depth and imagines stability—yet the necessity of move-ment between and across reminds us how inherently unstable and unfinished this exchange always is.

The stereoscope, a device required to illuminate the relational work of the stereograph, alerts us, as well, to the manufactured, though by no means in-sincere, character of diaspora. Indeed, stereographs function as much through similarity as through difference, and when we begin to scratch at and press the differences between the two pairings—differences in framing, in the direction of Garvey's gaze, in the changes in personnel who surround the leader, and dif-ferences between the two men and their divergent visions—we begin to better understand the image as a prop, a wedge that offers balance and unity. Brent Hayes Edwards avers that diaspora must be discursively propped up into an ar-tificially balanced state of racial belonging. Edwards employs the term *décalage* (translated as "jet lag"), borrowed from Léopold Sédar Senghor's own framing of diaspora, to "suggest a gap in time and space." Diaspora itself, then, serves as a prosthetic, smoothing out unevenness and stitching together Black peoples into racial alliances that are "temporary, artificial, and contingent, but no less real."[44] For Edwards, understanding diaspora as décalage is not a means to focus on the ways evocations of diaspora flatten out or erase contradictions. Rather, décalage helps us better comprehend what he calls "productive dissonances," that is, the notions of belonging and community such prostheses produce and how they produce them.

The distinctions between the two images of Garvey and between Garvey and Van Der Zee help to highlight the photograph itself as décalage, that which resists translation (but which is also the grounds for translation), that which asserts itself in the dissonance of the stereograph. The photograph—as docu-ment, as performance, and as relation—functions as the necessary prop meant to hold up these particular visions of diaspora, of "cultural and political linkage." Through the use of stereograph and stereoscope, I am attempting, then, to read not "for the efficacy of the prosthesis, but [for] the effects of such an operation," how the photographs are indeed necessary and "constitutive to the structure of [this] articulation of diaspora."[45] Reading stereoscopically—reading across images for their similarity and difference, reading between images for the tensions and silences, and reading chronotopically for their mutual translations and transformations—suggests a method of interpretation that suits a photographic practice of diaspora.

In the summer of 1926, Van Der Zee was asked to return to photograph the UNIA convention. His photographic services, the steadying frame of his camera, were needed more than ever in this moment, for the UNIA was indeed in chaos. Garvey had lost his legal appeal in the mail fraud case, in a decision that hinged on the modification of a photograph of the purchased Black Star Line ship from its previous name SS *Orion* to read *Phyllis Wheatley*; an act of aspiration on the part of the UNIA had proved a damning case of fabrication and fraud to the US government.[46] Now Garvey fought desperately to lead his organization from his cell in the federal penitentiary in Atlanta. He entrusted his writing, fundraising, and other business affairs to his "loving wife," Amy Jacques Garvey. Jacques Garvey remained one of the few whom Garvey still trusted, admonishing in his first published letter that he had been brought down by "liars," "plotters," and "idiots," white and Negro alike.[47] Though most members remained faithful to the UNIA's mission, a struggle ensued for control of the UNIA in which close associates George Weston and William Sherrill usurped Garvey's leadership. Garvey in turn deposed Sherrill and ousted him from the organization. By the time of the international convention in August 1926, two factions, one loyal to Garvey and the other allies of Weston and Sherrill, each claimed that its was the true organization and attempted to keep its rivals out of Liberty Hall. The two groups came to an uneasy truce for the duration of the convention only to later sue each other in court for the rights to Liberty Hall and, by extension, the control of the UNIA. So when Van Der Zee entered the meeting space, he would photograph the organization in the last throes of public unity.

Van Der Zee produced a collective studio portrait in which each individual is uniquely identifiable, a testament to the photographer's technical prowess (figure 1.15). Rather than a hindrance to his UNIA commission, here Van Der Zee's studio expertise works to create a truly compelling movement document: an image whose power lies in all those dark faces looking up in near-perfect unison, faces brightened by the hall's light from above—a photograph that evokes

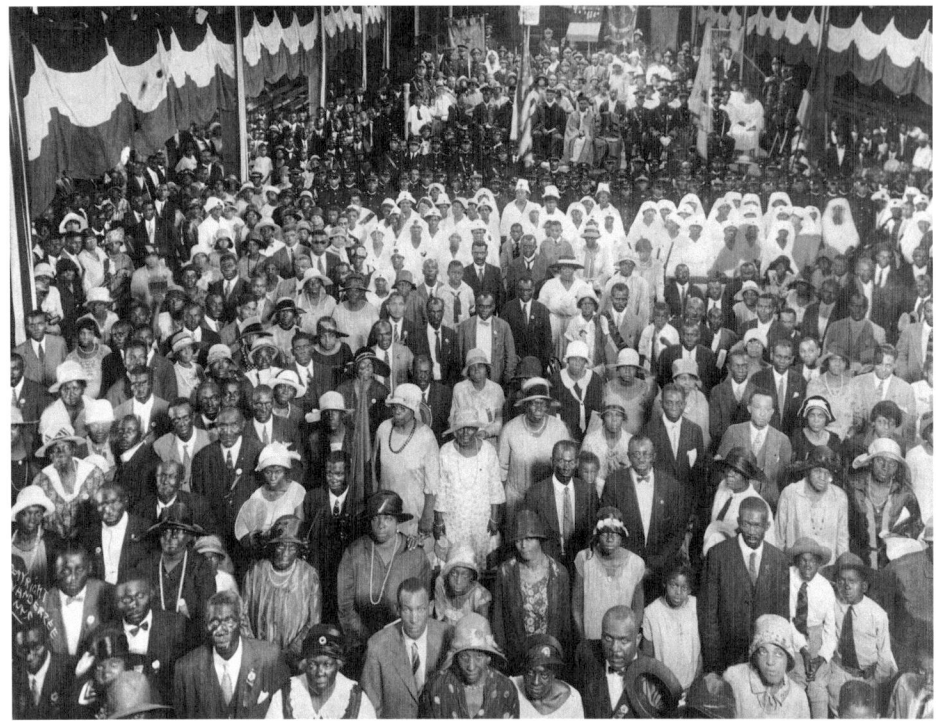

FIGURE 1.15. James Van Der Zee, *UNIA Assembly, Liberty Hall, 120 West 138th Street, New York*, 1926, printed later. Gelatin silver print, image: 7 9/16 × 10 in. (19.2 × 25.4 cm); sheet: 9 15/16 × 12 1/16 in. (25.3 × 30.6 cm). James Van Der Zee Archive, The Metropolitan Museum of Art; Gift of Donna Van Der Zee, 2021 (2021.446.1.41). © James Van Der Zee Archive, The Metropolitan Museum of Art. Image source: Art Resource, NY.

a three-dimensionality that comes in layers. The hall is still, and the members seem to hold a shared breath. Yet the flag buntings that undulate along the balconies provide a sense of motion. Van Der Zee captures in horizontal layers the UNIA assembly: the rank-and-file members who had purchased shares on the Black Star Line, the Black Cross Nurses who illuminate the image in their reflective white uniforms, and the African Legionnaires who anchor the space in front of the dais. He captures the leaders who sit erect in a row elevated above the front of the hall. Though in contention with one another, the leaders—variously dressed in scholarly robes and military uniform—echo Garvey's guises and presentations, suggesting at once a consistency of vision and the embrace of surrogacy. Van Der Zee's camera draws our eye to the empty chair at the center of the stage, draped with Garvey's professorial robes. The absent leader is the vanishing point in this Cartesian plane. With Garvey's presence marked only by an empty seat and Van Der Zee's presence known only by way of its afterimage, the photographer and the leader look at each other across the expanse of Harlem's black masses. As stereograph, Van Der Zee's mechanical precision and Garvey's mass movement come together. What comes into deep focus is hope.

2

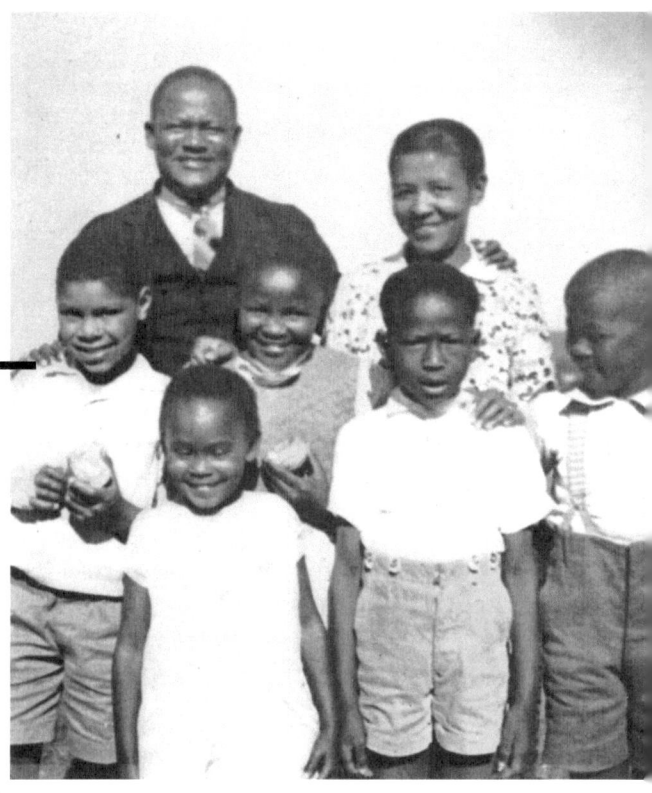

TO FEEL
PERFECTLY
AT HOME

ESLANDA ROBESON'S
ETHNOGRAPHIC LENS

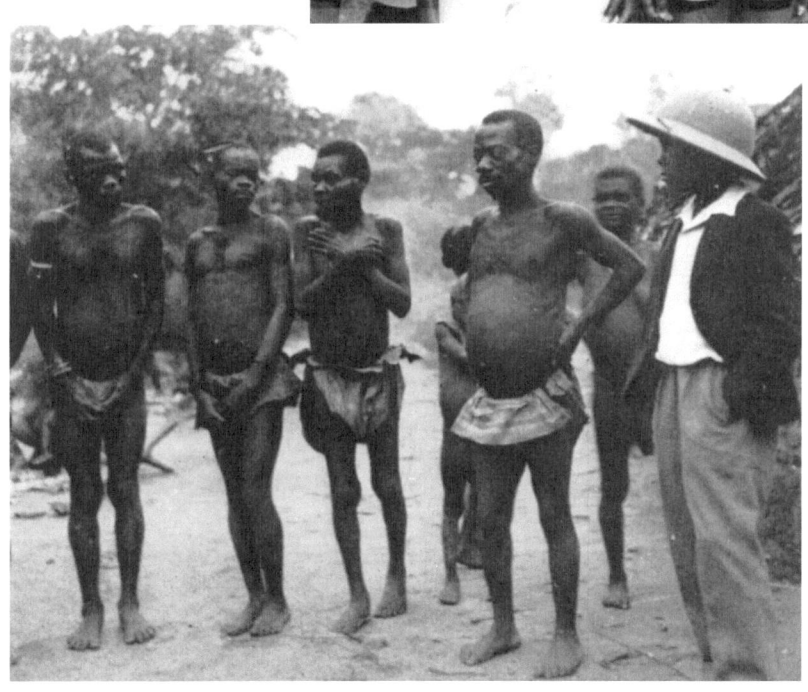

FIGURE 2.1. Eslanda Goode Robeson, photograph of Zach (Jack) Matthews, his wife, Frieda, and their four children with Paul Robeson Jr. From *African Journey*, folio 1. © Robeson Family Trust. Courtesy Robeson Family Trust.

FIGURE 2.2. Eslanda Goode Robeson, *Pauli with the Elders of Ngite*, 1936. From *African Journey* (1945). © Robeson Family Trust. Courtesy Robeson Family Trust.

My African trip was one of those grand dreams come true. It is certainly the most interesting thing I have done, and I will always be grateful for the opportunity. Its [*sic*] quite a different world, and I think every Negro who can, should go and look and listen and learn. We have a grand heritage from Africa, as a race, and it is shameful that we are not interested in it, and almost wholly ignorant of it.—ESLANDA GOODE ROBESON, letter to Harold Hackman, October 6, 1936

Pauli is enthralled.
—ESLANDA GOODE ROBESON, *African Journey* (1945)

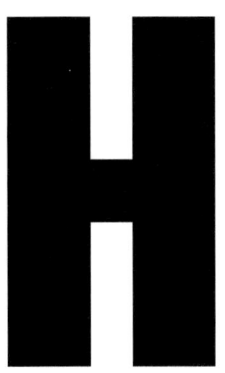

Here are two photographs we might loosely call "family portraits" (figures 2.1 and 2.2). Both were made by Eslanda Goode Robeson in 1936 during her three-month tour of South Africa, Uganda, and the Belgian Congo, as she was working toward a PhD in anthropology at the London School of Economics (LSE) and taking a pause from managing the career of her husband, the celebrated singer, actor, and activist Paul Robeson. Both photographs later appeared in Goode Robeson's published travel memoir *African Journey* (1945), drawn from her handwritten diary and ethnographic field notes from this earlier trip, the first of three she would make to the African continent during her lifetime. Both photographs present people of African descent in full or near-full body, facing the camera directly. In this context, what I seem to be describing are ethnographic images. Still, I want to call them family portraits because both photographs feature groups of people variously related by blood, by tribe, by filiation, by curiosity, and by proximity. More specifically, we might call them family portraits because they both include the photographer's eight-year-old son, Paul Robeson Jr., affectionately called "Pauli" by his parents.

In the first photograph Paul Jr. appears with Zach Matthews, his wife, Frieda, and their four children (figure 2.1). The Robesons stayed with the Matthews off and on in the last week of June 1936, at the Matthews's home on the campus of Fort Hare Missionary College in Alice, a small town in the Eastern Cape Province of South Africa, almost 150 miles northeast of Port Elizabeth. Zach, whom Eslanda had met in courses at LSE, was now a teacher of "Bantu Studies" in Alice. In the photograph, Paul Jr. (at far left) stands in line with the Matthews's three oldest children. Paul Jr. wears a button-down, short-sleeved, white shirt and khaki shorts, just like the two other boys. At the same height, Paul Jr. and the Matthews's older daughter stand side by side, with matching smiles and each holding half of a piece of fruit in their left hands. Their bodies squarely framed by Zach's shoulders, Paul Jr. and the girl twin each other. Similarly, Paul Jr.'s facial angle echoes that of Frieda as they both smile for Robeson's camera. Zach's right hand rests on Paul Jr.'s shoulder, his left hand appears on Frieda's shoulder. Frieda's hands rest on the shoulders of two of her children. With the photograph creating a series of circles, of visual rhyming patterns, Paul Jr. is successfully enfolded into the Matthews family (figure 2.3).

Eslanda made the second photograph on August 6, 1936, in Ngite, a Pygmy village and popular tourist site in the Ituri Forest of the Belgian Congo (figure 2.2). In this image, Paul Jr. stands to the far right side of the frame, which centers a group of village elders. The child and the village elders are all about the same height, probably around "four feet seven inches," which Eslanda notes as the "average" height of the village men.[1] They each occupy the same visual plane. According to Eslanda, "Pauli" and the "Headman of Ngite" regarded each other with curiosity, finding connection by way of their similar sizes but searching for clues about difference in age.[2] By photographing a dark-skinned child with a serious countenance and in adult-style clothing, Eslanda effects a contrast to popular safari photographs of the time: full grown white men and women visitors to Ngite, where towering whiteness emphasized dissimilarity, worked to ridicule the Pygmies and bolstered arguments for the fundamental distinctions (read: hierarchies) between races.[3] Yet Paul Jr.'s pith helmet—a hat commonly worn by British officials in the tropics—and his hands thrust into his khaki pants mark him as foreign and highlight difference and distance. This distance is underscored by the gazes that Paul Jr. and the Ngite elder train on each other across the full plane of the image, rather than on the photographer. Indeed almost no one in this photograph seems to be looking in the same direc-

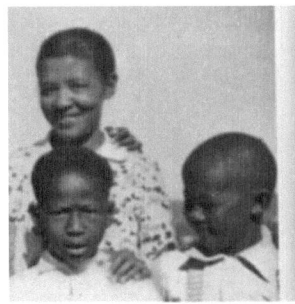

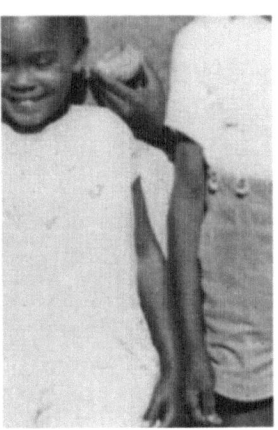

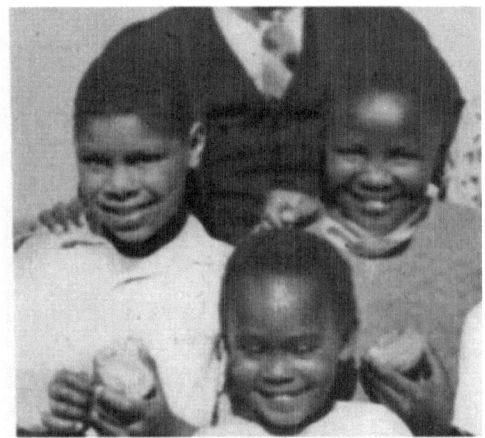

FIGURE 2.3. Three details of Eslanda Goode Robeson's photograph of Zach (Jack) Matthews, his wife, Frieda, and their four children with Paul Robeson Jr. (figure 2.1). From *African Journey*, folio 1, details. © Robeson Family Trust. Courtesy Robeson Family Trust.

tion (and one person in the background is a moving blur). In the photograph with the Matthews family, Paul Jr.'s inclusion draws fictive, though still heart-felt, bonds of kinship between the African American Robesons and the Bantu Matthews, visually reconnecting the Black family broken by and scattered in diaspora. Conversely, the Ngite photograph is an image of first encounter (albeit full of respect and curiosity), rather than established connection. Paul Jr. and the Ngite people are all here in this photograph, we might say, but they are not together.[4]

Taken together, these two photographs featuring Paul Jr. made on a trip that was at once research and tourist excursion impel me to ask what exactly is the distance between family portraiture (of beloveds and blood ties) and ethno-graphic photography (of others and objects of study)? And in an era of colonial entrenchment, what distinguishes a colonial image, by which I mean an image in service to imperial projects, from an image made in the context of colonialism, that is, an image made in a historical moment not under conditions of its own choosing? Is it the photographer's selection of subject, their choice of framing, their orchestration of the scene, or the absence of direction altogether? Is the difference found in the photographed person's gaze, pose, or posture, whether an imagined insistence on self-fashioning or tense stasis?[5] Is the difference in the conditions of collaboration, that is, how these two or more people found themselves facing one another, at once separated and joined by a camera? Does the distinction lie in the terms of their exchange? Perhaps we parse the difference in the captioning of the photograph, the language of description that draws attention to a type, a landscape, a natural order, or an individual with a name and perhaps a story? Or perhaps the contrast between family portraiture and ethnographic photography, and between photographs *of* versus photographs *for* colonialism, is in their circulation and usage—books or postcards or government reports or family albums. But if, say, a single photograph for a single archive functions in all of these ways, well, that means these distinctions are never stable and always in motion.

This chapter explores the wide-ranging, sometimes contradictory role photography played in elaborating Eslanda Robeson's anthropological vision and political platform as expressed in *African Journey*. I ask, How did Eslanda Robeson *see* Africa, in and as image and text? How did Robeson's deployment of the camera navigate—that is, variously express, refuse, or fabulate—the expectations and conventions of these genres to present colonized Africa to her audiences not merely as homeland but homeplace? Moreover, what forms of diasporic identification and belonging might have been nurtured through the presence of her son Paul Jr. as a photographic subject, himself a beloved curiosity and matter of study to his mother?

African Journey is an effusive, unconventional, and even undisciplined mix of ethnography, travelogue, family narrative, photography, and Pan-Africanist politics. Published by the John Day Company in 1945 (figure 2.4), *African Journey* presents an affirming understanding of Africa and its people from the unique vantage point of an African American woman, one perhaps best known for her marriage to Paul Robeson, one of the most famous and globally recognized men of the time. Of course Mrs. Robeson, or Essie as she was called by friends and family (and to whom I refer as Eslanda throughout this chapter), was also an anthropologist, the author of three nonfiction books (*African Journey* was her second), and a committed anticolonial and antiracist activist.[6] Thus the trip marked Eslanda's efforts to experience Africa firsthand, at once outside of and through the framework of dominant anthropology, and *African Journey*

FIGURE 2.4. Cover of the book *African Journey* (1945) by Eslanda Goode Robeson, identified also as "Mrs. Paul Robeson." © Robeson Family Trust. Courtesy Robeson Family Trust.

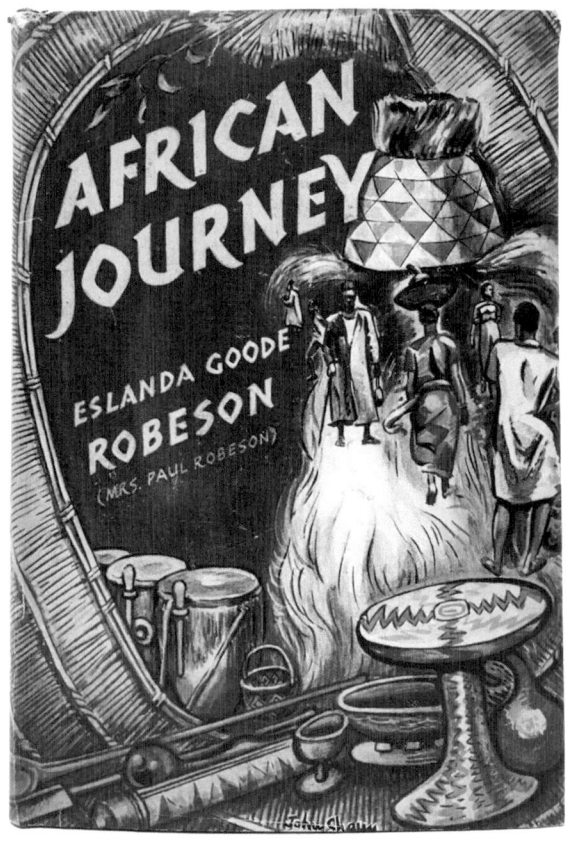

reflects a commitment to fostering political and cultural connections among Black diasporic subjects.

African Journey accomplishes this work not only through writing that is at turns elegant and assertive, droll and acerbic, but also through the proliferation of Goode Robeson's own photographs. The book is further distinguished by the presence of her son, Paul Jr., who plays a central role in the narrative and appears in nearly a quarter of *African Journey*'s sixty-six photographs. As one reviewer described the work: "Ostensibly the experiences of the wife of Paul Robeson on an African tour in 1936, this book develops a special interest far beyond that of the usual travel book because of the character of Pauli, the Robesons' small son. Then eight years old, Pauli is revealed as a percipient, charming boy whose mature observations and reactions to the unknown are perpetually satisfying."[7] Eslanda's own research trip is filtered in part through Pauli's eyes and experiences. Eslanda records Paul Jr.'s observations nearly as often as she records her own. This is their shared journey.

African Journey was well reviewed in Black and white US periodicals alike, and "the first printing was sold out on the day of publication."[8] Audiences responded favorably to the unconventional mix of intellectual fieldwork, political reconnaissance, and family vacation, set against the backdrop of brewing anticolonial struggles and Eslanda's increasingly sharpened Pan-African consciousness. Reviewers appreciated the book as a "starting point of real study" of Africa (*New York Herald-Tribune*), the book's assertion of "pride in . . . African origin" (*Pittsburgh Courier*), and its illumination of Africa as "a land in which people live who are like many all of us know" (*Amsterdam News*).[9] The great enthusiasm for *African Journey* among Black press reviewers, especially, suggests the hunger for real-time access to contemporary African people unmediated by Western racism and for routes to express pride in the "dark continent" and imagine a future for Africa beyond and after colonialism.

Through its mix of anthropology, travel narrative, and family photography, *African Journey* employs what we would now call "interdisciplinarity," an approach that disrupts the confining and backward-looking impulses of each of the three genres. By "backward-looking," I mean here a fixation with finding primitives, with romanticizing the past, with feverishly documenting and recording, and with pursuing the racial projects—anthropology, diaspora, and photography in the early twentieth century—that bound these together. Robeson writes against a dominant strain of academic anthropology, and of racial science more broadly, that understood racial hierarchies as the natural outcome of the arrested development of groups deemed culturally and biologically inferior. *African Journey* also does not fall prey to burgeoning Harlem Renaissance–era expressions of "diaspora" and "homeland" that embraced Africa solely as a site of cultural heritage and prelapsarian glory rather than as a living, breathing place in struggle and in formation.

In her experimentation with different registers of photography, ranging from individual and family portraiture, to still lives of everyday objects, to landscape, Robeson calls on the medium to push beyond its ability to record what theorist of photography Roland Barthes has called the "that-has-been," and seeks instead to document a diasporic encounter in the present.[10] For the most part, Robeson's photographs in *African Journey* refuse an anthropological imperative to photograph primitives, in this case Africans, as biological subjects whose bodies function as "visible signs" of transhistorical racial essences. Her images wrestle as well with a tendency to photograph other cultures "in the past," in a fixed timeless but not present place.[11] Similarly, by focusing her camera on modern technology and Western dress as well as traditional tribal artifacts—and by including herself and Paul Jr. within her African frames—Robeson resists African American ideas about their "eternal bond" to an unchanging Africa that "is always there."[12] If we may follow literary scholar Kenneth W. Warren, rather than "mak[ing] coincident only an African past to an African American present," Robeson's photographs open space to consider "the relationship of Africans to black Americans" in the real time of 1936 and 1945.[13]

It is the presence of Paul Jr. as traveling companion, interlocutor, photographic subject, and ward that brings the genre-crossing work of *African Journey* into focus, both its achievements and its limitations. Paul Robeson Jr. was born in Brooklyn, New York, in 1927, and for the first decade of his life lived primarily in England and Moscow, attending elite schools and largely isolated from other Black children. For much of his life up to the moment of this trip, Paul Jr. had been looked after primarily by Eslanda's mother, Ma Goode, while Eslanda traveled with her husband and managed his business affairs. Eslanda often expressed enormous guilt about her extended absences as a mother. She did, however, have very clear ideas about how she wanted Paul Jr. to be raised and what kind of person she hoped he would become. She committed these ideas to paper in lengthy letters of instruction to her mother. In one letter, composed a little over a year before the Africa trip, Eslanda wrote that she wanted Paul Jr. to come to be as confident of his place in the world as she was of her own,

> to feel perfectly at home and at ease in any company . . . to consider myself a pretty swell human being, and to look for human beings everywhere, in any walk of life . . . to open up my mind and to think with it . . . to do impossible things . . . to be as good as I could . . . never to think I am being looked down upon. I unconsciously feel I'm top dog. That's the reason I am at home in any society. I want Paul to have that.[14]

Though not part of the original plan for this momentous trip—Paul Sr. had contractual obligations in London, thus Paul Jr. took his place—it would seem that taking Paul Jr. along on this journey fit neatly into Eslanda's broader vision for her son. "If some Africans on a film set open up a new world to the child, a trip to the heart of Africa itself will be a revelation. He will see millions of other brown and black people, he will see a black world, he will see a black continent."[15] By intertwining her narrative of Africa with the experiences of her son, a dark male child, Eslanda alerts us to the fierce urgency of her vision for the African continent now and in the future.

African Journey is structured as a day-by-day diary of Eslanda and Paul Jr.'s summer abroad. Over the course of three months, Robeson encountered a broad range of people. She shared meals, observed everyday activities, asked questions, and listened intently as they revealed their suffering and resistance, their dignity and degradation, their joys and fears. *African Journey* is bookended by Robeson's italicized assertions of African humanity. The book is dedicated to "*the brothers and sisters, who will know whom I mean.*" And the narrative's concluding paragraph is a single sentence: "*Africans are people.*" In a global political and cultural climate that dismissed African peoples as primitive and eminently exploitable, this contention bordered on the revolutionary. What lies in between the opening dedication to a self-selected family and the closing affirmation of African humanity are Robeson's descriptions of modern cities, ancient yet complex native lifestyles, and African locals both educated and worldly, and poor and dignified. Her hope for the book was that it would "take folks right out to Africa with me, talking all the way there and all the way back. So you could know the folks, hear them talk, and see what I saw."[16] Eslanda did not want to shy away from what she saw. Nor did she want to embellish suffering. Rather, she chose to look and write with political commitment and human solidarity, aware of her unique and privileged position.[17]

Leaving London on Friday, May 29, 1936, mother and son took the train, "[sitting] close together and [holding] hands all the way to Southampton"[18] (figures 2.5 and 2.6). There, on the southern coast of England, they boarded the steamship *Winchester Castle* on May 30 and traveled the full length of the African continent to Cape Town, South Africa. The passage from Southampton to Cape Town took two full weeks; they disembarked only once, on the island of Madeira, far off the coast of Morocco, for a day visit. They anchored in Table Bay early in the morning of June 15 and spent the next three weeks traveling through South Africa, hosted by numerous friends and acquaintances they had met in England, mostly through academic and activist circles, African and white alike. Eslanda and Paul Jr. visited African mission schools and colleges, saw the mines in Johannesburg, and toured townships and "reserves." Eslanda also attended the All-African National Convention in Bloemfontein, a gathering of four hundred delegates from all over South Africa organizing against new legislation aimed at further depriving the native populations of citizenship rights.[19]

On July 7, the Robesons boarded a train in Johannesburg for the coast of Mozambique where they took another ship to Mombasa, Kenya, stopping at Dar-es-Salaam and Zanzibar for a day each. From Mombasa, they traveled by

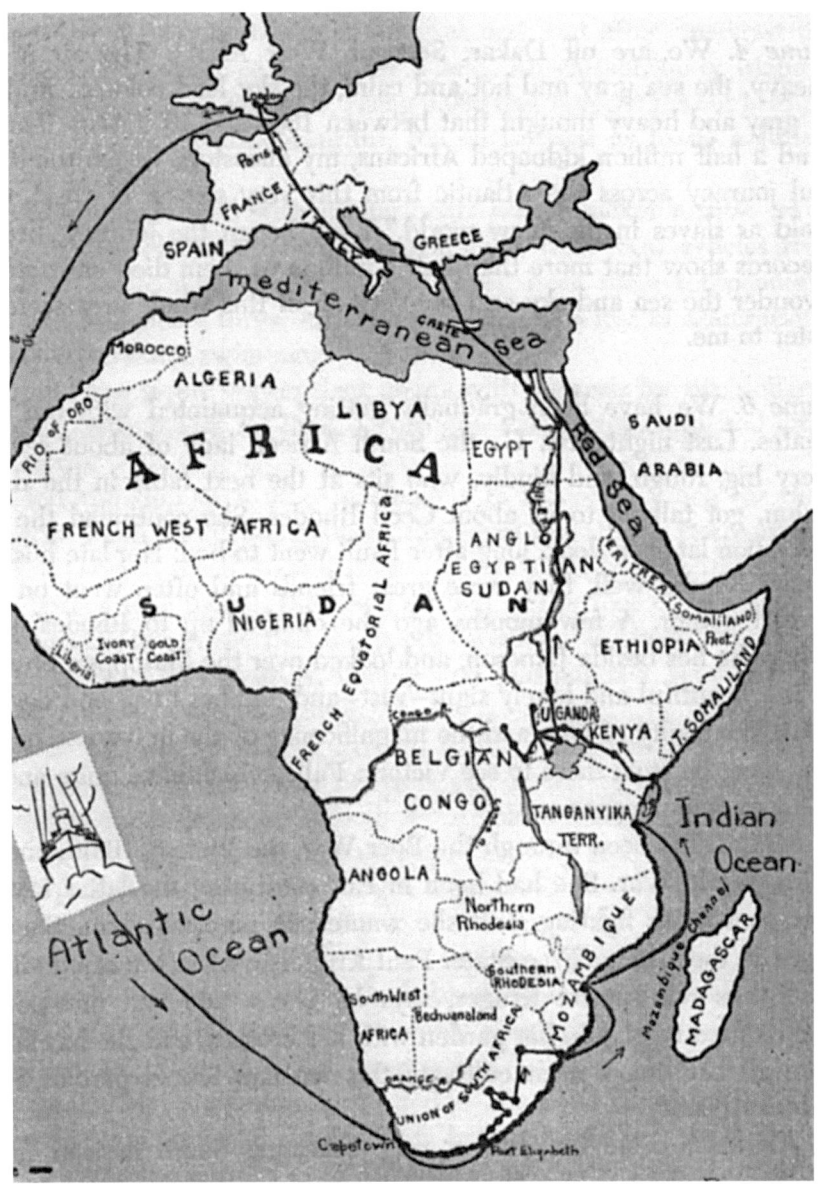

FIGURE 2.5. Full continent journey map, from *African Journey*. © Robeson Family Trust. Courtesy Robeson Family Trust.

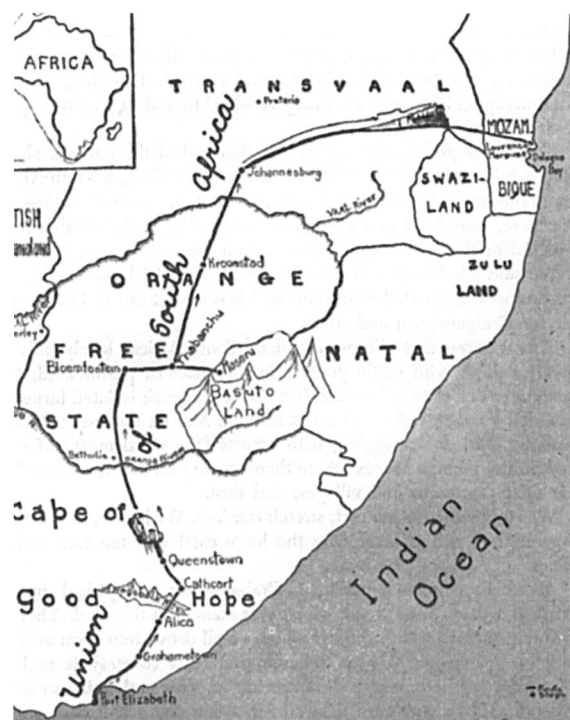

FIGURE 2.6. Southern Africa journey map, from *African Journey*. © Robeson Family Trust. Courtesy Robeson Family Trust.

train to Kampala, Uganda. There, they were fetched by their contact and friend Akiki Nyabongo, a fellow anthropologist Eslanda had met in England and also a cousin of the *mukama* (king) of Uganda's Tooro province. Nyabongo and his driving companion drove the Robesons to Kabarole, Tooro, where Eslanda conducted her "anthropological field work on cattle culture in Uganda" from July 19 through August 16. During their time in Uganda, they made a number of trips by car to visit each of the five Ugandan provinces, as well as venturing into the Belgian Congo to see the "Pygmy village" of the Ngite people (figure 2.7). Their time in Uganda drew to a close as Eslanda and Paul Jr. traveled to Entebbe, the seat of the colonial government at the time, where they dined as guests of the British governor. The next day, the colonial official insisted that they take his government car to the airport. The final journey home to London by airplane, seaplane, and train took them across Sudan and the Nubian Desert to Luxor and Alexandria, then "Crete, Athens, Brindisi, Paris, London. All a dream and a nightmare," writes Eslanda, "because I was ill."[20] When they arrived in London on August 25, Eslanda was taken off the airplane on a stretcher and removed immediately to the hospital but recovered relatively quickly.[21]

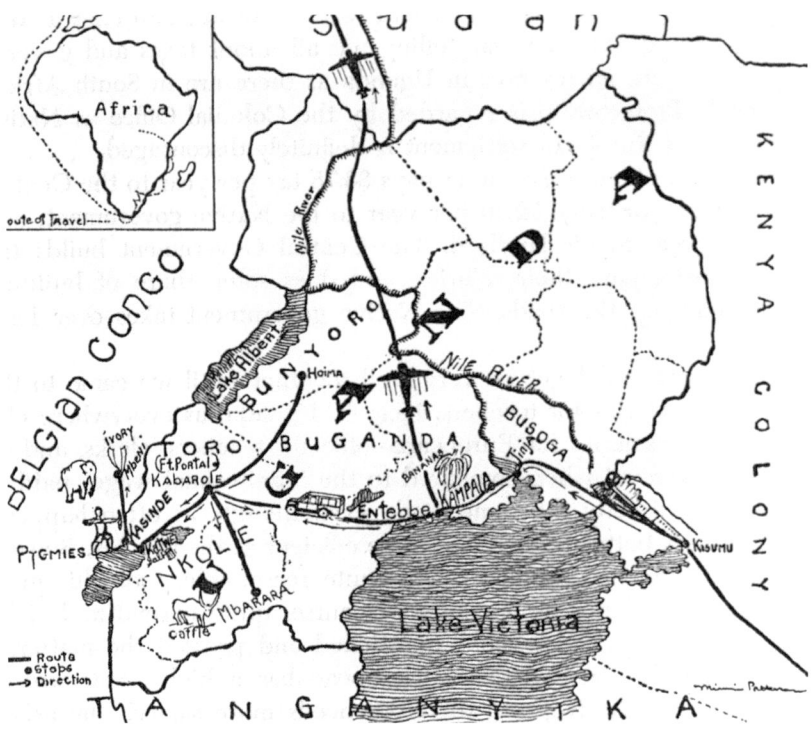

FIGURE 2.7. Uganda and Belgian Congo journey map, from *African Journey*.
© Robeson Family Trust. Courtesy Robeson Family Trust.

This was an ambitious trip to be sure—a trans-African Grand Tour. The challenges of traveling through Africa during this time were made more difficult because Eslanda was a Black American and a woman with her only child. The challenges began before they even departed as Eslanda faced difficulty securing visas. "It seems if you are a Negro, you can't just make up your mind to go to Africa, and just go," she writes. "Oh, no. Not unless you are a missionary. The white people in Africa do not want educated Negroes traveling around seeing how their brothers live; nor do they want those brothers seeing Negroes from other parts of the world, hearing how they live."[22] The British Colonial Office in London feared exactly the kinds of exchange that Eslanda was pursuing, contact not for the purposes of religious pacification ("the Gospel always helps to keep people quiet and resigned") but to better understand the structural conditions that beleaguer Black peoples globally. Eslanda finally got visas for Swaziland, Basutoland, Kenya, Uganda, and Egypt by brandishing her university credentials and describing her anthropology course of study. The visa for South Africa arrived after Eslanda and Paul Jr.'s departure.

Some of these challenges were offset by the privilege they enjoyed as the wife and child of one of the most internationally recognized and beloved Black men of the moment, and by the social and political connections such status afforded them. However, while these perks certainly eased Eslanda and Paul Jr.'s journey, they by no means prevented physical illness or racist encounters, nor did the pair's status ensure safe passage or accommodation. For example, on their visit to Mbeni in the Belgian Congo, Eslanda, Paul Jr., and their traveling party were initially denied rooms at a Belgian-owned hotel. "After considerable pressure from our D.C. [district commissioner], and a lot of '*distingue*' and 'important' on his part against the '*noir, noir,*'" the owner relented and escorted the group to what Eslanda described as rooms "scarcely fit for animals." Paul Jr. recognized this as a pyrrhic victory and remarked, "This is what we get when we are black and important. Wonder what we'd get if we were unimportant."[23] We might understand Eslanda as navigating the bounds of her own mobility: traveling as a free Black person to South Africa where "natives" could not move without official papers, journeying as an American of means on roads traversed by desperately impoverished displaced Africans, or entering spaces designated for men only as a woman, who still often required the intervention of colonial officials or "big men."

Anthropology

If the Robeson name somewhat eased the journey through Africa, it was the field of anthropology that provided Eslanda a route into the African continent. While this entrée may seem strange, the approach was born of Robeson's own political disposition and "New Negro consciousness," with its attention to understanding African American culture's connections to Africa. Further, the New Negro movement had a vibrant and active wing in the social sciences (built by the likes of W. E. B. Du Bois, Charles Johnson, St. Clair Drake, and Horace Cayton). While the social sciences broadly offered African American intellectuals a framework for addressing "race problems," anthropology in particular presented "a way of documenting and celebrating their African heritage."[24] The field provided a certain critical distance and perspective while enabling its practitioners to travel to Black communities near and far. In this way, Black anthropologists across the diaspora, including Zora Neale Hurston, Arthur Fauset, Katherine Dunham, Jomo Kenyatta, and Eslanda Robeson, were able to study and experience both themselves and the breadth of Black cultures, while forging diasporic connections in an "objective" manner, "validated" by academic sciences.

Robeson's methodology was further nurtured by her training at LSE under Bronisław Malinowski. Malinowski, like Franz Boas in the United States, emphasized "cultural relativism," whereby, rather than studying cultures as representing stages in human evolution, anthropologists should approach each culture on its own terms; accordingly, through detailed ethnographies not only might "we" Westerners learn from "other" peoples, but investigators might be able to find patterns and draw connections across cultures.[25] Even more compelling, the anthropology program at LSE offered a rigorous course of study in African languages, history, culture, and geography. For her part, Robeson embraced anthropology for the real world encounters it enabled and relied on. Understanding the field as a form of "dynamic interpretation," Robeson described anthropology "as the study of man and his relation to his fellow man, and to his changing environment. Thus it includes the study of primitive man under primitive conditions, of modern man under modern conditions, of human relations, race relations, of education, of social institutions."[26] She recognized it as a field that encouraged one to truly engage human existence both synchronically and diachronically.

Robeson also recognized the limits of anthropology, particularly as it had been practiced by her (white male) predecessors. In Kabarole, Uganda, Eslanda asked her hosts directly "what they thought of visiting anthropologists, and how they liked being 'investigated.' They smiled and said they were vastly amused, and would often take the searching and impertinent questions as a game, giving the most teasing, joking, and fantastic answers they could think of." As one chief declared, "White people are not interested in us. They only want to take away our land and our cattle, and make us pay taxes. Why should we tell them our sacred history, and the details of our social organization?"[27] Such an admission invites readers to question some of anthropology's truth claims and underscores the discipline as helping to build European empires and as a "handmaiden of colonialism."[28] Simultaneously, Eslanda positions herself here as an insider, a foreigner but a diasporic subject, one who might be trusted with "tribal knowledge." She reveals the "hidden transcripts" of her Ugandan interlocutors, who possess a very clear understanding and critical analysis of their colonial subjugation.[29]

Her political identifications, coupled with her firsthand experiences, led Robeson to resist some of anthropology's claims. First, she flat-out rejected popular notions, alive and prevalent among her teachers and peers at LSE, that fixed African peoples as outside history and tied to an eternal premodern past. Her own experiences in the rich Black diasporic community of London, where she and Paul were active in the political, social, and cultural organization, the West African Students' Union, and regularly hosted African students and expatriates at their home, gave her firsthand knowledge to the contrary.[30] Eslanda's formal and informal meetings with natives in their homelands reveal a critical understanding of the ways colonial ideology fixed them as "primitives" unfit for self-governance. For example, in Kabarole, a gathering of "young, eager, and intelligent" schoolteachers ask Eslanda a range of questions about educational policy and opportunities for Black people in England and America, and they are excited to hear about successful integration efforts of nomadic tribes in the Soviet Union. In the course of the conversation, the group challenges the label of "backwardness" levied against them by the colonial government. "'What do they mean by this "backward"?' Before I could answer, or try to answer, a fellow teacher said: 'They mean people they have kept back, and continue to keep back.'"[31] "Backwardness" is a condition imposed by white colonizers rather than an organic state; "primitive" is a fiction Europeans tell themselves to assuage and justify hierarchy and inequity. Similarly, when meeting with a group of chiefs in Mbarara, the capital of the Nkole province of Uganda, Eslanda was "surprised and impressed" by their inquiries about the conditions of Indigenous peoples in the United States, "the Indians in America," alongside more expected questions about Negro life and politics in her country of birth.[32] Such conversations reveal Robeson's interlocutors as actively seeking information about antiracist struggles against settler colonialism globally and challenging the racial logics of those systems.

On a lighter note, *African Journey* highlights the here and now of her subjects by consistently noting their engagements with technology and the vitality of their cities. Eslanda gushes over host Dr. Alfred B. Xuma's "gorgeous new 1935 Buick, complete with balloon tires, shock absorbers, special springs, etc," which brought Eslanda and Paul Jr. from Sofiatown (as she spells it) in Johannesburg to Bloemfontein.[33] The lights of Johannesburg were "like Detroit"; Kampala, Uganda, was a "colorful town with good roads, shops, smart African police, markets, and handsome African women."[34] Orderly cities, flashy amenities, and up-to-date technologies offer evidence of modernity, especially when peopled (and patrolled) by Africans. And even if Black Africans are segregated and sequestered into certain parts of the city or country, they still traverse these spaces, working in homes and mines that constitute them as a modern proletariat.

Further, rather than taking the anthropological tack that the non-European other was different from the ("Western") researcher yet still worthy of scholarly interest, Robeson deemphasized difference and distance, highlighting instead similarity. This was a key tack in her descriptions of Kabarole, the capital of Tooro in southwestern Uganda and the site of her fieldwork. Here, she drew the lines of similarity through the category "women." Broadly, Eslanda came to study the herdspeople of this region, a connection made through Akiki Nyabongo, a student of anthropology at Oxford originally from Kabarole. Once arrived, Eslanda soon focused on "the herdswomen in the dairy." In working with them, she not only learned a lot about *bisahi*, "the handling of milk after it is collected from the cattle . . . [which] is women's business," but also about custom, tradition, home management, community gossip, general medical practice as "women's work," and "a great deal about the very important business of living." Eslanda also received and recorded the herdswomen's analysis of dwindling herds and diminished livelihood caused by the colonial government's vaccination of cattle, which caused a number of cattle to die. "We understand that needles are helpful for some diseases," Eslanda quotes the women collectively, ". . . but one must also study and understand the cattle."[35] Eslanda valued the women's cultural, political, and professional knowledge and understood them as a gendered proletariat.

Textually, Eslanda found commonality in the experiences of Black peoples under global white domination, in the analogous ways, for example, colonialism and Jim Crow segregation defined the textures of Black life in South Africa and the southern United States. For example, Eslanda notes that the network of safe houses developed by black travelers on the roads of southern Africa echo the informal systems throughout the US Deep South: "You are passed from friend to friend, from car to car, from home to home, often covering thousands of miles without enduring the inconveniences and humiliations of the incredibly bad Jim Crow train accommodations and lack of hotel facilities for Negroes." Likewise, she identifies the vibrancy of Black townships, segregated spaces cast off as dangerous slums but made into communities by their residents, rich and complex in their diversity. Friedasdoorp (also known as Ferreirascamp), the oldest township in Johannesburg, developed from a mining camp, was considered "the roughest section." But it reminded Eslanda "very much of Lenox Avenue in Harlem on a summer Sunday afternoon," full of people enjoying themselves and each other.[36] The promotion of likeness over difference also emerges where *African Journey* takes the form of travelogue rather than formal anthropological study: whereas the latter purports the objectivity of the social scientist, the former situates the writer-traveler at the center of the narrative.[37] *African Journey*'s form eschews the anthropological trope of the "ethnographic present," a literary device that wrote subjects of study in the present tense even as those descriptions might have been primitivist, freezing cultures in time such that the past is written *as* present.[38] Rather, through its attention to African modernity in highlighting Africans' engagement with colonial politics as well as emergent technology, *African Journey* claims Africa's and Africans' presence and *presentness*, over and against anthropology's tendency to place the continent and its peoples outside history.

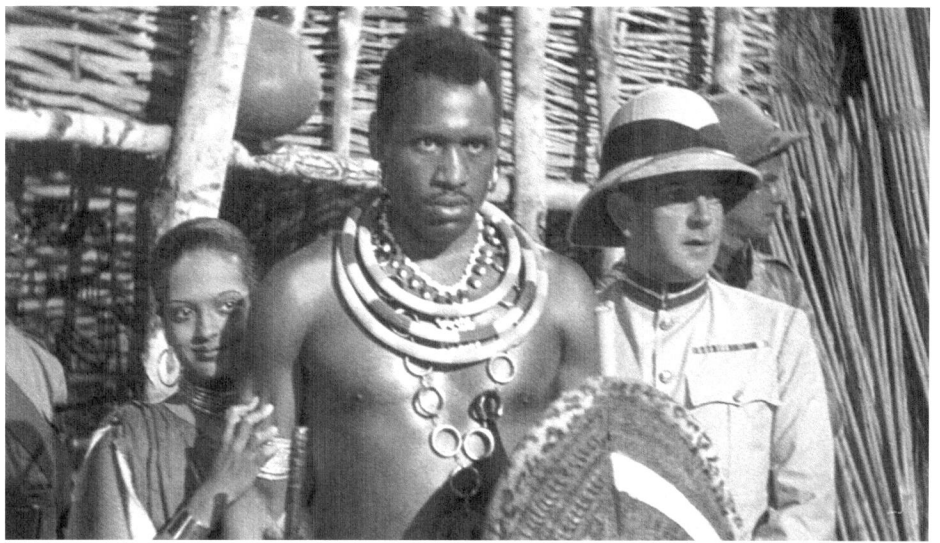

FIGURE 2.8. Nina Mae McKinney and Paul Robeson with Leslie Banks. Film still from *Sanders of the River*, Zoltan Korda, dir., 1935.

Photography

"I blush with shame," Eslanda reflected after her fulsome stay in Alice, "for the mental picture my fellow Negroes in America have of our African brothers: wild black savages in leopard skins, waving spears and eating raw meat. And we, with films like *Sanders of the River*, unwittingly helping to perpetuate this misconception. Well, there will be no sequel to *Sanders*!"[39] Eslanda was of course referring to the 1935 film that starred Paul Robeson as an animal skin–clad Nigerian chief who, with his wife (played by Nina Mae McKinney) at his side, loyally serves the British colonial regime (figure 2.8). Eslanda had negotiated a handsome contract for this film, to be produced in London, but could not secure the right to approve the final cut. The Robesons advocated for a movie that would portray African peoples in a more culturally complex manner, including an appearance by Eslanda's LSE classmate and future president of independent Kenya, Jomo Kenyatta, as an extra, as well as footage of dances and ceremonies filmed in Africa. However, in the ultimate edit of *Sanders of the River*, Africans remained simple background players to the colonizing white heroes. The film's degrading images and procolonial sentiment pained and embarrassed the Robesons (and opened them to criticism from Black leaders). Moving forward, both Paul and Eslanda became sensitive to their roles in future depictions of African and African-descended peoples.[40]

Sanders of the River was intended as a departure from 1930s "jungle films" like *King Kong* and the Tarzan series, as well as from popular expedition films like those of Martin and Osa Johnson and *Africa Speaks!* (1930), directed by Walter Futter (in which the director intentionally drove a local Masaai villager in front of a lion and included the footage of the villager's murder in the final cut of the film).[41] Even with Black protagonists, *Sanders*, like the other "jungle films" made in Britain, Europe, and the United States, relied heavily on the visual tropes of colonial photography. This archive, which includes all genres of photography—ethnographic photographs, postcards, cartes de visite, magazine illustrations, and the like—often featured fearsome scantily clad men and bare-chested women, posed at every angle in every form for study. Images were contextualized and framed by accompanying captions that quickened their meanings to legitimate imperial projects.[42] Anthropology, in particular, wielded "the camera like a measuring instrument," profoundly influencing the visual terrain of photographing Africa and its peoples in the colonial era(s), especially in the years prior to World War II.[43]

Yet, even as this archive offers a record of photography's alignment with colonialism, it remains vast and complicated and, as such, raises a number of challenges for contemporary study. On one hand, the study of ethnographic and other kinds of photography in, of, and adjacent to colonial projects must contend with the often tense relationship between the photographer (whether anthropologist, Western tourist, or colonial bureaucrat) and the Indigenous photographed persons; between the extractive work of the photographer as handmaiden of colonialism and the colonized nonsubjects attempting to navigate an uneven exchange; between the powerful and powerless, between white and nonwhite, between male scientist and female objects of often prurient study. On the other hand, scholars, artists, archivists, and curators have tried to pry open space for the range of relations and contingencies within these various photographic events, across collaborations from coerced to freely given. They have also sought to highlight engagements or stage encounters with these archives by unintended viewers, either in the moment of the image taking or in later moments after colonialism has ended and reasserted itself in other guises.[44]

Burdened by "Manichean opposition" (Garb) and strangled by a "flattening" "discursive grip" (Edwards), writers have called the colonial archive "tense," "vexing" (Campt), vacillating between "distance and desire," and marked by "ambivalence" (Hayes and Minkley). I take these calls and interventions as invitations to imagine what other stories can be told with this archive. Is the colonial story the only one available to us (Colard; Azoulay)?[45]

Given this terrain, what choices did Eslanda make as an anthropologist, a photographer, a Pan-Africanist, and a parent?

Eslanda's cultural politics become evident in the photographic work and practices of *African Journey*. Though somewhat new to photography and filmmaking—that is, as a camera operator—at the time of the trip, Eslanda brought a Cine-Kodak (16 mm) camera and a Rolleiflex twin-lens reflex camera gifted to her by Paul right before departure. "'You can't take too many pictures,' [Paul] said wisely."[46] Eslanda took this advice to heart and over the course of the trip made hundreds of photographs and some twenty reels of film.[47] Her camera work became integral to her fieldwork. According to biographer Jeanne Moutoussamy-Ashe, Eslanda "often used photographic note-taking methods to describe situations, especially at times when pencil and paper could not adequately describe her experience."[48]

With a wealth of both words and images, Eslanda took great pains while putting the book together in choosing the most evocative photographs for *African Journey*'s publication. The images cross genres: portraiture, ethnographic evidence, landscape, casual snapshot, family portrait. The trajectory of the photographs—not only from the beginning of the book to the end, but across the span of her stay in each successive location—suggest that Eslanda was learning her equipment and developing her eye as the trip progressed. The opening folios of *African Journey* (there are seven in all) feature many photographs taken from a distance and devoid of people. For example, photographs like "Typical Basuto village" and "Palace of Mukama of Toro [Tooro] at Kabarole" reflect an effort to take in as much of the scene as possible (figure 2.9). Panoramas such as "Basutos and Basuto house at Matsieng, typical of Basutoland" aim to present "a context of situation," as her teacher Malinowski endeavored to provide in his own anthropological photography.[49]

As *African Journey* progresses, and as Eslanda settles into a particular place and establishes a rapport with the people she's met, her camera gets closer and closer to her subjects. Some of these photographs reflect the parameters of her fieldwork, a study of "cattle culture in Uganda," and present careful visual categorizations that aim to catalog and index. But they also reflect her real enthusiasm for the beauty of everyday objects. For example, a series of photographs detailing "the making of banana wine [in] Kabarole" ends with a carefully framed image of a "wooden vessel for finished wine" (figure 2.10). At another home stay, Robeson woke early to "photograph . . . the 'old things' around the house." Similarly, Robeson's images of people also start out in an ethnographic vein (e.g., "A Pondo miner having his hair 'wrapped' in the compound at Robinson Deep [South Africa]") (figure 2.11) but work to produce insightful portraits in which her subjects smile back comfortably (figures 2.12 and 2.13).

When I first encountered this archive, and indeed in my first writings about Eslanda's photography, I thought I could see in the images themselves direct

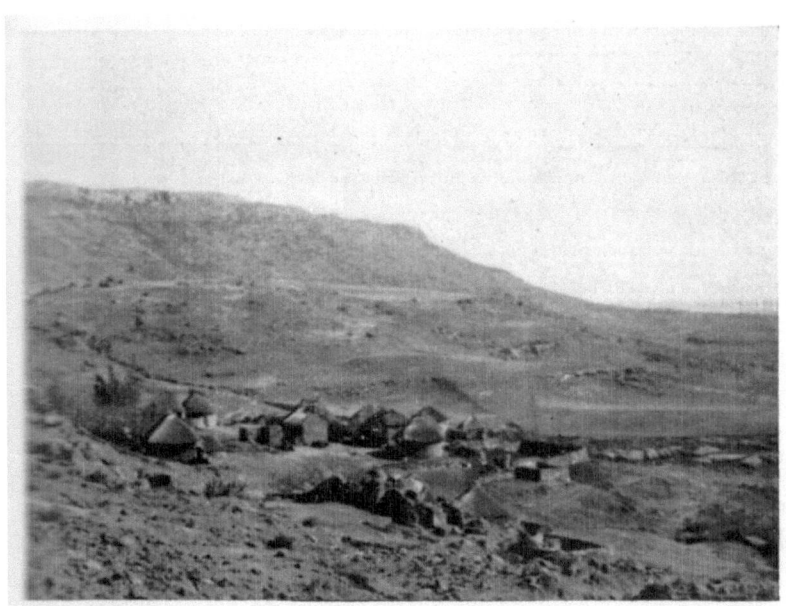

Typical Basuto village.

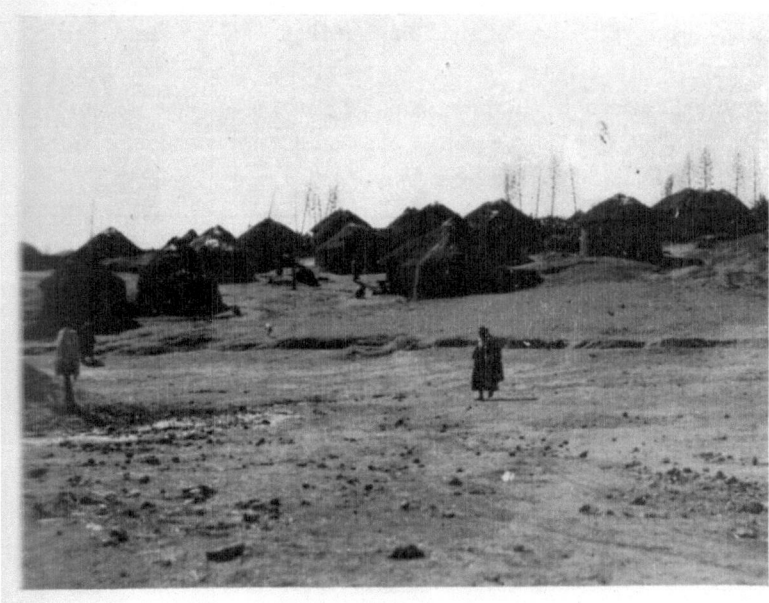

FIGURE 2.9. Eslanda Goode Robeson, "Typical Basuto village," from *African Journey*, folio 2. © Robeson Family Trust. Courtesy Robeson Family Trust.

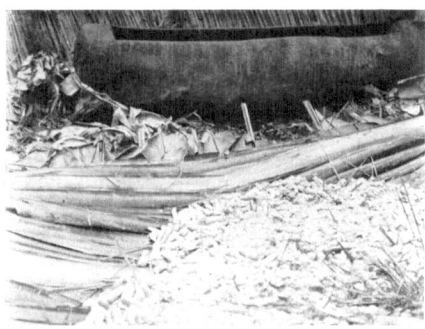

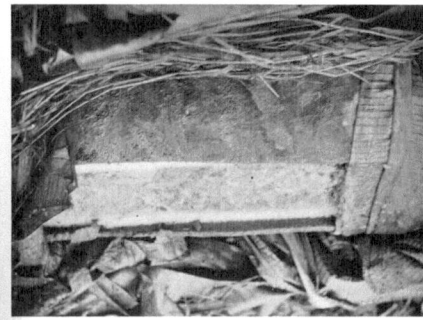

The making of banana wine, Kabarole.

Banana wine fermenting in trough. Below, wooden vessel for finished wine.

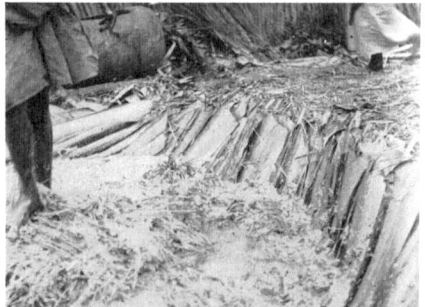

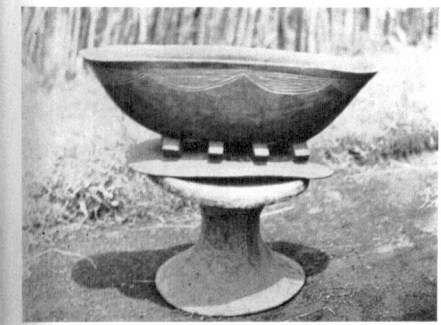

FIGURE 2.10. Eslanda Goode Robeson, (*left*) "The making of banana wine, Kabarole"; (*right*) "Banana wine fermenting in trough. Below, wooden vessel for finished wine." From *African Journey*, folio 5. © Robeson Family Trust. Courtesy Robeson Family Trust.

counters to the colonial project. She certainly does not traffic in the most outrageous kinds of colonial photographic tropes. For example, in her treatment of women, Eslanda practices a modest gaze (figure 2.14). Women almost always appear clothed, in contrast to the majority of photographs, postcards, films, and other visual ephemera that has constructed native African women as savage and sexually available through visually equating nudity with lewdness (figure 2.15). Such framing might suggest a "politics of respectability" whereby Eslanda imagines that a way to "elevate" African women in the eyes of American and European audiences is to visualize them as modestly and chastely as possible. (She may also have made these choices because this trip took place during winter in the Southern Hemisphere, thus requiring more layers of clothing for warmth.) But we might also understand these photographs, like many others (e.g., "The schoolteachers of the district come to see us at our home in Kabarole"; "Some

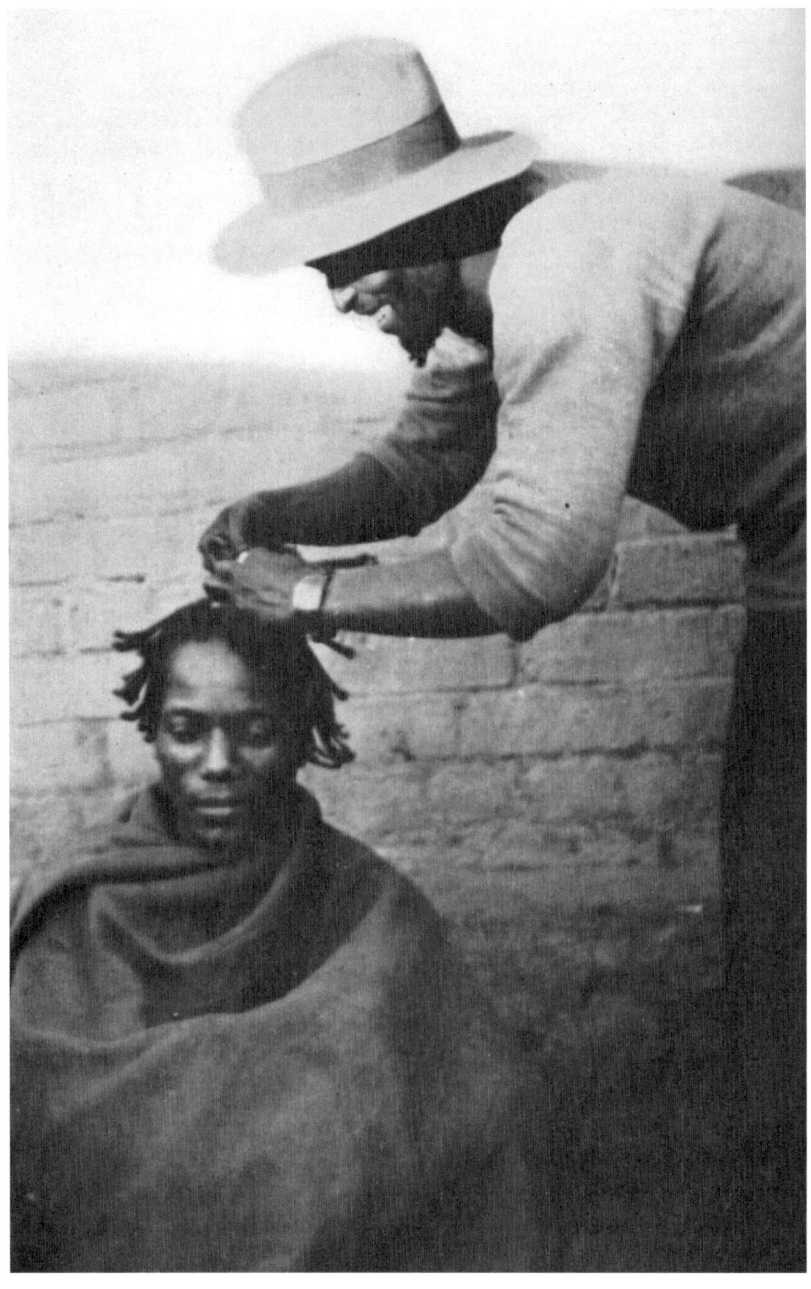

FIGURE 2.11. Eslanda Goode Robeson, "A Pondo miner having his hair 'wrapped' in the compound at Robinson Deep." From *African Journey*, folio 3. © Robeson Family Trust. Courtesy Robeson Family Trust.

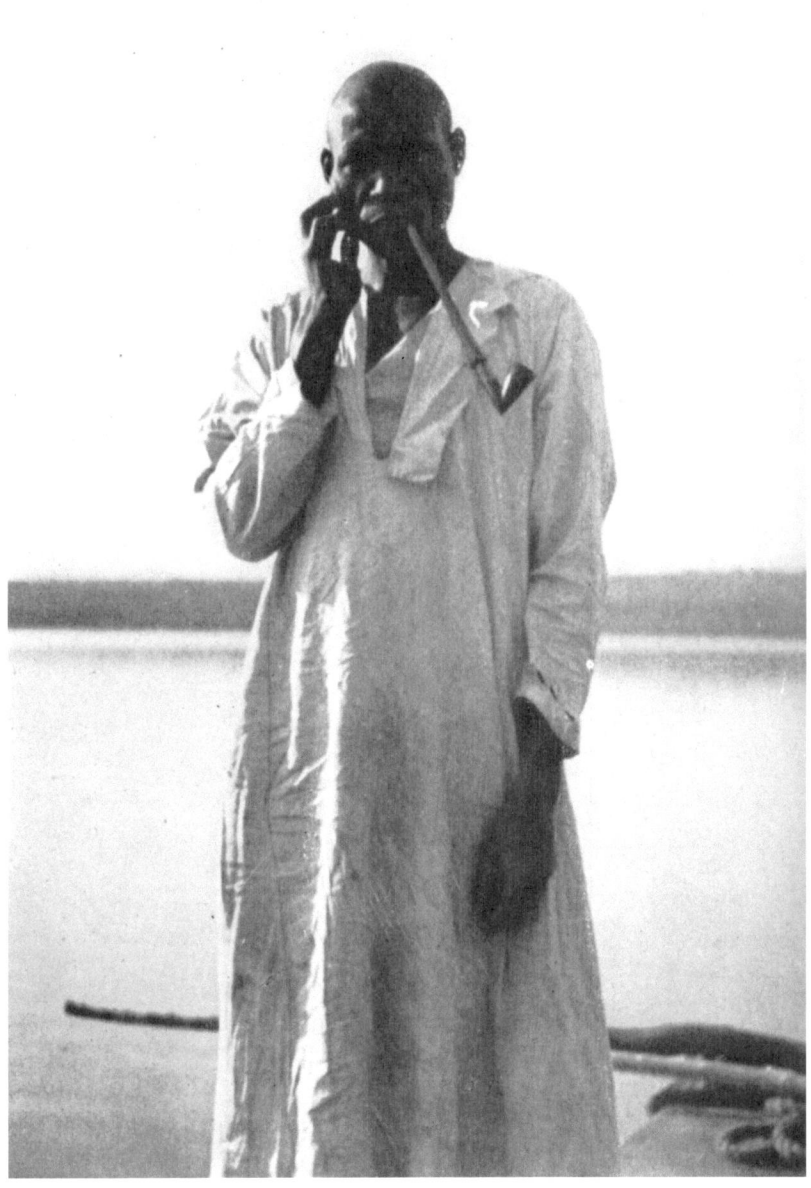

FIGURE 2.12. Eslanda Goode Robeson, "Passenger on Nkole ferry." From *African Journey*, folio 7. © Robeson Family Trust. Courtesy Robeson Family Trust.

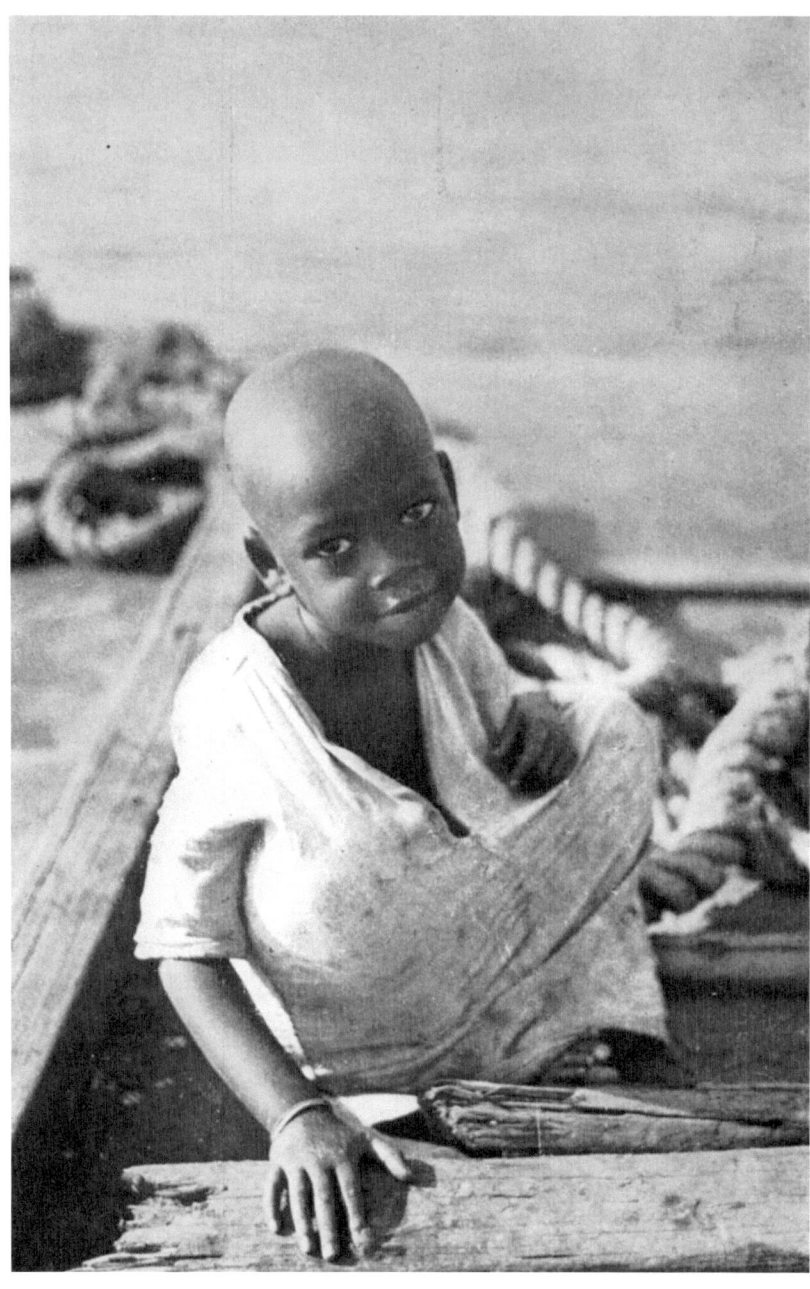

FIGURE 2.13. Eslanda Goode Robeson, "Passenger on Nkole ferry." From *African Journey*, folio 7. © Robeson Family Trust. Courtesy Robeson Family Trust.

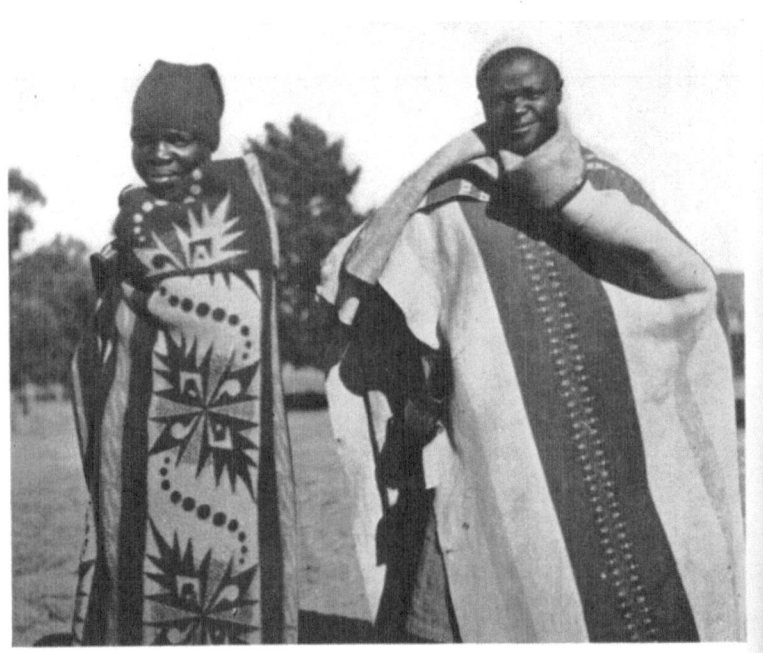

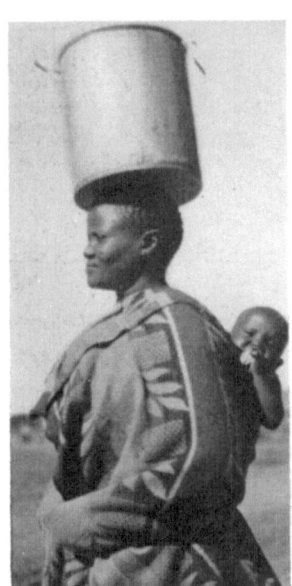

Basutos at Maseru, Basutoland.

FIGURE 2.14. Eslanda Goode Robeson, "Basutos at Masero, Basutoland." From *African Journey*, folio 2. © Robeson Family Trust. Courtesy Robeson Family Trust.

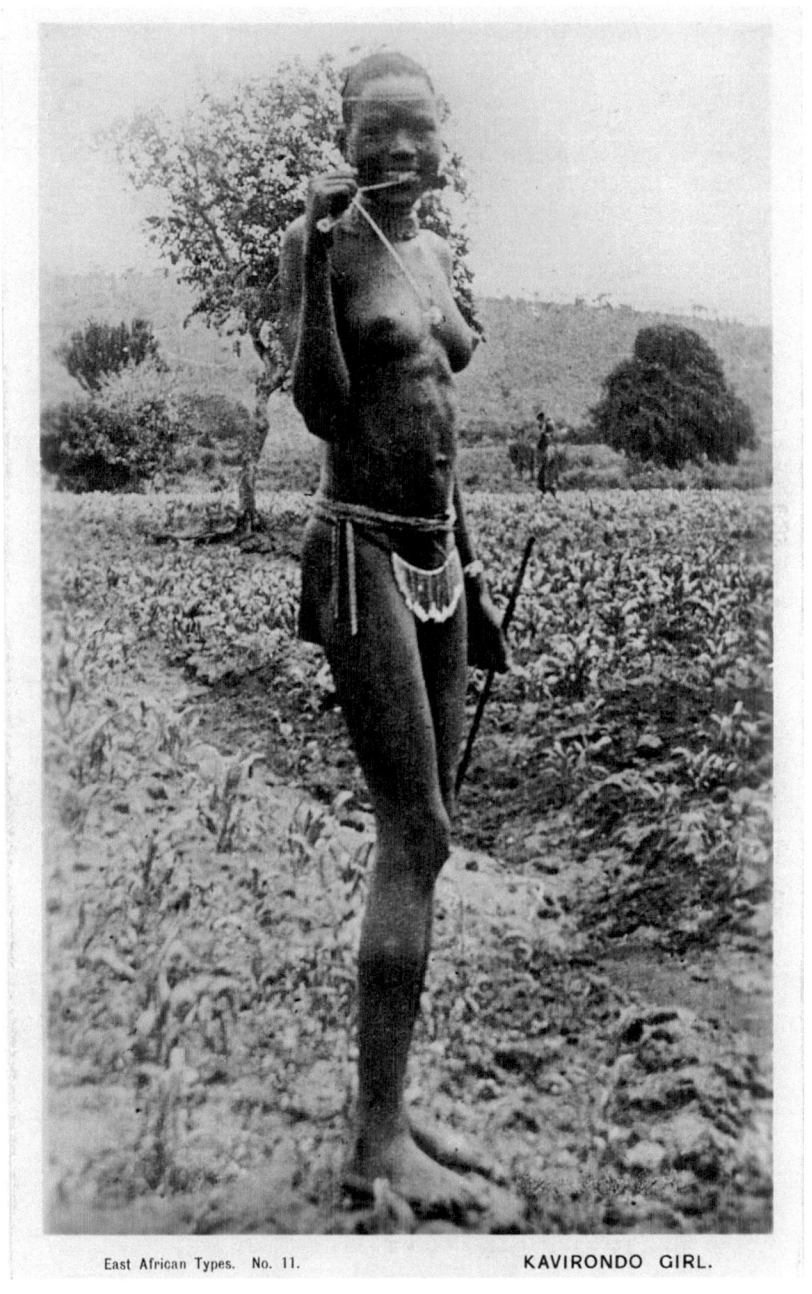

East African Types. No. 11. KAVIRONDO GIRL.

FIGURE 2.15. "East African Types, No. 11, Kavirondo Girl." Postcard collected by Eslanda Goode Robeson, mailed to Carl and Fania Van Vechten, ca. 1936. James Weldon Johnson Memorial Collection in the Yale Collection of American Literature, Beinecke Rare Book and Manuscript Library. © Robeson Family Trust. Courtesy Robeson Family Trust.

members of the Nkole family who visited us at Kabarole to persuade us to come and see their country"), as reflecting relationality and exchange, the encounters that were at the heart of this trip.

Robeson photographs many of her African subjects in a manner that directly counters visions of empire and Hollywood sensationalism that sought the primitive and the iconic, the authentic and the timeless.[50] In contrast, Robeson's photographs feature weddings, schools, and people in combinations of Western and traditional local dress. In these images, especially favoring the poses of portraiture over the surveying gaze of ethnography, Africans emerge as modern individuals, navigating both precolonial histories and colonial exigencies.

Robeson does not take camera work lightly. Throughout the text, she reveals that she is highly sensitive to the ways the camera as an anthropological tool can lay bare the unevenness in the relationship not only between anthropologist and her subjects but also, and more important for the political commitments of the project, between Black American and Black African. Robeson repeatedly asks permission to pull out her camera and take photographs—whether of people, objects, or workspaces—and waits until she has established a rapport: "I never bring [my camera] out unless I am sure no one will mind."[51] And she often offers something in return, whether photographs staged by the sitters themselves, as she did at the behest of the house staff in Kabarole, or simply money, as in the case of the Maseru in Basutoland in South Africa when Robeson paid the hospital fees of those folks she photographed outside the dispensary (clinic).[52]

In each of these ways, Robeson describes and practices photography as part of a diasporic civil contract in which photography is a tool that emphasizes mutual recognition between African diasporic subjects. Here, I am borrowing Ariella Aïsha Azoulay's compelling concept of "the civil contract of photography," in which Azoulay encourages us to envision the role of photographic spectatorship as one of "civic duty," specifically in the case of images of the abused, the violated, the dispossessed.[53] As Azoulay writes, "The nation-state (re)territorializes citizenship. . . . Photography, on the other hand, deterritorializes citizenship, reaching beyond its conventional borders and plotting out a political space in which the plurality of speech and action . . . is actualized permanently by the eventual participation of all the governed. These governed are *equally* not governed within this space of photography where no sovereign power exists."[54] In Azoulay's formulation, the civil contract of photography reinvigorates the radical political and liberatory potential of the medium of photography.

One aspect of this political relation appears when we recall that the photograph is not merely the product of a technology but also evidence of a set of relations. In the case of Robeson's African images, the photographs record an encounter between two (differently) marginalized people, the photographer and the photographed, who have shared a space and a time. In the making of the image, the "partner-participants" enter into a contract with each other and also with the users (later viewers) of the photograph, a contract in which we all agree to speak to, of, and on behalf of the image and its subjects. The photograph, then, is never simply a record of the past but, in its ability to travel physical and temporal distances, is persistently extending viewing communities and reminding us that the "effect" and "meaning" of any photograph is never "sealed off" or determined in the final analysis. Photography's work is always in the present, in the here and now.[55]

Diaspora

We might understand Robeson's commitment to photography as pronouncing her a "citizen in the citizenry of photography[, which] entails seeking, by means of photography, to rehabilitate one's citizenship or that of someone else who has been stripped of it."[56] This disposition is underscored by the presence of Paul Jr. throughout the photographs, her young son who, like Africa, she wants the world to see on his own terms. Robeson's usage of photography in *African Journey* draws on, and blurs the line between, ethnographic photography and family snapshots; a desire to note the familiar unknowingly slips into recording the familial. If anthropological photography finds pleasure in difference, family snapshots locate joy in sameness, in the filial and the familiar. In her dedication to "the brothers and sisters," Robeson is clearly hailing Africans as family and locating her Pan-Africanist political vision in the space of kinship. Paul Jr.'s presence in both text and image, bring this conjuncture into sharp relief.

Photography scholar Marianne Hirsch asserts that the camera functions as "the family's primary instrument of self-knowledge and self-representation . . . the primary means by which the family story is told."[57] In the Matthews family photograph described at the start of this chapter (figure 2.1), as well as in the three other family portraits in which Paul Jr. is featured, we might consider Eslanda Robeson as attempting to tell a new "family story," of "Africa, 'my old country,' my background, my people, and thus about myself."[58] Paul Jr. serves as the link between Africa as anthropological research site and Africa as ancestral homeland. Paul Jr.'s presence also works to diminish the "intrinsic distance" between the Western observer occupying modernity and the "authentic African" fixed in a "backward" past. In doing so, Robeson asserts the "here" and "now" of African peoples, the urgency and exigency of African struggles in real time, a new "truth" and "authenticity" of African subjects.

Familial looking, however, can be deceptive and divisive. The identifications such imagery engenders, as Hirsch reminds us, "can be too easy . . . and can also draw . . . lines of exclusion and disidentification." These problematics also become clear in Eslanda's photos of Paul Jr. As one African woman proclaims of Paul Jr. on their trip, "That boy belongs to us—see his mouth, eyes, nose, the shape of head—pure African. Oh yes, that boy belongs to Africa, to us."[59] But, as Eslanda stresses, the Pygmies are from another time and another place. She quotes white American author Grace Flandrau's description of the Pygmies as "not Negro," and Eslanda further describes them as having "an oriental cast." In the Ngite village photograph, Paul Jr.'s Western clothing and his place at the edge of the frame alert us to a series of questions about *African Journey* and Eslanda Robeson's documentary project.

Indeed, the Ngite photograph has always sat uncomfortably with me and forced me to look a bit more closely at those photographs that seemed to suggest mutuality, to assert a distinct "Pan-African gaze" over a colonial one. Yet, in attempting a Black American photographic practice that aims to be a visual counternarrative that reframes global Black subjectivity, could such a Pan-African gaze also reinscribe hierarchies of power in looking and the unevenness of looking relations between differently positioned diasporic subjects, and if so, how?

Take, for example, the number of Eslanda's photographs that repeat colonial image tropes. She was no doubt familiar with the cliché poses, framings, and descriptive language through her anthropological research, as well as through the circulation of cartes de visite and postcards, some of which she herself purchased and mailed to friends and family. Mother and child images and images depicting hair braiding appear frequently in the colonial archive, and such images are included in Eslanda's archive. Or consider who receives the courtesy of naming in her captions and who does not. Or, what about Eslanda's use of "typical," a word that reduces individuals to types and squeezes complex peoples into neat boxes?

While I no longer feel certain that we can see in Eslanda's images an unequivocal colonial counterarchive, I also no longer believe that such an archive exists, so entangled are the accumulations of meanings and uses of these images, and as Zoé Samudzi reminds us, so "un-decolonizable" is the camera itself.[60] I do argue, though, that Eslanda strove within and against the colonial image archive as she encountered it to find a mode of communication for her personal and political commitments.

Here are an image and its verso, a postcard Eslanda purchased in the middle of her trip to send to her dear friends Carl and Fania Van Vechten in New York City (figures 2.16 and 2.17). The slightly sepia-toned photograph on the

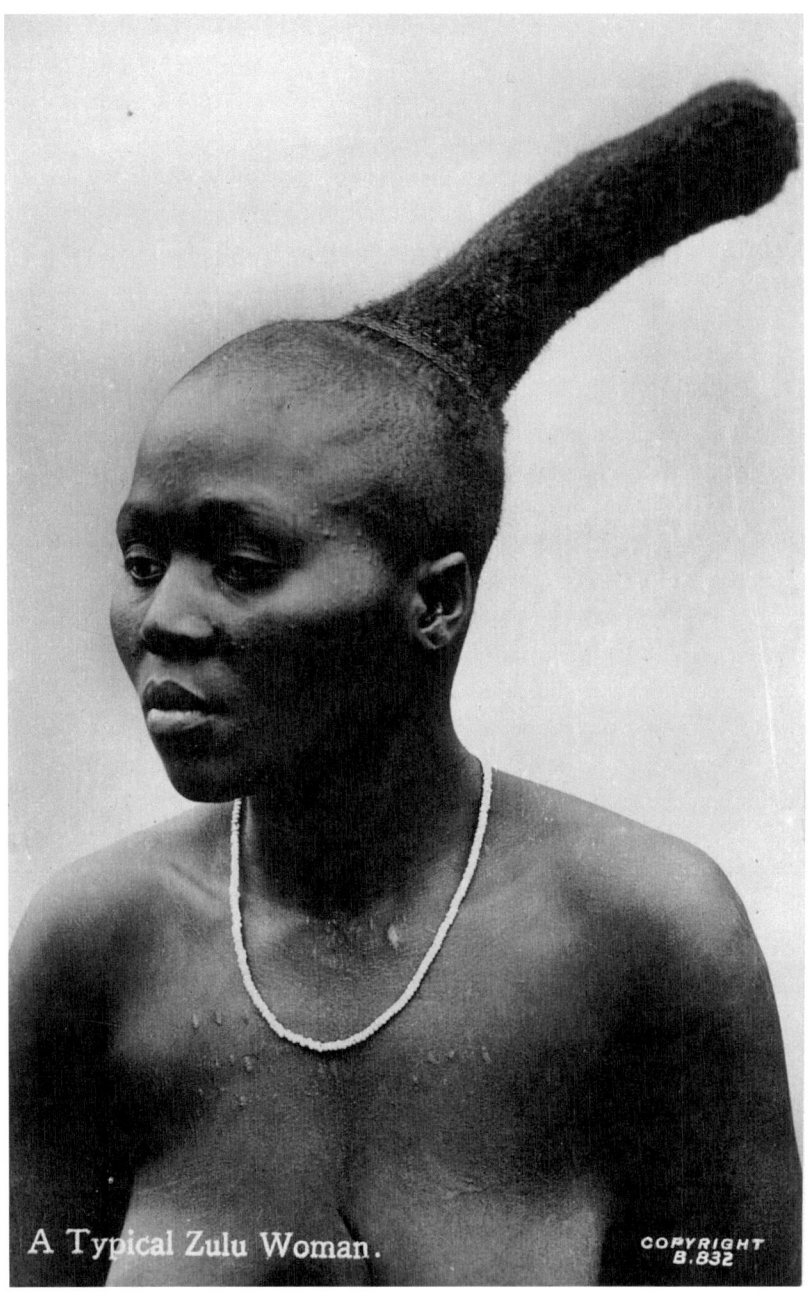

A Typical Zulu Woman.

COPYRIGHT
B.832

FIGURE 2.16. "A Typical Zulu Woman." Postcard (front) sent by Eslanda Goode Robeson to Carl and Fania Van Vechten, July 4, 1936. Robeson Correspondence, James Weldon Johnson Memorial Collection in the Yale Collection of American Literature, Beinecke Rare Book and Manuscript Library. © Robeson Family Trust. Courtesy Robeson Family Trust.

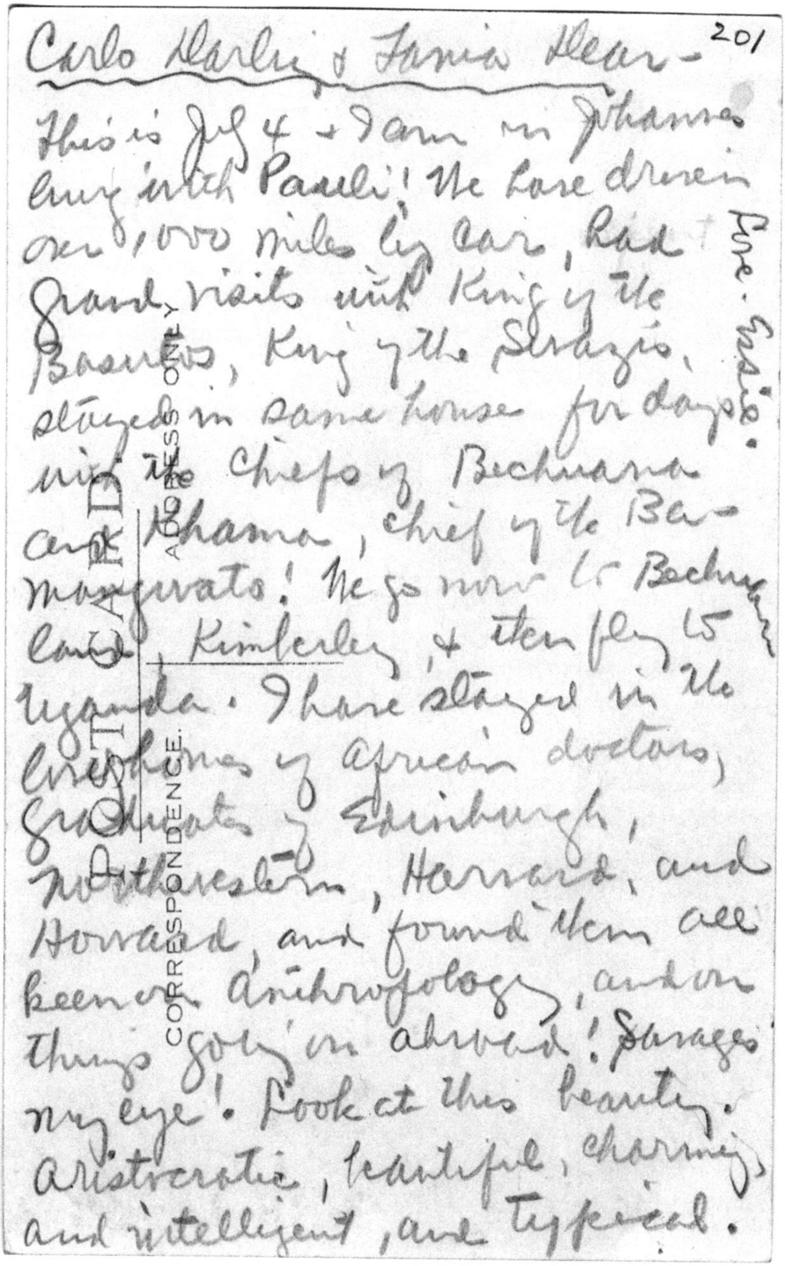

Carlo Darling & Fania Dear—
This is July 4 & I am in Johannesburg with Pauli! We have driven over 1,000 miles by car, had grand visits with King of the Basutos, King of the Swazis, stayed in same house for days with the Chiefs of Bechuana and Khama, chief of the Bamangwato! We go now to Bechuanaland, Kimberley, & then fly to Uganda. I have stayed in the homes of African doctors, graduates of Edinburgh, Northwestern, Harvard, and Howard, and found them all keen on anthropology, and on things going on abroad! Savages my eye! Look at this beauty. Aristocratic, beautiful, charming, and intelligent, and typical.

FIGURE 2.17. Postcard (verso) sent by Eslanda Goode Robeson to Carl and Fania Van Vechten, July 4, 1936. Robeson Correspondence, James Weldon Johnson Memorial Collection in the Yale Collection of American Literature, Beinecke Rare Book and Manuscript Library. © Robeson Family Trust. Courtesy Robeson Family Trust.

front of the postcard features a dark-skinned woman visible from the chest up against a flat white background. While her torso is directed almost fully to the camera, her head is in partial profile, somewhere between the 45-degree angle of the venerated portrait and the 180-degree angle of the scientific or criminal study. Her gaze is directed to her right, the viewer's left, and slightly downward. The framing enables us to see the impressive height of her *isiqholo*, a traditional hairstyle indicating that a woman is married and no longer available for courting. Her shoulders are exposed and she is bare-chested; a string of white beads hangs around her neck, adding an elegant contrast to the field of dark-brown skin marked by scarification. The image stops before her full breasts come into view. The caption reads "A Typical Zulu Woman."

It is not clear who took this photograph originally, but Herbert Hutchinson and J. W. Nankivell, two academic geographers trained in England who held teaching positions in Cape Town in the early twentieth century, included the image in their 1934 book *Southern Africa: The Land and Its Peoples*.[61] Published in Cape Town two years before Eslanda's trip, *Southern Africa* offered a geographic study focused on the history, geology, demography, and economic and agricultural history of southern Africa (South Africa, Zimbabwe, Mozambique, and Namibia, all referred to in this publication by their colonial names), interspersed with travel commentary and buoyed by maps and "several delightful photographic studies."[62] The photograph is the second in the book, is captioned there "Zulu Woman," and is the only uncredited photograph in the book.

Eslanda was an enthusiastic correspondent and sent letters and photographic postcards to friends and family from every part of the world. No doubt drawn to the beauty of the image, Eslanda also had something to say about the description. On the back of this postcard, she wrote:

Carlo Darling & Fania Dear-

This is July 4 & I am in Johannesburg with Pauli! We have driven over 1000 miles by car, had grand visits with King of the Basutos, King of the Swazis, stayed in same house for days with the Chiefs of Bechuana and Khama, chief of the Ba-Manguato! We go now to Bechuanaland [present Botswana], Kimberley and then fly to Uganda. I have stayed in the homes of African doctors, graduates of Edinburgh, Northwestern, Harvard and Howard, and found them all keen on Anthropology, and on things going on abroad! Savages my eye! Look at this beauty. Aristocratic, beautiful, charming, and intelligent, and Typical.

Love, Essie

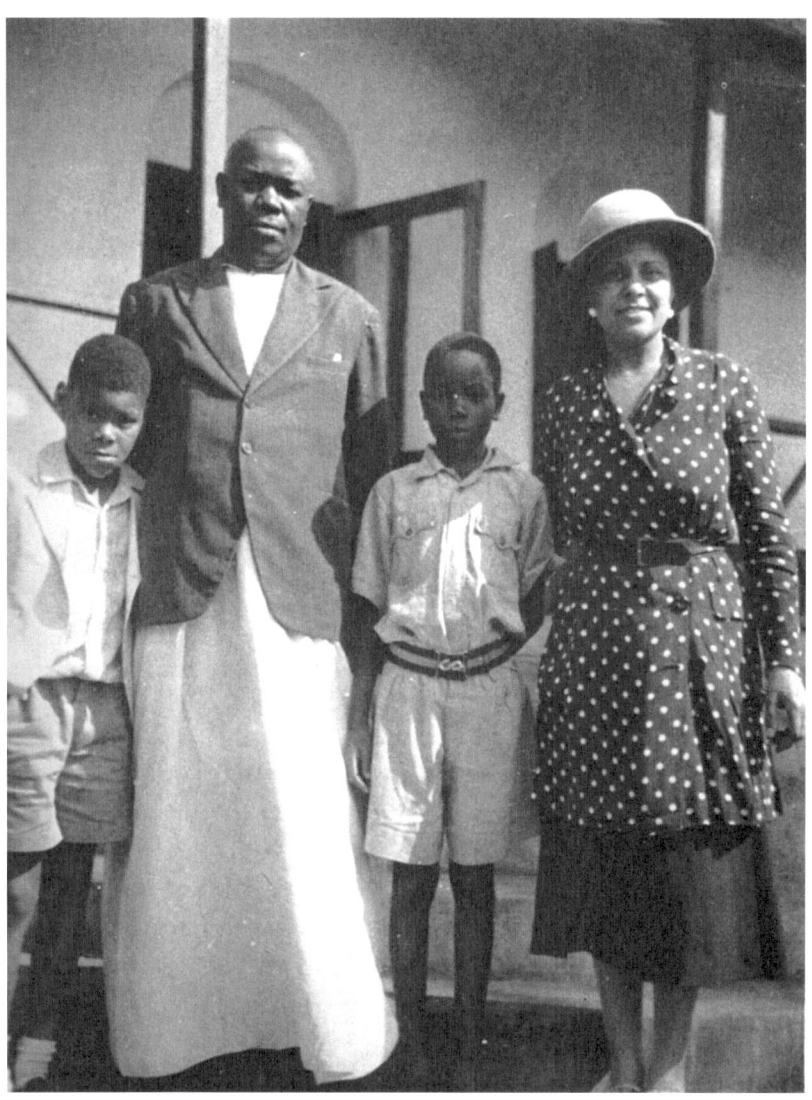

FIGURE 2.18. Eslanda Goode Robeson, "Pauli and I (left and right) visit with the Mulamuzi, the chief justice of Buganda (next to Pauli), at his home in Kampala," 1936. From *African Journey* (1945). © Robeson Family Trust. Courtesy Robeson Family Trust.

Eslanda has taken a tourist postcard, an image made in service of colonialism, and subverted the language and logics that reduce this photographed person to a racial and ethnic type. While she remains nameless, the woman's typicality is now enfolded into a more fulsome and complex picture of Black African life.

It is difficult to overstate the uniqueness of *African Journey*. While it is "like" political tracts, "like" travel memoirs, "like" ethnographies, *African Journey* is also unlike any of these forms. Certainly neither in 1936 nor in 1945 was there a book like this, nor did a form exist to describe the personal and political aspirations of a Black American woman for global Black futures, from her only child to Black peoples on the other side of the world. No form to contain the wealth of sights and smells, of experiences, or the complex relations between people variously linked (and divided) by race, gender, class, and status (figure 2.18). No form to describe feeling at home in a world that despite Jim Crow, colonization, and enclosure, only grows larger with each encounter. There was no form, so Eslanda invented it.

3

MAKING HOME IN EXILE

KATHLEEN CLEAVER'S
BLACK PANTHER
FAMILY ALBUM

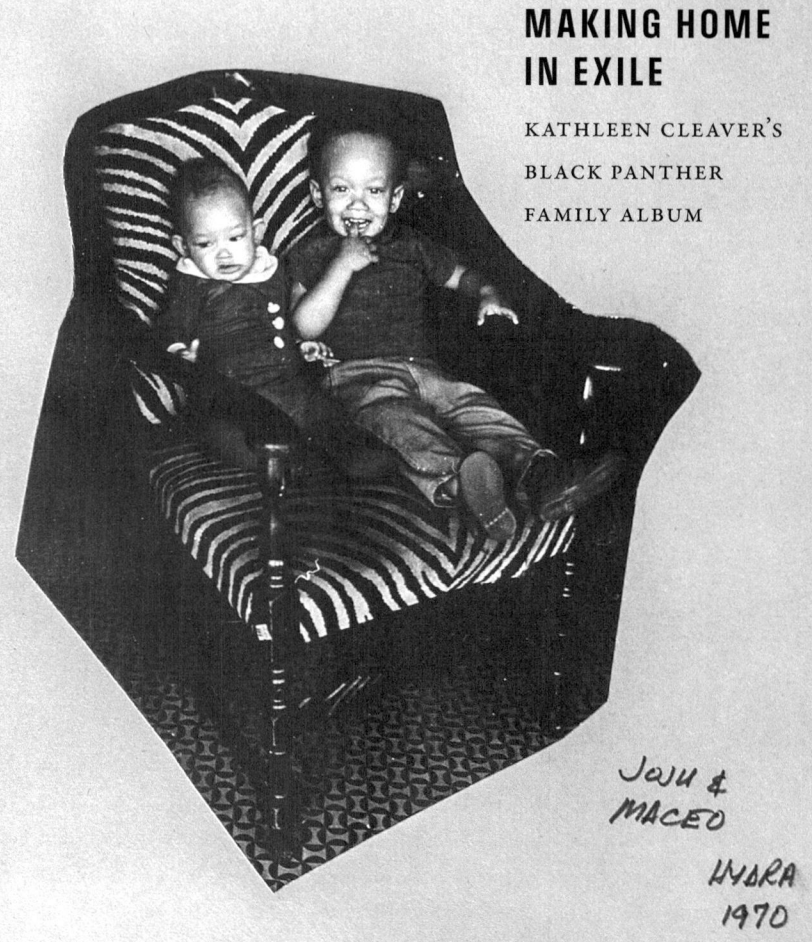

JOJU &
MACEO

HYDRA
1970

FIGURE 3.1. "Joju & Maceo [Cleaver], Hydra 1970." From Kathleen Cleaver family photo album. Photograph of album by John Stephens. Courtesy and © Kathleen Neal Cleaver Archive.

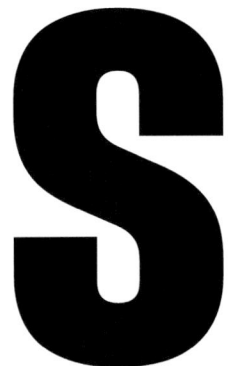

Sometime in the early 1980s, Kathleen Neal Cleaver, former Black Panther, former political exile, (almost) former wife of the FBI's most wanted revolutionary, and now a thirty-something Yale undergraduate mother of two, sat down to compile a family album.

Although her children, Maceo and Joju, were now adolescents, there were no albums that gathered photographs of their infancy and early childhood (figure 3.1). Maceo Eldridge Cleaver was born in Algeria on July 29, 1969, a little over a month after Kathleen arrived there to meet Eldridge. Eldridge had fled the United States in late 1968 after engaging in a shootout that ended in the police slaying of seventeen-year-old Bobby Hutton, the Panthers' first recruit. Facing attempted murder charges, which would surely have resulted in a death sentence for an ex-convict and outspoken radical, Eldridge jumped bail and fled first to Cuba and then Algeria.

When Kathleen became pregnant with their second child the following year, 1970, Eldridge urged Kathleen to travel to North Korea. According to Kathleen, Eldridge was not satisfied with the quality of medical facilities in Algiers. But there were political motivations as well. During the first year of Maceo's life, Eldridge cultivated strong ties with North Korea, a socialist nation-state that offered both a model of Third World independence and *juche,* or "self-reliance," and, as part of Eldridge's "Asian strategy," also provided legitimacy for the fledgling Panther embassy in Algeria. Formally invited by the North Korean Democratic Women's Union, Kathleen, with Maceo in tow, arrived in Pyongyang on June 2, 1970. Eldridge followed and arrived not long before Maceo celebrated his first birthday and Kathleen gave birth to their daughter, Joju Younghi, on

July 31, 1970. The children's names in part chart the path of their parents' journey in exile: Maceo, for the nineteenth-century Cuban revolutionary Antonio Maceo, and Joju Younghi, a "Koreanized" name that roughly translates to "rare heroine" or "young hero born in Juche, Korea." Kathleen testified in *The Black Panther* newspaper, "I have received while here the most excellent and thorough medical attention in my life, and been afforded the most pleasant and comfortable living conditions for myself and my family."[1]

The Cleavers returned to Algiers the following month and began the work of what we might call revolutionary homemaking. The children spent their early years romping in the Mediterranean and running around the three different apartments in which their family resided (figure 3.2). They were held and entertained by visiting Black Panthers, foreign dignitaries, and an international host of comrades and allies. In an "organized communal nursery" in their various homes, Maceo and Joju were looked after alongside the young children of other Panthers, who had joined Eldridge and Kathleen in Algiers either in voluntary or forced exile. This nursery included the young children of Donald and Barbara Easley Cox, Emory and Judi Douglas, Charlotte and Pete O'Neal, and Sekou Odinga and his wife, Yaasmyn Fula. Maceo and Joju played underfoot while their parents established the International Section of the Black Panther Party (BPP), eventually recognized by the Algerian government as an official "liberation movement," which provided the Party with an embassy, telephones and telex, and a monthly stipend (figure 3.3). Then, when the Cleavers split from the Party in 1971, those who remained with the Cleavers reorganized into the Revolutionary People's Communications Network (RPCN).

Kathleen was responsible for packing and unpacking and packing up again the Party's and the family's belongings. It was her job to make a comfortable home while keeping it mobile and ready to move. She packed up the house on Pine Street in San Francisco and then in Algiers, from the apartment at Point Pescade on the Mediterranean, to the two-story home in the formerly French suburb of Hydra, to the "elegant villa" that served as the BPP embassy in El Biar, and the subsequent move to France when the Algerian government had grown tired of the motley crew of hijackers that found their way to Eldridge and the RPCN.[2] Kathleen carried what photographs she could from Algeria to France and eventually back to the United States. But these items represented only a small portion of a much larger archive reportedly lost in the move. "I was livid," she recalled, "because one of the biggest trunks we had in Algiers was filled with books and photographs. I had made arrangements for someone to ship it but it never made it. The CIA took it," she laughed. "French intelligence or US intelligence have it."[3]

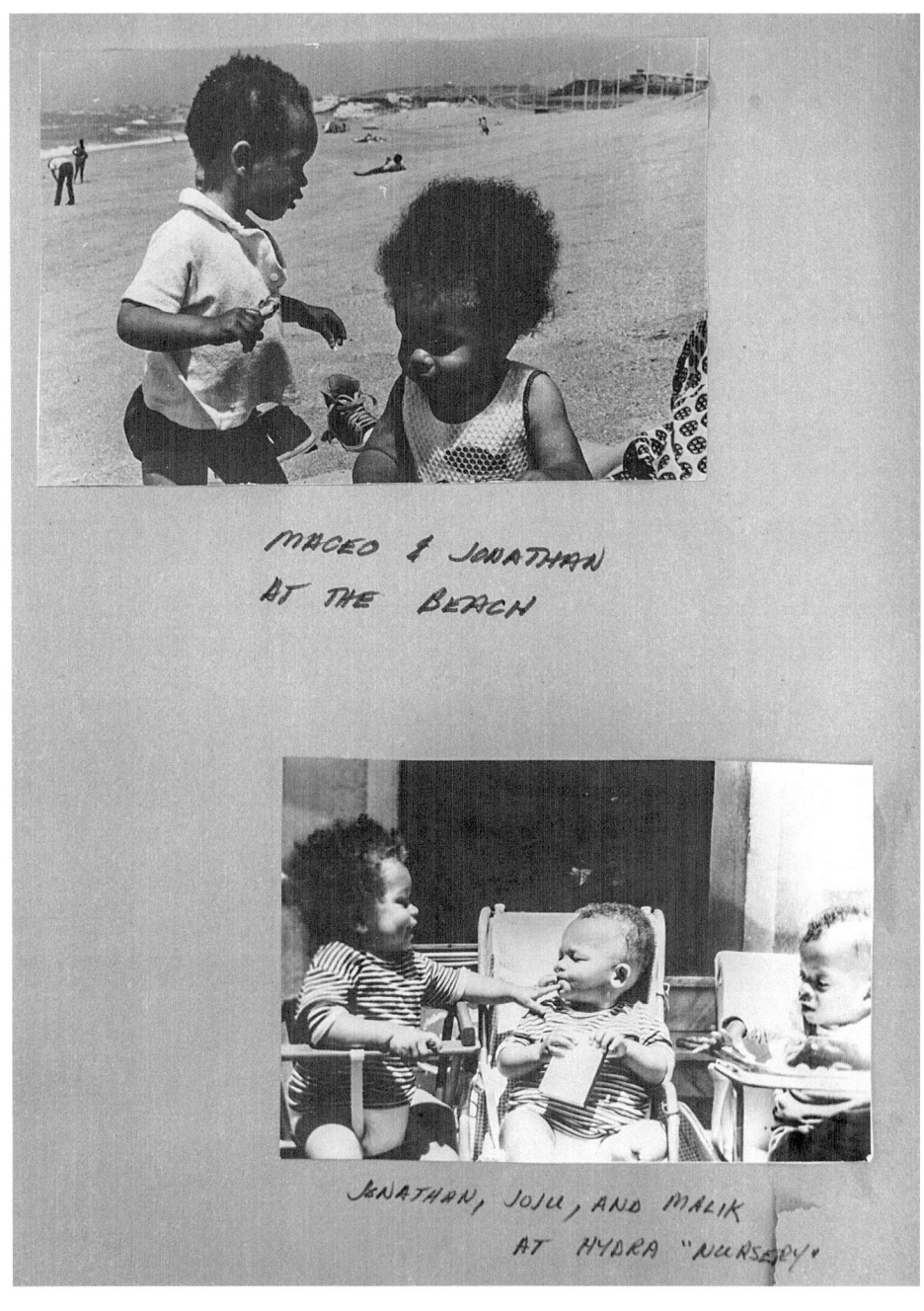

FIGURE 3.2. "Maceo [Cleaver] & Jonathan [Cox] at the Beach" and "Jonathan, Joju and Malik at Hydra 'Nursery.'" From Kathleen Cleaver family photo album. Photograph of album by John Stephens. Courtesy and © Kathleen Neal Cleaver Archive.

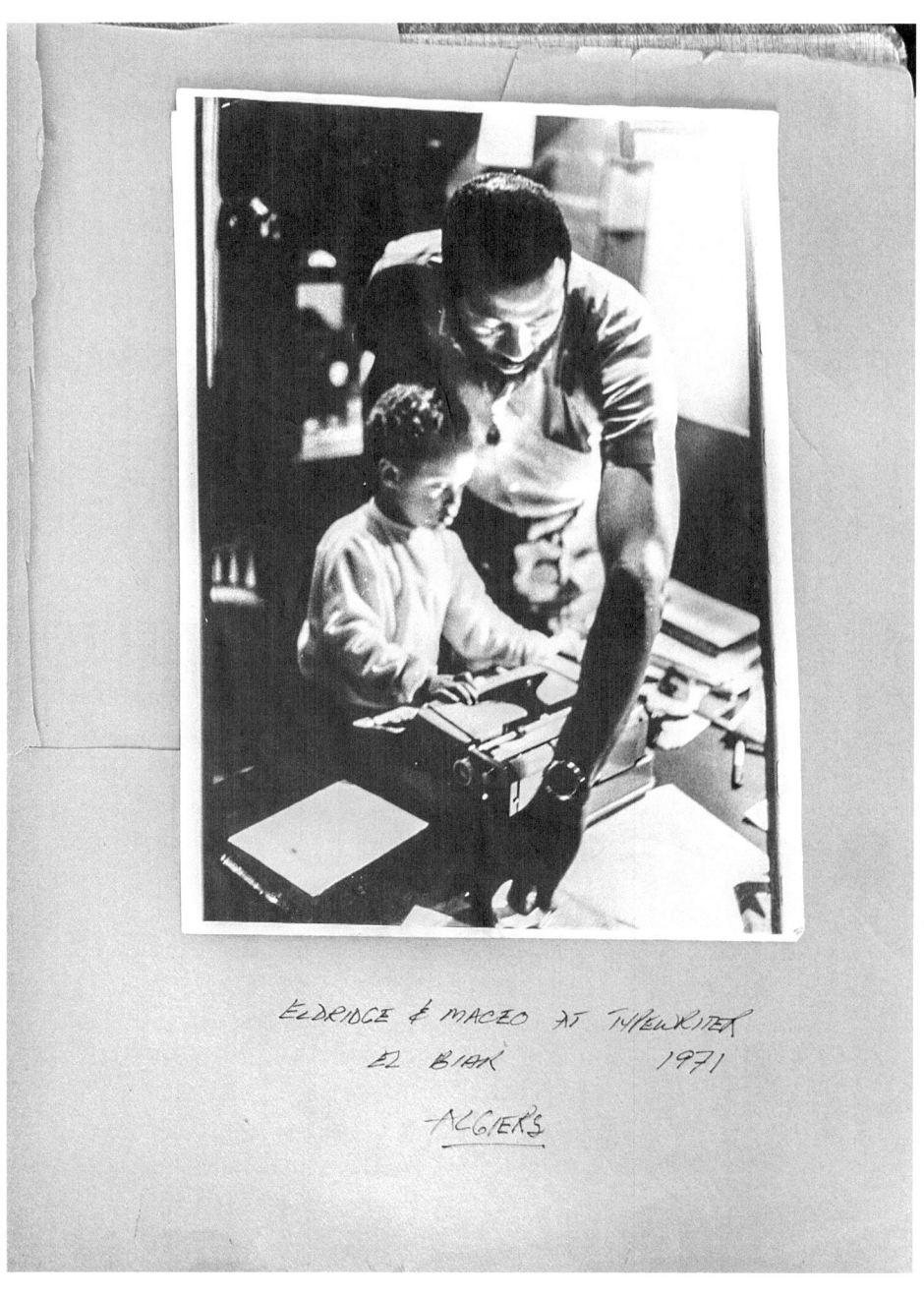

ELDRIDGE & MACEO AT TYPEWRITER
EL BIAR   1971
ALGIERS

FIGURE 3.3. "Eldridge & Maceo [Cleaver] at typewriter, El Biar, 1971, Algiers."
From Kathleen Cleaver family photo album. Photograph of album by John Stephens.
Courtesy and © Kathleen Neal Cleaver Archive.

For the repository and assemblage, Cleaver chose a standard, fairly unremarkable album intended for a scrapbook, about eleven by fourteen inches with marbled dark-green covers, containing beige paper pages to which "snaps and scraps" could be affixed with glue. Here, in the relative calm of her New Haven, Connecticut, apartment, no longer parenting two children under the age of five, no longer living as a declared enemy of the US state in fear of her husband being extradited, imprisoned, or assassinated, Kathleen Cleaver assembled and memorialized the story of their family's years living in Algeria.

The album is composed largely of photographs that others made of the Cleavers (with some images made by Eldridge): amateur snapshots by visiting friends and supporters; professionally made images taken by movement photographers and photojournalists; outtakes and stills from the RPCN-made guerrilla propaganda films that Eldridge referred to as "voodoo"; commissioned government portraits executed by various Second and Third World state employees in Vietnam, China, North Korea, the People's Republic of the Congo, as well as Algiers. This range of photographs was initially intended for state diplomacy or propaganda, or both; for reproduction in *The Black Panther* newspaper or later the RPCN publications, *Voice of the Lumpen*, *Right On!*, and *Babylon*, and other radical movement media outlets; for movement mobilization and fundraisers; or for inclusion in other people's family albums. Now they were being curated by Cleaver in a nondescript mass-produced album to tell the quotidian story of a family living under most extraordinary circumstances.

This album is one particularly rich artifact in Kathleen Cleaver's personal photography collection. Before this trove of images was acquired by Emory University's Special Collections in spring 2020, the collection resided in Cleaver's home in Atlanta, Georgia.[4] At around two thousand images, this archive includes snapshots and formal portraits, contact sheets and family albums, made by professional photographers, amateurs, and Cleaver herself; they also include posters, flyers, book and magazine clippings and outtakes, and more than a dozen photo albums made by Kathleen Cleaver; her mother, Juette Johnson; her aunt Dorothy Johnson, an avid traveler; and Geronimo Ji-Jaga Pratt, a BPP member who spent twenty-seven years in prison on false charges (Cleaver served as a member of Pratt's legal team). After his release from prison in 1997, Pratt married Kathleen's daughter, Joju, with whom he had a son, Kayode. The collection thus includes Pratt's photographs as well.

The collection is coextensive with the Cleavers' period in the BPP. Kathleen joined the Party in late spring 1967 and was soon thrust into the maelstrom created by the incarceration of BPP cofounder Huey P. Newton that fall. She rose to prominence as one of the Party's key leaders and organizers, as well as one of

Black Power's most recognizable icons.[5] Professional and personal photographs in the archive chronicle this period, especially the Cleavers' years in exile in Algeria and France (1969–75). During this time they greeted thousands of visitors as the US contingent of the first Pan-African Cultural Festival, headed the International Section of the BPP (until their expulsion from the Party in 1971), and traveled throughout socialist Africa and Asia. Many images document the afterlives of the Party and its participants.

The collection also chronicles Cleaver's life before she joined the Panthers and provides a window on the making of a unique figure in Black social movement history. A third-generation African American college student, Cleaver lived with her family in Asia and Africa before finishing high school, dropping out of Barnard, and joining first the Student Nonviolent Coordinating Committee (SNCC) and then the Black Panther Party. The collection includes materials from the erudite Neal and Johnson families, dating as far back as the 1850s, indicating that these Black families recognized the power of the medium in its earliest years. Cleaver's father, Ernest Neal, was a professor of sociology and her mother, Pearl Juette Johnson Neal (called Juette), was the first African American woman to earn an advanced degree in mathematics from the University of Michigan. Juette's father, J. Spurgeon Johnson, held advanced degrees, and Juette's uncle Charles Spurgeon Johnson was the first Black president of historically Black Fisk University. In 1948, when Kathleen was three, the family moved from Dallas to Alabama where her father took up the directorship of the Rural Life Institute at Tuskegee Institute. In 1954, Ernest Neal joined the US Foreign Service and over the next half-dozen years, the family lived in India, the Philippines, Liberia, and Sierra Leone, countries each newly independent or working to throw off the shackles of colonialism. Photographs in the collection document the Neal family's participation in Black and brown nation building and transnational freedom dreaming: from contributing to administrative meetings to hosting diplomatic events and attending schools with students of many colors and cultures.

Thus, while this photography collection has great political and historical significance, it is perhaps best understood as a family archive. The fascinating Algiers album, in particular, enriches our knowledge and contributes significantly to the growing scholarship centered on the International Section of the Black Panther Party, the work of Black internationalism in the era of Black Power more broadly, and gender politics in the context of Black revolutionary struggles. And it does so through the specific lens of a Black woman–authored text.

To return to one of the key questions animating this book: What does family photography as a genre, and the specific form of the family photo album, reveal, delimit, and engender? Bell hooks has reminded us that family photography—

portraits, snapshots, albums—held a place of significance for many Jim Crow–era African American families as they sought to carve spaces of validation and recognition.[6] This was no less true of Kathleen's family. Family portraits and documentation were important to the Neal and Johnson families, no matter their geographic location, whether the American South or the Global South. "My family always had pictures," Kathleen emphasized. "My mother had photos and albums. When I was growing up pictures were accessible to everyone. [Especially] with Brownie cameras."[7] Kathleen is particularly proud of the commissioned family portrait by famed African American photographer P. H. Polk, taken at his Tuskegee studio. The collection as a whole, and the Algiers album specifically, provides insight into a life marked by diaspora in its many iterations and constellations: transnationalism, Pan-Africanism, migration, exile.

Scholar Marianne Hirsch's assertion that the camera functions as "the family's primary instrument of self-knowledge and self-representation . . . the primary means by which the family story is told" prompts me to ask, How is the Black diaspora articulated through the rubric of family photography?[8] What kind of story does a family album tell? How can a family album help us understand the fullness and complexities, the failures and promises of Blackness in the world? How might it teach us to read and see and feel Black radicalism otherwise? To read and see and feel Black women's lives otherwise?

Increasingly, I've come to think of Cleaver's capacious family photography collection and the Algiers album through the lens of curation. In recent years, it has become popular—some might say overused, played out even—to call something "curated." And, equally, I think there is a fetishization of the figure of "the curator."[9] Both terms have come to stand in for an individual brand rather than a community-based practice. Calling Kathleen's work curatorial has offered me an umbrella term for author, leader, activist, caregiver, scholar, and icon. By "curatorial," I mean the process of organizing, arranging, and looking after the items in a collection—the early vocational meaning of the term. I also invoke the curatorial in the turn from its "vocational" iteration to the process of selection and "exhibition-making practice." In this sense, I am also referring to the necessity of collaborating with others, especially artists, to realize a community or what bell hooks might call a "homeplace."[10] I am thinking here of what it means to build community with and through art at the center. To hold space and engender a sense of belonging knowingly impermanent and contingent, ephemeral but no less real. And to develop, intervene in, or control a narrative. In these meanings, my use of *curatorial* returns the role of curator to its Latin root *curare*, as someone devoted to the practice and model of caretaking, and connects us to a Black feminist ethics of care.[11] The late Koyo Kouoh, a curator and arts leader who called herself an "exhibition maker," offers a model for my own thinking when she described her curatorial practice: "to defend sites of criticality and dreaming, to care for the health and vitality of our society, [and to engage] with new and undervalued artistic practices."[12]

First, we may consider the photographs at the moment of their creation as a project of *curating home*.[13] As the family lived in exile and birthed and raised their children while also serving as US "ambassadors" for the global Black liberation movement, photographs and photography demonstrated Cleaver's efforts of making a way, of creating and holding a space where her children and community could thrive. Kathleen also made it a priority to collect and keep photographs from this time, effectively building an archive and assembling a collection. Second, in the assemblage of the album in the early 1980s, we can see the work of *curating memories, memorializing the past*: pursuing a commitment to documentation, a registering of loss, an act of celebrating a time and place of her life that was gone, a marriage ending, a laying to rest. The family album functions as both elegy and eulogy and offers Cleaver another way of telling history. Finally, we may understand Kathleen Cleaver's act of compiling the album as one of *curating photography*. Here we come closest to the common usages of *curating*, as both care for a collection and tasteful selection. Thus, I would like to offer Cleaver's collecting and assemblage as creative acts of radical caretaking.

One particular photograph, the photograph that opens this chapter, can draw us into the work of curatorial *homemaking, memorializing*, and *curating*: a black-and-white photograph of Maceo and Joju made in 1970 by visiting BPP photographer Jeffrey Blankfort, a close friend of the Cleavers (see figure 3.1).

Curating Home

This photograph by Blankfort is one of the few images in which Maceo and Joju appear alone together as siblings, without one or both of their parents. They are nestled into a single chair side by side, their arms touching. Even so, there is room to spare, which gives a greater view of the chair.

I turn to the chair's very cute occupants in a moment. First, let's talk about the chair itself (figure 3.4). A relatively straightforward piece of furniture, this carver chair (an early American design) sports a seat and back upholstered in zebra print fabric. According to Kathleen, this chair was one of her favorites and featured prominently in the San Francisco home she shared with Eldridge from 1967 until she left to join him in Algiers. It was one of many "African-themed" items in their house: animal prints, carved masks, shields and spears. The zebra print is reminiscent of course of the iconic image of BPP minister of defense Huey P. Newton, a photograph staged by Eldridge Cleaver in May 1967. Keenly aware of the power

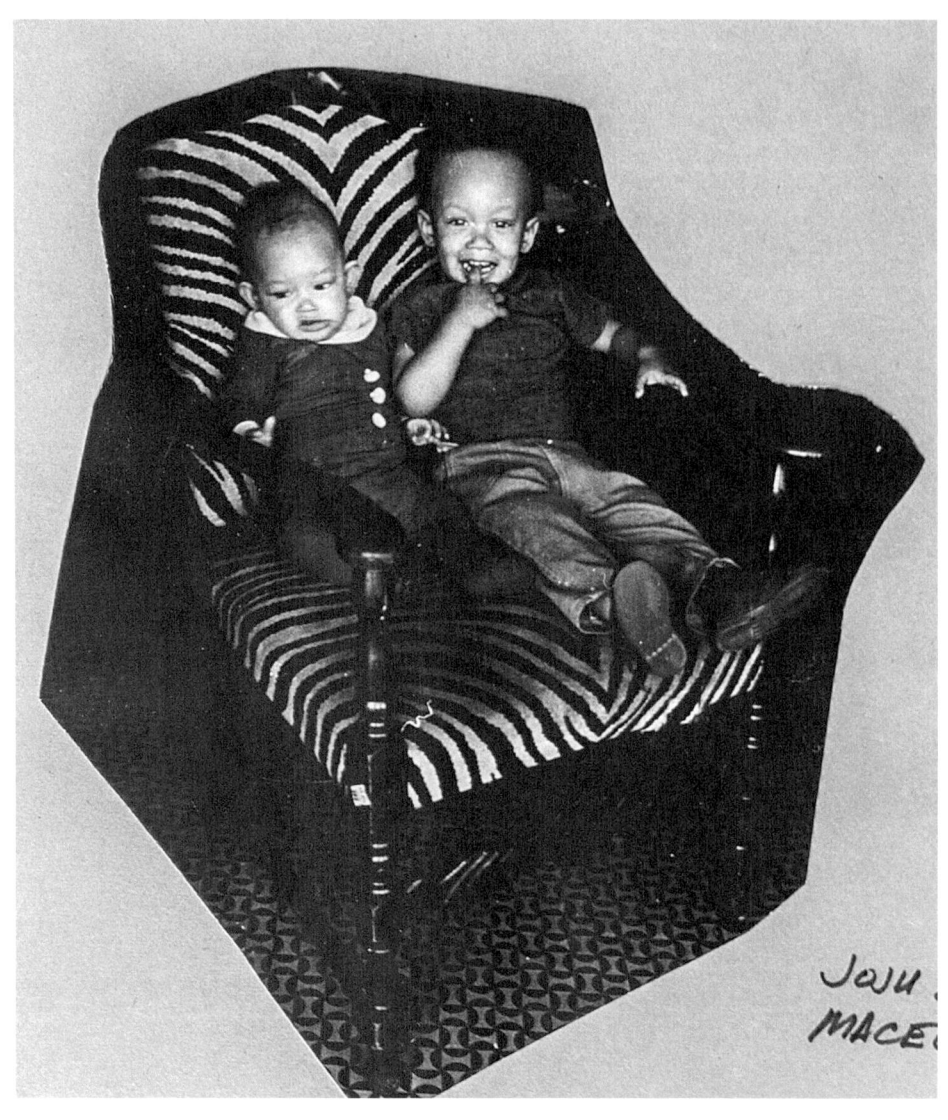

FIGURE 3.4. "Joju & Maceo [Cleaver], Hydra 1970" (figure 3.1), detail.

of image and of personality, Cleaver felt it necessary to orchestrate a publicity photograph of Newton as the Party was gaining national and international attention after its takeover of the California capitol building only a few days before this photograph was made. I described in my first book, *Imprisoned in a Luminous Glare*, how, through its visual dramaturgy, the photograph captured and clarified many of the ambiguities and competing strains of "Black Power" that had adhered around the discourse. The African artifacts—the spears, the shields, the zebra skin rug—symbolized cultural nationalism, a philosophy defined by a glorified African past and the unifying force of a monolithic Black culture.[14]

Knowing, however, that those "artifacts," or replicas, as was more likely, came from the Cleavers' home encourages us to think more carefully about how quotidian objects become powerful conduits of diasporic connectivity. In her essay "Back to Africa: The Evolution of the International Section of the Black Panther Party (1969–1972)," Cleaver wrote of the significance of such connection, specifically in the context of a trip in 1972 to Congo-Brazzaville of a Panther delegation, a group yearning to be hailed as family by their African hosts: "The desire to return to Africa was always a powerful undercurrent in the Afro-American experience. The hunger to see the land where their ancestors were captured and brought as slaves to America remained ever present among Blacks struggling to express their identity in a White-dominated world."[15] The possession of diasporic resources, to use Jacqueline Nassy Brown's term, in one's living space can offer a sense of movement and mobility, an expression of connection across space and time, especially in a condition of immobility and stasis.[16] The spears, shields, and masks were items that one admired as art and lived with. But the chair, a place of rest and momentary settling down, was something to be lived *in*.

The centrality of the chair has implications for how we read the photography of Black liberation writ large. Tina Campt is instructive here. Following Kevin Quashie, Campt urges us to consider quiet "as a modality that surrounds and infuses sound with impact and affect" and "the quotidian as a practice rather than an act/ion,"[17] as hermeneutics capacious enough, acute enough to track refusal and not just resistance, stasis and not just mobility. In doing so, we are able to "rethink foundational approaches to diaspora studies."[18]

On one hand, we can read this photograph and the album overall for a certain confirmation of these foundational approaches; that would mean considering the photograph for its visualization of the forced mobility of some of the most iconic figures of the Black radical tradition. But the album also offers a depiction of homemaking that is itself a kind of aspiration to the quiet and stillness of the domestic quotidian and the tension between rest and motion (figure 3.5). Taken together we are forced to contend with how, in Campt's words

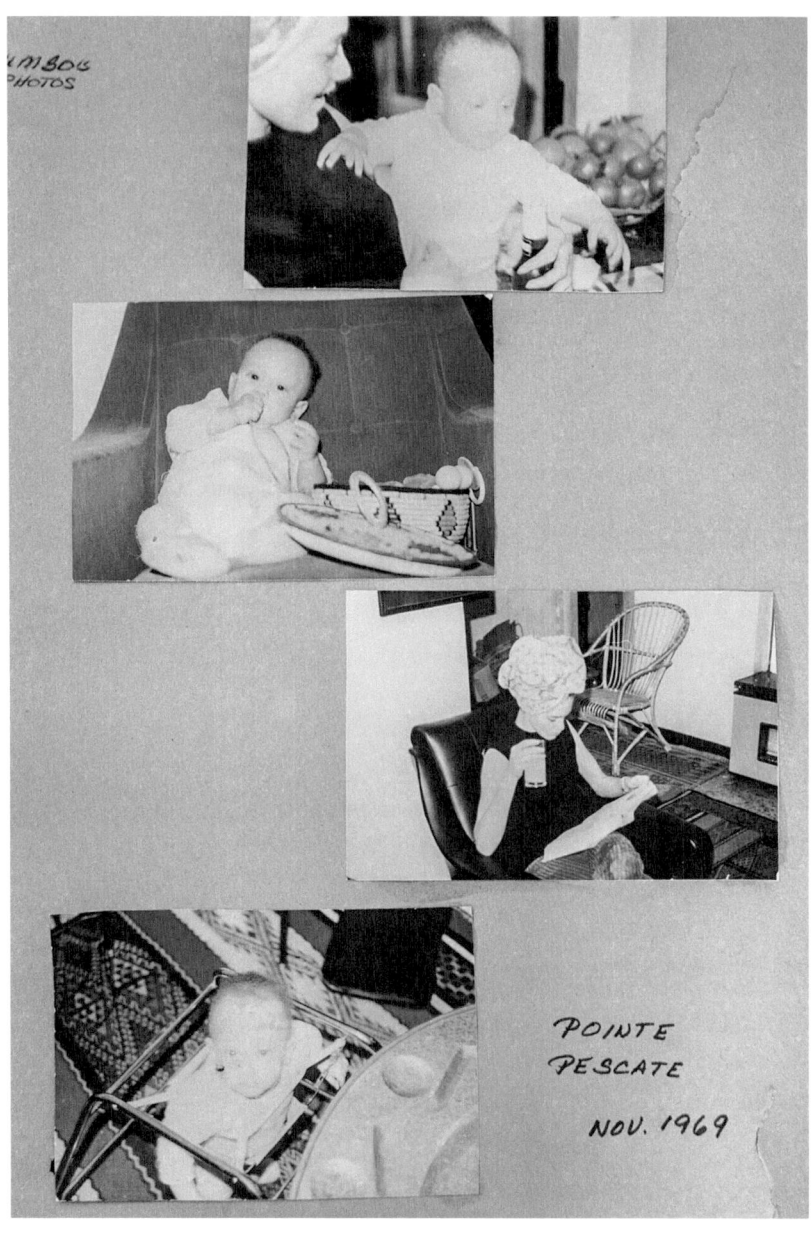

FIGURE 3.5. Four photographs of Kathleen and Joju Cleaver, "Point Pescate, Nov. 1969." From Kathleen Cleaver family photo album. Photograph of album by John Stephens. Courtesy and © Kathleen Neal Cleaver Archive.

again, "the black quotidian [functions] as a signature idiom of diaspora culture and black futurity" for even those who are the most recognizable, most vocal, and most resistant figures in our political culture.

Kathleen loved this chair so much that she had it shipped from San Francisco to Algiers. According to Kathleen, this photograph of Maceo and Joju in the zebra print chair was made the day the shipment arrived from the States and into their second home in Algiers, in the suburban area of Hydra. They were unpacking the boxes, and Kathleen placed the children in her favorite chair. The chair, we might say, is as much a subject of this photograph as the children.

For the subject-citizen who lives under conditions of uncertainty and hostility, home is always in motion, necessarily has to be here and elsewhere; home is respite and retreat that necessarily has to be mobile. Kathleen was no stranger to making a home internationally. She'd witnessed her parents, her mother especially, settle the family into living quarters in India, the Philippines, Liberia, and Sierra Leone. This upbringing as ambassadors (agents?) of the Cold War United States was of course a far cry from living in exile as an enemy of the United States. But one commonality for Kathleen was the need to create a familiar environment amid persistent newness.

This proved no easy task. Although Kathleen writes that the Panthers were thrilled to be in Africa because of the place the continent held in their political and cultural imaginaries, the reality of living in exile, and the complexities of Algeria in particular, made their experience a difficult one. Of the thirty Panthers living in Algiers at the height of the International Section, only Kathleen spoke French, and no one spoke Arabic. None were able to comprehend the complex political situation or the histories that bound and divided Algeria's various ethnic, tribal, and religious groups. And for the women, as Kathleen remembered, "we came with our big hair and our big hoop earrings and our short skirts," styles deeply iconic and celebrated in the United States but largely in transgression of expectations for modest female dress in Islamic Algeria.[19] The exuberance for Black liberation that brought the Panther contingent to Africa was dampened by their ignorance of Algeria.

Returning to the photograph, we can see a kind of complicated color story at work in which the zebra print competes with the typical Islamic tile pattern of the floor. In the home she loved and protected in San Francisco, the chair was meant to invoke an "Africanness," a diasporic resource that imagined and thus forged a (one-sided) connection to an elsewhere beyond Babylon, a diaspora desire iterated through a material object. Now, in real Africa—real, complicated Africa—the chair was a symbol of home and what had been left behind. The photograph's elevations depict an imagined Africa sitting atop a real one,

FIGURE 3.6. "Joju & Maceo [Cleaver], Hydra 1970" (figure 3.1), detail.

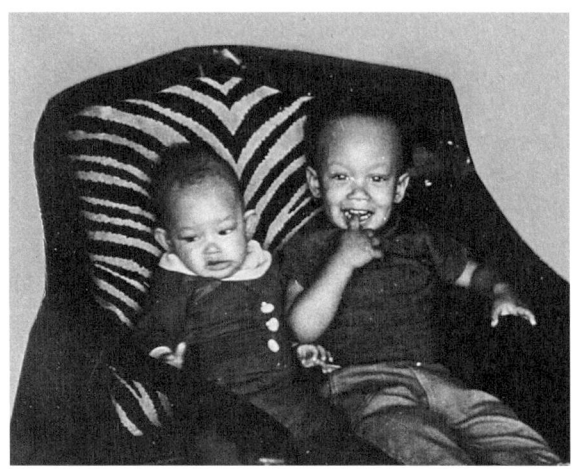

Curating Memories

an idea that hovers above solid ground. Ideas of home are here nested within each other. And each supports her children.

Let's return to the human subjects, the photographed persons of this image (figure 3.6). Joju, on the left, is less than a year old. Her body is mushy; she hasn't too much in the way of hair or teeth that we can tell. She appears new to the work of sitting up, and her position in the chair feels a bit precarious, as if she might tip over or slide off in the direction of her gaze. Indeed, she is a small human in motion, her legs and feet disappear into a blur. The blur in turn casts a shadow over the seat. Maceo, on the other hand, is still enough, the finger of one hand in his smiling mouth while the other hand holds onto the chair. At almost two years old, he looks directly at the camera with a kind of delight that suggests a growing knowledge of how to pose for the camera. In the archive of images of Maceo—whom family members observed as a serious child—this is one of the few in which he is smiling.[20]

Joju's blur and Maceo's smile remind us of the impulse to memorialize childhood and an idea of family by way of the photograph, but also the limits of that prospect. It is limited not just because children are notoriously difficult to photograph as they are generally incapable of, or simply refuse, stillness. The blur casts a dark spot, a limit to visibility caused by a small body not fully in possession of itself. The smile asserts a happiness that in retrospect was fleeting and complicated. These two gestures open up for us a consideration of different kinds of memorialization, beyond commemoration or celebration, into narrative forms that, wittingly or not, allow for incompleteness, hold space for the unspoken and unsayable, and concede to the "simultaneity of joy AND trauma" rather than one OR the other.[21]

When I ask her, "What prompted you to put the album together?" Kathleen has no answer. However, in 1982–83, Kathleen was writing her senior thesis in history as a nontraditional college student at Yale University.[22] That essay, "The Evolution of the International Section of the Black Panther Party in Algiers, 1969–1972," was later revised and published in one of the first academic volumes on BPP history, *The Black Panther Party Reconsidered*, edited by African American studies scholar Charles E. Jones and published by Black Classic Press in 1998. I think it is no accident that these two narratives of the Cleavers' time in exile emerged at the same time, and we may even think of them as mutually constitutive. Art historian Cheryl Finley has characterized the work of photo albums as mnemonic aids and observed that "the very act of 'reading' the visual narrative of a photographic album can itself construct and produce memories."[23] Indeed, in working with Cleaver to organize the family photography collection, I witnessed the way memory cathects, and history adheres to, individual photographs for her. The process of engaging with photographs—holding them, looking at them, and (to follow Campt) listening to them—emerged as critical to Kathleen's narration of her own life. I imagine that this hapticity was as true in the 1980s as it is now.

In "Back to Africa: The Evolution of the International Section of the Black Panther Party (1969–1972)" (the published version of her thesis) Cleaver offers a detailed overview of a facet of BPP history about which little had been written.[24] In the italicized preface to the essay, Cleaver emphasizes the difficulty of writing an underground history: "The clandestine, or otherwise nonpublic, events that led to the creation of the Black Panther Party's International Section made the existence of extensive documentary records improbable. Fortuitously, the initial obstacles to traditional research did not deter me since my personal involvement in the International Section's formation gave me a basic understanding of its chronology, its main personalities and the extraordinary political dynamic that sustained its existence."[25] Although she intended initially to write a political–foreign policy–foreign relations history focusing on "the unfolding drama of the Black Panther Party during 1969–1971, the relationship between Algeria and the United States during those same years, and finally, the policies of the United States intelligence services towards the International Section of the Black Panther Party," Cleaver found it difficult to find ample documentary support. Thus she "channeled" her work into a narrative history with the hope that future scholars with greater access might delve further into the subject.

The writing style is scholarly, yet clear and direct. While Kathleen does not shy away from what might be deemed controversial assertions, including that Huey Newton and David Hilliard may have been compromised by the FBI, there is little in the way of sentimentality. Each of her conclusions is supported by evidence, buoyed by "traditional sources" (newspaper and magazine articles, declassified COINTELPRO [Counter Intelligence Program] documents, oral histories), and properly footnoted, as was no doubt emphasized as part of historical disciplinary training. The most substantive mention of family life, which, as we know from Kathleen's oral testimony, both structured and impacted political life in Algiers, is a paragraph that describes the "expanding community of fugitives...[and] community of families" as one of a series of "complexities" that demanded a creative response—most specifically, the organization of a "communal nursery"—but that inadvertently hampered the political activities and efforts toward "people's diplomacy" that the International Section hoped to achieve.[26] That is, children were there, day-to-day family concerns happened, and sometimes they got in the way of the "real work" of revolution. On the whole, "Back to Africa" recognizes how high the stakes were (in 1983, in 1998, and continue to be) in recounting the history of the Black Panther Party, an organization derided still, well into the twenty-first century, as terrorists and thugs by local, state, and federal forces, and whose members have aged in prison, such as Mumia Abu-Jamal, or aged (and died) in exile, such as Assata Shakur, for alleged crimes attached to their participation in the movement more than two generations ago.

Juxtaposing the Algiers album with the thesis-cum-article helps us think more effectively about what different photographic genres reveal, delimit, and engender. If the article is effective history, then the album offers affective history, one that must reckon with "complexities" and that does not—cannot—deny negative affect or bad attachments like boredom, exhaustion, laziness, or betrayal. In doing so, the album holds out the possibility of acknowledging the personal and political failures of the Cleavers' time in exile, failure without the political impulse of redemption that, in the words of African diaspora studies scholar Ianna Hawkins Owen, is so central to the Black left's "revisionist narratives of resistance." The article teaches us, but the album, as Owen would say, "refuses to counsel us."[27]

In his stunning book, *Ordinary Failures: Diaspora's Limits and Longings*, Owen argues that recitations of failure in diasporic memoirs by Saidiya Hartman, Langston Hughes, Jamaica Kincaid, and others need to be attended to if we are to actually undo the binary logics of success and failure in which Blackness is always on the losing side and, even when successful, only underscores the logics of anti-Black structures. The failures here are those in which Black people betray and cheat one another, misrecognize and refuse one another, shame and are ashamed of one another.

One of the failures of that era and, I believe, in much of our subsequent scholarship about the BPP has been a kind of oblique address of, but ultimately a redemptive narrative about, gender relations. In the movement's own moment this looked like an attempt to call out "male chauvinism" and to create new models of gender engagement and equity. In the historiography, this attempt has taken the form of acknowledging shortcomings, mapping contradictions, and yet ultimately praising the efforts of an organization trying to undo centuries of white supremacist patriarchy, to make a new world under the most harrowing of conditions.[28] I consider my own work as having made this attempt as well. Taken together, our endeavors at nuance and generosity have for more than fifty years created conditions of soft silence around ~~and apology for~~ one of the most egregious forms of intraracial failure: sexual violence and domestic abuse.

The violence in the Cleaver homes—from San Francisco to Algiers to Paris and back to the United States—is perhaps one of the greatest open secrets of BPP history and historiography. The secret became a front-page headline in the March 6, 1971, issue of *The Black Panther*: "Free Kathleen Cleaver and All Political Prisoners," which frames an isolated photograph of Kathleen, donning sunglasses with fist raised and mouth open mid-speech (figure 3.7). In a four-page supplement, Deputy Minister of Information Elaine Brown declares that Eldridge is holding Kathleen hostage in Algiers and recounts in detail Brown's "whispered conversations" with, and concerned observations about, Kathleen during Brown's visit to Algiers in July and August 1970. Brown writes that Kathleen had been living in a state of terror since leaving the United States and that she was subject to Eldridge's anger and his persistent physical and verbal assaults, including an incident Brown observed in which Eldridge slapped Kathleen in her hospital bed in North Korea in the weeks before she gave birth to Joju. Eldridge further abused Kathleen by flaunting his lovers in front of his wife (presumably, including Brown herself). More broadly, Brown decried "the double-standard [of the Cleaver marriage] manifested to the highest degree: A man can run from woman to woman; but a woman must be his and his alone." She detailed the romantic relationship between Kathleen and one of the hijackers, Clinton Smith, also called Rahiem (and sometimes Rahim). Smith escaped from the California State Penitentiary at Chino along with Bryon Booth, and the two followed Eldridge from Havana and then to Algiers, becoming part of the extended cadre of exiles living with the Cleavers.[29] Brown concludes her account with Eldridge's brutal disallowance of "a freedom of choice" that he en-

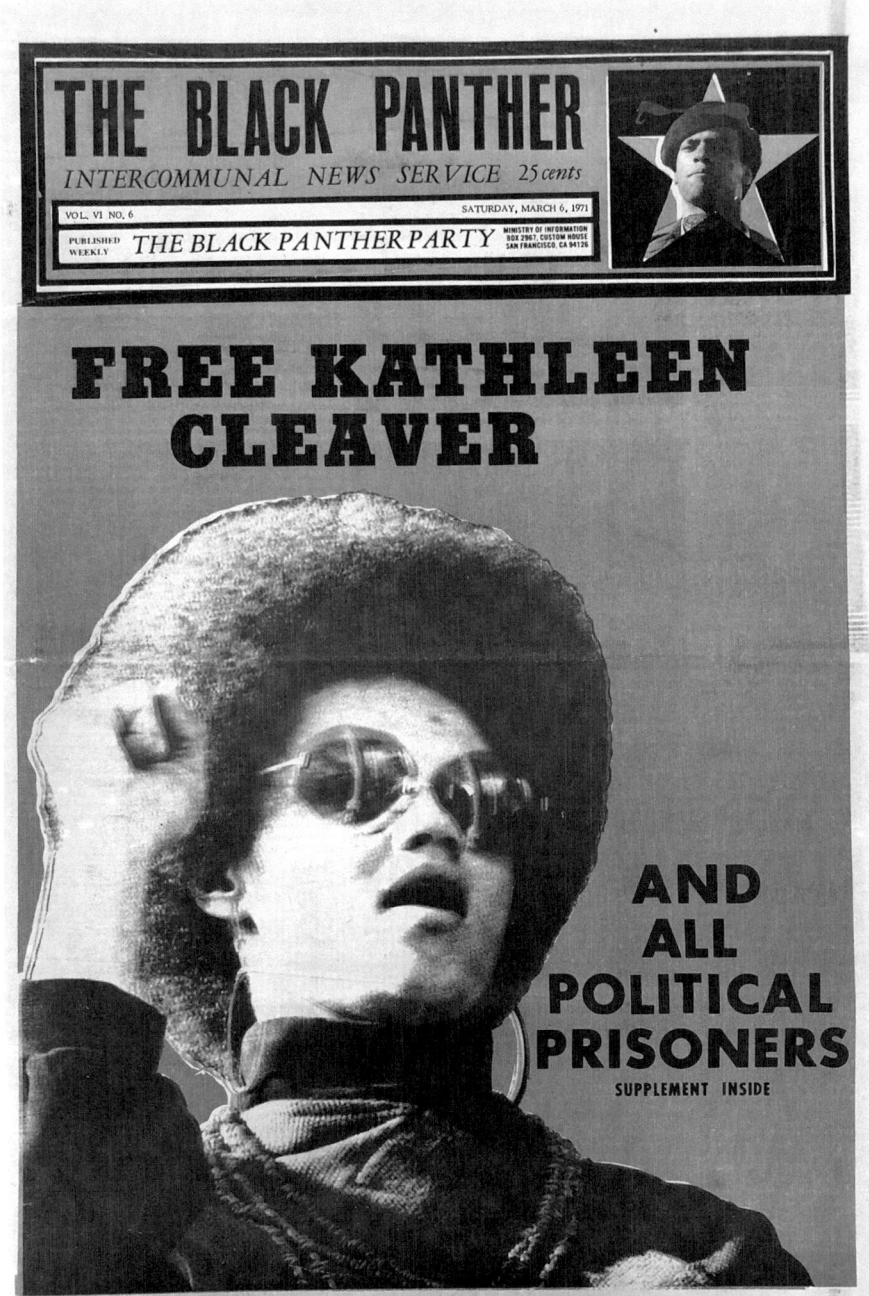

FIGURE 3.7. "Free Kathleen Cleaver and All Political Prisoners." Cover, *The Black Panther*, March 6, 1971.

joyed but would not grant Kathleen: Eldridge allegedly murdered Smith and buried his body in Algiers. Algerian police, unhappy with the unruly hijackers, reluctantly looked the other way.[30]

Brown later recounted an abridged version of this story, along with her own fear of being beaten or killed by Eldridge, in her 1992 memoir, *A Taste of Power*. The 1971 *Black Panther* article—difficult, sensational—was accompanied by three photographs: one of Rahim (captioned "The man Kathleen Cleaver loved. The man Eldridge Cleaver killed."); one of Malika, Eldridge's young Algerian mistress; and one of Kathleen "with an eye blackened by Eldridge Cleaver." It is this last that offers the most corroboration of Brown's story—not necessarily of sexual intrigue and marital infidelity but certainly of physical abuse. And it is the photograph that is perhaps the most damning of the subsequent historiographic silence: A failure to acknowledge our radical heroes at their most vulnerable. A visual erasure of our most embarrassing personal and political failures.

Brown's piece, which concludes with a direct message to Kathleen to "PLEASE BE STRONG, FOR THE PEOPLE WILL SET YOU FREE!" appeared at the height of the tensions between the Cleaver and Newton factions of the Party. And the split between the two groups would be announced as a cover story on March 20, 1971, only two issues after the "Free Kathleen Cleaver" supplement. Historian Robyn C. Spencer writes that "accusations of mistreating women became a potent weapon in these factional struggles" within the BPP, as well as within the Young Lords and other Panther affinity groups. Spencer thus seems to downplay this invocation of domestic violence issues and other forms of "chauvinism," casting it not as a pressing concern but as a cover story for power struggles between different constituencies. In her discussion of the "Free Kathleen Cleaver" supplement, Spencer quickly moves past Brown's accusations and takes Kathleen's dismissal—"a claim she quickly denied"—at face value.[31]

Significantly, Brown frames domestic violence as a political crime and a crime against the Revolution. She places the issue in line with the political prisoner work the BPP was deeply engaged in and sees it as just as important and life threatening as the trials faced by a number of other Panthers simultaneously. In doing so, the highest-ranking woman Party officer highlights the ways that gender violence (misogynoir specifically) is an impediment to, and its undoing inseparable from, the "progress of our glorious struggle."[32] Indeed, Black women were coming to power in new ways in the Party and with that power came an avowal of what historian Danielle McGuire has called "black women's bodily integrity." This power also meant embracing the possibilities of revolutionary sexual autonomy, including Black women taking lovers of all genders, not adhering to patriarchal gender roles, and fully inhabiting all of the freedoms that were held out to, often promised to, or even expected of and for cis-heterosexual Black male revolutionaries.[33] Thus, rather than discount Brown's supplement as merely a very clever move in a high-stakes game for the future of the Party, we might *also* consider it an assertion of Black women's leadership that necessarily acknowledges that the Party must actively create the conditions—of safety, of parity, of respect—that enable Black women to continue to take up the bulk of the Party's work. We might consider the expulsion of Eldridge Cleaver from the Panthers as inevitable for a host of ideological reasons and modes of praxis beyond just armed revolution versus service pending revolution. Brown suggests Eldridge's ideological crimes are patriarchal as well. They include a toxic masculinity that manifested in a reckless shootout with the Oakland Police Department that got beloved recruit Bobby Hutton killed, and further manifested as violence and terrorism enacted against his wife, who also happens to be one of the foremost architects and formidable organizers of the Party. Brown throws down the gauntlet and in one deft move makes a play for the more effective, less volatile Cleaver, and a future Party with more Black women at the helm and Black women's equity at the core.

We may imagine that Brown's article only made an already stressful and difficult situation more precarious for Kathleen. On a most basic level, Brown presented Kathleen with the choice to leave her husband in Algeria or leave the organization that she had worked so hard to build. To leave her husband would be to dissolve her family, replicating for her children Kathleen's painful experience of her own parents' divorce. However, though history often points to the leadership of Newton and Seale, Kathleen's imprint on the BPP is undeniable. Since joining in spring 1967, Kathleen had built the Party up in its most dire hour, recruiting members, raising funds, and igniting awareness during a period of siege and, when faced with exile, drawing on the experience of her international upbringing as the child of diplomats to enact a viable international office. By choosing her immediate family, then, she risked another kind of exile. Becoming even more isolated, she would have to remake her political connections and professional world.[34]

Kathleen managed to recharge her political relevance while gaining space from Eldridge by leaving Algiers, depositing Maceo and Joju with her mother, and embarking on a months-long speaking tour of the United States to build the new Revolutionary People's Communications Network. In an interview with *Jet* magazine (one of many publicity engagements she undertook while in the United States), Kathleen described the Cleavers' post-Panther endeavor as "a structure linking up the national and international organizations and movements of people engaged in revolutionary work. This new [aboveground] organization would not engage in guerrilla warfare or armed struggle," as Eldridge would have it, but instead "furnish true and factual information among people who are engaged in armed struggle or other forms of revolutionary or progressive activity."[35] In this way, Kathleen reprised her work as communications secretary in a global context. In doing so, she announced her ongoing commitment to her family, to her husband, and to the Revolution while also asserting her own mobility—"I wasn't a fugitive, so I could come back to the States whenever I wanted"[36]—and carving out space for choices as limited, as disappointing, and as difficult as they might be.[37]

I am not prepared to argue that Kathleen deliberately recites failures of the International Section and of herself and her family in the album in the way the memoirists do in Owen's study. I suspect that Kathleen is herself unprepared to make such an admittance. But I believe that the family album as a form is too messy, too obstreperous, to withhold, externalize, or deny entirely the failures and disappointments of familial relations. I'm thinking of family here as at once the Cleaver nuclear family, the growing community of Black American exile families that lived under the Panther banner in Algiers, family as a metaphor for nationalism, and family as a map of intergenerational kinship and affective ties.[38]

Take, for example, a page that appears early in the album with only two photographs; page tears and glue stains indicate that some photographs have been removed (figure 3.8). At the center right is a photograph of Kathleen in a mustard-colored dress on a terrace overlooking Algiers. Close to the right edge of the frame, Kathleen's attention is not on the city view that sprawls behind and around her, but directed softly at the newborn in her arms. From the captions to the left of and beneath the image—"Hotel Aletti July 1969" and "Pan African Cultural Festival"—we can deduce that the baby is Maceo. Mother and child are in their own enclosed circle. They are turned away not only from the city and the sea but also from the photograph at the bottom left, which features a white-presenting woman in a maroon caftan standing in front of a wall of flowers, smiling directly at the camera. Beneath the photograph, Kathleen has written "Friend," but on the image itself, Kathleen has drawn a thick cartoon moustache. She does not recall the woman's name but remembers that this "friend" was "in love with Eldridge" and made her way to Algiers to be close to him. In one retelling, Kathleen mentions that this was not the only "friend" who came to visit them in exile.[39]

It would seem a memory that a scorned wife might want to forget or excise. Instead, Kathleen chose to include this photograph in her family album, on the same page as a tender mother and child portrait, and to deface it in such a way that calls attention to a cascade of betrayals. As affective history, the Algiers al-

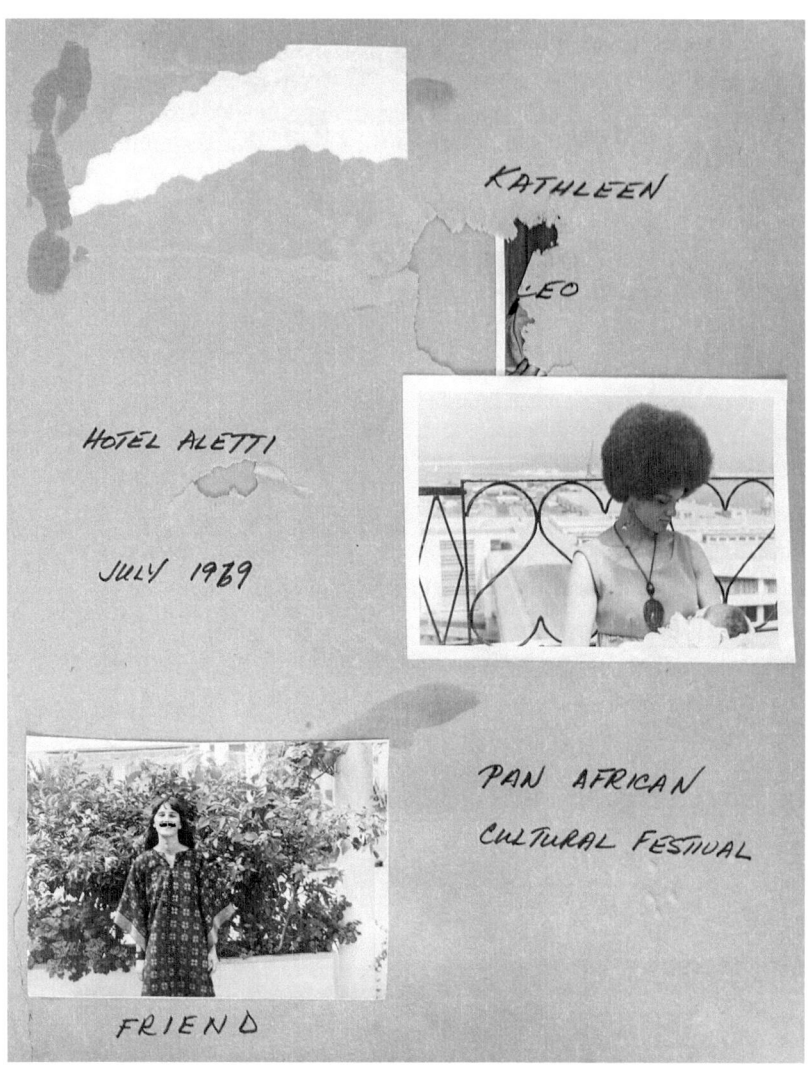

FIGURE 3.8. "Friend" (left) and "Kathleen [illegible]eo" (right); missing: "Hotel Aletti, July 1969," "Pan African Cultural Festival" (?). From Kathleen Cleaver family photo album. Photograph of album by John Stephens. Courtesy and © Kathleen Neal Cleaver Archive.

bum offers an "archive of feeling," to borrow Heather Love's term in the context of queer histories of loss and injury. Love writes, "Taking care of the past without attempting to fix it means living with bad attachments, identifying through loss, allowing ourselves to be haunted."[40] On this album page with its absent images and paper scars, Kathleen at once tends to her newborn baby and allows the image of her husband's infidelities (marked by a belated clapback) to hover in close proximity.

We might also consider the photograph of the new family of four, also made by Jeff Blankfort, one of the few images in which the Cleavers appear *as* a family of four (figure 3.9). Kathleen has expressed her dislike of this image: "We look so bored with each other."[41] It's not difficult to see why: Kathleen and Eldridge sit side by side on a couch or day bed, their bodies leaning heavily onto the wall behind. The children fill all the space, it seems, between their parents and the camera: Kathleen is mostly obscured if not practically buried by the bundle of blankets that holds Joju on her lap. Eldridge makes a lackluster attempt at holding Maceo, who, slightly blurry, seems to be moving away from something outside the frame and further into his mother. Or perhaps he is trying to get space from his father's lit cigarette, which Eldridge holds in his other hand. His long arm holds that smoke and rests on the couch's armrest, taking up nearly a third of the image—a framing that gives the impression of the family crowded on top of one another. The parents look exhausted, one child looks worried, and the other child is a heavy weight. It is a photograph that stands in stark contrast to the glamorous image made by Gordon Parks of Kathleen and Eldridge in Algiers, a different sort of family photograph that has become iconic, one that imagines the young couple as unencumbered, bolstered by their love for each other; their imprisoned leader—and, by extension, the Revolution—hovers in an image on the wall behind them (figure 3.10).[42] The moody shadows in this photo contain mystery, whereas the family photo is brightly lit against an empty wallpapered backdrop. The Algiers album offers public images of Kathleen's strength and power. It also does not deny private fear and disempowerment.

As Hirsch, Martha Langford, Thy Phu, Jo Spence, and other scholars of family photography have pointed out, the family album provides a narrative, albeit one that is "unruly and eclectic," of multiple genres, and is both repetitive and chaotic. A form that more often than not loses the plot. Indeed, we might understand the production of the family *as* the plot, the driving force and the album's reason for being.[43] What is more, if we understand the family album as an act of communication whose "suspended conversations," to use Langford's term, are reawakened by subsequent engagements, then the album allows for the possibility of different tellings each time it is opened. The tattered pages

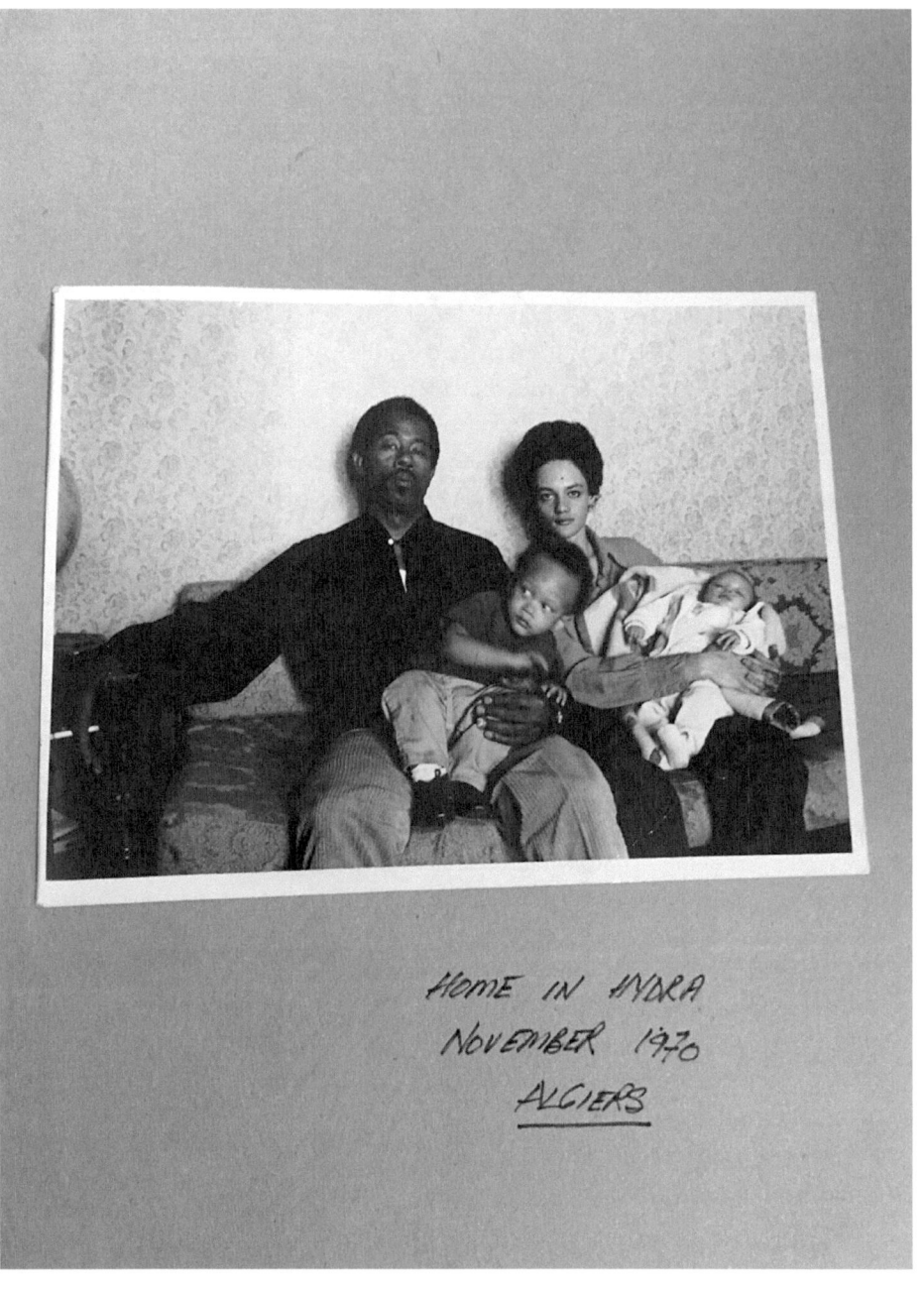

HOME IN HYDRA
NOVEMBER 1970
ALGIERS

FIGURE 3.9. "Home in Hydra, November 1970, Algiers." From Kathleen Cleaver family photo album. Photograph of album by John Stephens. Courtesy and © Kathleen Neal Cleaver Archive.

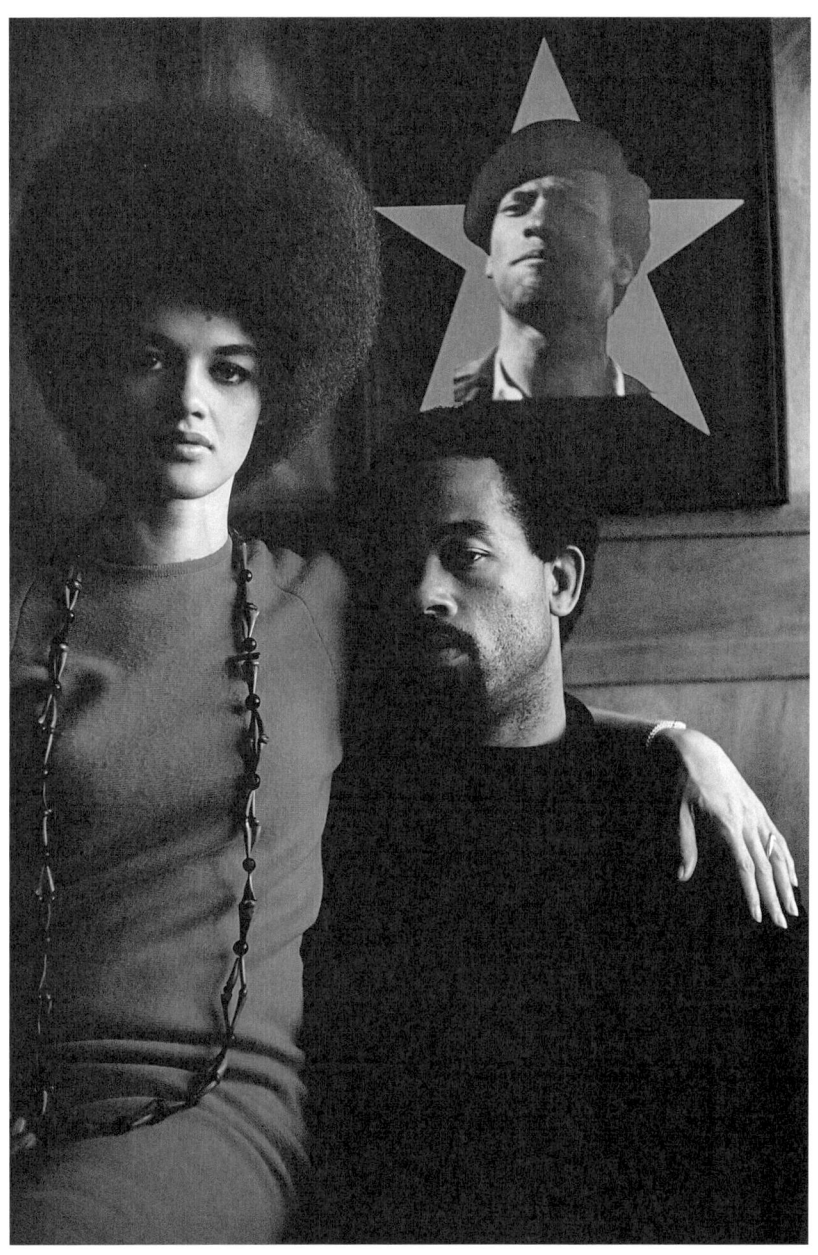

FIGURE 3.10. Gordon Parks, *Eldridge Cleaver and His Wife, Kathleen, Algiers, Algeria, 1970*. Courtesy and © The Gordon Parks Foundation.

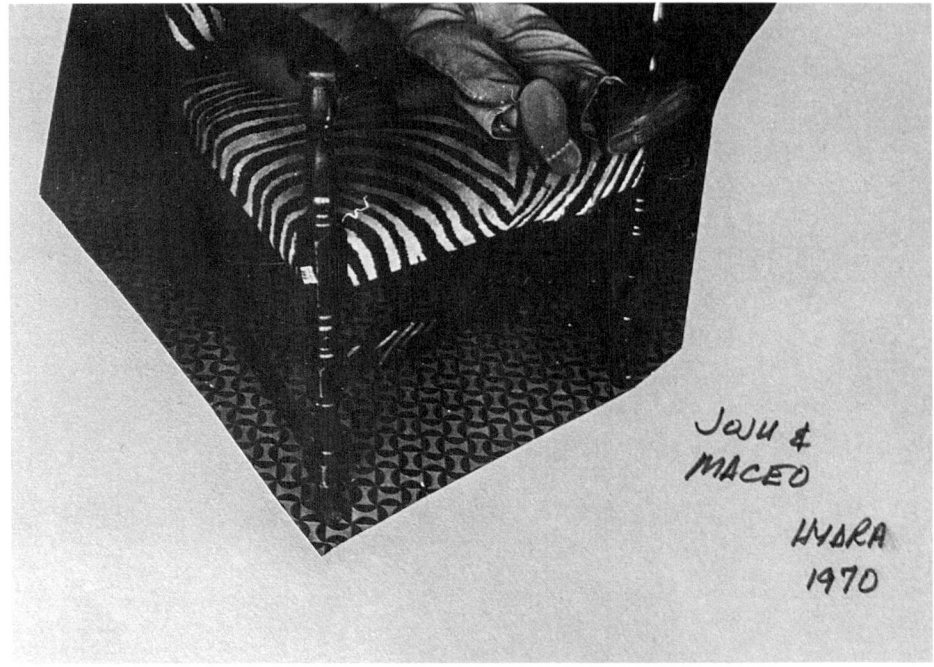

FIGURE 3.11. "Joju & Maceo [Cleaver], Hydra 1970" (figure 3.1), detail.

and loosely affixed photographs suggest as much. Here, in the Algiers album, nothing is fixed, not in the sense of having been cemented or of having been repaired. Indeed, any attempt to fasten a meaning or to resolve a story only proves fruitless, only invites more questions than it might answer.

The impossibility of holding the girl child still or of keeping the other one happy alerts us to the impossibility of a closed or complete narrative.

Curating a Life

Let's return one last time to the photograph of Joju and Maceo in the zebra chair to consider the diasporic work of curating (see figure 3.1). While the children are seated in the chair and the chair rests on the tile floor, the image itself seems to float in the center of the album's page (figure 3.11). The photograph sits on its own page, and no other images appear on the one facing it. It is clear the photograph has been cut with the effect of emphasizing the chair and children, and excising the room around them. In fact, in another photograph from this same series, which Kathleen has kept framed on the piano in her living room, Kathleen has excised herself. It is Kathleen's own handwriting that disrupts the sense of the children in a universe of their own: just to the lower right of the image she has identified this photograph as "Joju & Maceo," and just below that "Hydra 1970." In this way, she provides a written anchor to the visual balloon.

It is the cut-and-paste detail, the negative space, and Kathleen's handwriting that remind us of the work of assemblage and authorship of the album. And the very selection of a scrapbook with paper pages, rather than a photo album with sticky pages and designated plastic sleeves, alerts us to Kathleen's intention to compose and not just compile, to narrate and not merely document. But rather than that of artist or author, here we can think of Kathleen's process as curatorial, as selecting, organizing, arranging, and looking after the items in a collection. We need to consider curating as a key feature of her personal and political work.

Kathleen is herself a lover of photography and is finely attuned to the power of the visual in social movements. When she began working with the Black Panther Party officially in November 1967, she "created the position of Communications Secretary based on what I had seen Julian Bond do" during her time with SNCC. "I sent out press releases, I got photographers and journalists to publish stories about us, . . . I designed posters," though she never put her name on the posters she created.[44] It was Kathleen who, as BPP communications secretary, enlisted husband-and-wife team Pirkle Jones and Ruth-Marion Baruch to make intimate portraits of Panthers and their supporters to counter the blustering, swaggering images circulating in the mainstream press, a commission that resulted in the book and photography exhibit *Black Panther 1968* and in many ways set the terms for subsequent Panther portraiture. It was Kathleen who saw freelance photographer Jeffrey Blankfort's photographs in a San Francisco newspaper and invited him to photograph for the Party. Gordon Parks's visit to Algeria that resulted in the iconic image of Kathleen and Eldridge (and Huey) sparked a friendship between Kathleen and Parks until the latter's death in 2006, a relationship nurtured during the time that Kathleen's former longtime partner, documentarian St. Clair Bourne, produced *Half Past Autumn*, a film about Parks. Kathleen served on the board of the Gordon Parks Foundation for many years and was honored by the foundation at its gala in 2016. This lifelong penchant for identifying images and aesthetics she liked, and transforming that enthusiasm into political commitment, I believe enables us to think about collecting, curation, and assemblage in potentially radical or, at the very least, transformative terms; that is, to understand the significance of visual representation for narrating one's own story.

We might think of collecting as doing similar work. Although she rarely took up the camera herself, Cleaver noted that "when I was in California, people kept taking pictures of me, so I started to collect them." Collecting photographs of herself as she watched herself become an icon—a phenomenon she has described as simply "weird"—was a way of inventorying and asserting control over the proliferation of her own image.[45]

Paying attention to the differences between the image of Maceo and Joju as it appears in the album and as it appears framed in Kathleen's home helps us make sense of the latter pages of the album, where Eldridge makes fewer appearances. With Eldridge no longer a central or primary figure, these later pages feature more professional photographs of Kathleen, as well as a number of large-group snapshots and pictures of unidentified people. Many of these photographs were made during Kathleen's tour of Europe and the United States after the split from the BPP and her making space from Eldridge. At first, I thought these selections were a bit random, somewhat odd, and I could not make sense of how they fit into the story of the Cleavers in exile. But their inclusion in a family album, in *this* family album, pushes the parameters of both *who* constitutes family—whether by blood, by skin, or by choice—and *what* constitutes a family photographic archive, from snapshots and formal portraits, mugshots and posters, to personal albums and public websites. The album suggests that these are fluid concepts yet are mutually reinforcing. These photographs suggest the beginning of Kathleen building a life after the Party and after Eldridge. In the early 1980s, we can see Kathleen putting together a "dream book for existing otherwise," reminding herself that she had been doing so even a decade earlier.[46]

The curatorial may not return Kathleen to the center of her life narrative, but it reaffirms her architectural work, her work as an organizer and as a creator. It enables us to celebrate her political, intellectual, and cultural labor while respecting her "right to opacity." Caribbean philosopher Édouard Glissant famously called for the "right to opacity" as a way to hold space for the unknowable, as a means to challenge the Enlightenment precept that one must be "legible" to be regarded as human. And, indeed, "visibility" for marginalized peoples has been the route to recognition by the state. Yet we know that visibility, access, and transparency can present their own traps and dangers. This is especially so for Black women, whose lives and bodies are not simply or only ignored but are subject to heightened civic and state exposure, intervention, surveillance, and distortion. Reading the album as a curatorial project directs us to take seriously that which is included in the album, what is cut and pasted, marked and torn, removed and replaced. It opens a pathway to thinking about Black women's leadership, organizing, and world-building, to holding the public and the private, the spoken and the withheld, not in opposition but as concomitant forces in the production of a radical imagination. And it does so without demanding an uncritical visibility.

Conclusion—On Archival Abundance

How do we tell the stories of Black women's lives when the records are scant or nonexistent, misleading if not outright lies, registers of the state or of capitalist domination that invoke Black women only as fungible commodities? This work feels urgent because we know they are there in history because we are here.

Black feminist scholars have urged caution in the archives, especially when it comes to centering the lives of Black women subjects. Saidiya Hartman, Ula Taylor, Hazel Carby, Tera Hunter, Tina Campt, Daphne Brooks, Farah Jasmine Griffin, Sarah Hayley, Marisa Fuentes, and Françoise Hamlin, to name only a few, have taught us to read for, against, and with archival silence. They have taught us how to write through the development and employment of methodologies like "reading against the bias grain" (Fuentes) and "critical fabulation" (Hartman).[47] They have reminded us that new theories require new histories. And they have alerted us to the ways our own desires for subjects' "agency" or narrative "wholeness" are at once powerful and dangerous impulses.

The Cleaver archive reminds us of the rarity of such records, those made by and about Black women themselves. And yet such an archive still runs the risk of misinterpretation, especially when utilized to uphold foundational and familiar stories of Black life, stories that eschew complexity in favor of heroism, that smooth over contradiction for the sake of a tidy ending. Instead, following Marianne Hirsch, we might consider this an "archive of possibility," one that in Hirsch's words "makes space for countermemories and potentially disruptive memories," that "asks us to rethink what constitutes an event" or a "life of value." In this way, an archive of possibility has the power to "shift the structures of knowledge and intelligibility" that archives presume in their institutionalization of knowledge.[48] The Cleaver collection also impresses on us the importance of archive making and caretaking, especially of a generation still with us though dying, and of movements whose histories are still being shaped. In these ways we might understand a curatorial practice as part of what Cedric Robinson called the Black radical tradition, the ongoing cultivation of "an ideology of liberation" that seeks the *could be* of life outside the "systemic privations of racial capitalism."[49] The Algiers album, and the photographic archive from which it comes, reveals a life of radical commitments that does not deny life itself.

4

SHELTER IN PLACE

DAWOUD BEY, SADIE BARNETTE, AND
THE PHOTOGRAPHY OF UNCERTAINTY

Looking Back

Here's a random sampling of photographs from my phone, March through September 2020:

- An image of a cruise ship out in the San Francisco Bay taken from the hill where I walk my dog.
- My spouse at the dining room table, speaking intensely into his laptop, one arm raised above his head mid-gesticulation.
- Our family eating dinner at the same dining room table.
- Industrial-size containers of Aveeno lotion, Lysol wipes, and Mixed Chicks leave-in conditioner (a still life).
- My younger kid in a graduation cap and gown in front of our house, standing next to a lawn sign that reads "Congratulations Class of 2020."
- The backs of dozens of protesters and their signs marching through Berkeley (no faces).
- iPhone images of Zoom sessions before I started taking screenshots.
- A seemingly endless array of photographs of the sky from my bedroom window.

I am an image hoarder who doesn't delete their phone photos (70,928 as of this writing). And now, looking back—and it doesn't matter when I'm writing this because it is always "looking back"—I am trying to make sense of these assorted images. I'm wondering what I thought I was seeing. Wondering what it is I thought I was saving, capturing, documenting. What knowledge did I think I was producing? What was I trying to learn through the act of making these photographs?

When I took them, we were in the midst of at least one pandemic. I couldn't have told you (nor could anyone else) whether this was the opening foray of a soon-to-be-contained crisis, the soft side of a flattened curve, or the pernicious creep of a coming storm. I could tell you that we were surrounded by imminent and immanent death.

On March 17, 2020, six counties in the Bay Area, where I call home, were ordered to shelter in place. "Shelter in place" is the term used at the onset of a storm or tornado, a school shooting, a rampant fire, or an earthquake (disasters man-made and naturalized): an order to stay put where you are and wait out whatever emergency threatens. "Get inside, stay inside" said the Centers for Disease Control website. Stop. Drop. Hold. Do your best to get to safety as fast as you can and hold on. Be still, breathe. Be kind, hold your breath. If you must go outside, wear a mask. Learn to breathe through this new behavior.

I made thirty-nine photos that day.

My photos from March to September 2020 reveal the tight circuit of my everyday life: kitchen, bathroom, front yard, dog walk, dining room, bedroom. These photos also demonstrate my privilege: a healthy family, a job that could be transitioned online and its correlate, strong Wi-Fi, not to mention access to good hygiene products in overabundance, and above all, a safe home.

"Home" it seemed was the best defense against an indifferent virus we could not see, a malignant federal government that refused to see, and the persistent vulnerability to premature death that we had seen for far too long. And yet, even as we came to rely on home so intensely, we were also reminded that home is permeable, fragile, and precarious. Whether by virtue of the people we share it with (take, for example, the rise in instances of domestic abuse), the neighborhoods we live in (consider the rise in rates of homelessness), or the unrelenting demand for the rent or mortgage we owe. Or maybe it was Breonna Taylor's murder by Louisville police while she slept in her bed, as she sheltered in place, that reaffirmed for you, as it did for me, that home, especially Black home, is nothing more than a notion in or to a society structured in white supremacy. (Reader, are we still waiting for all three of the police officers who participated in her murder to be fired, arrested, indicted, convicted? And if those officers have faced charges, would we call it "justice"?)

What is photography in the context of volatility and doubt?

From the emergence of the medium, we in the Euro-American context have been taught to think of photography as proof.[1] And certainly proof has been photography's mode of being in the Western world and its call to service. We have been disciplined to engage photographs as assertive, detail-oriented, confident in their gathering up of the past, self-assured in their framing of right now, and even in their function as a medium able to document other worlds and other dimensions.

Yet when I look at these photographs from the first year of the pandemic—mine and others'—all I see is a true picture of uncertainty. Photo after screenshot after photo persistently asking questions about the future.

But really has there ever been a photography that *didn't* emerge from volatility and doubt? That *didn't* hope to contain the mercurial, settle a debate, or fix a problem? If, since the advent of colonialism, imperialism, and the transatlantic slave trade, we are always already in the midst of catastrophe as Aimé Césaire, Walter Benjamin, and so many others have reminded us, can photography's world-making capacity be anything other than world-proposing?[2] We want photography to be a period, but it's really just a question mark.

Increasingly, theorists and lovers of photography have called on us to explore photography's unknowns. Shawn Michelle Smith has encouraged us to consider what lies "at the edge of sight" outside the photographic frame, what a photograph does not, will not, or cannot register whether by virtue of the limits of the medium or by the biases of the mediator that Sylvia Wynter calls our "inner eyes."[3] Stanley Wolukau-Wanambwa directs our attention to "art that interrogates the notional transparency, the efficacy and intelligibility of the visual, as a site through which we encounter but at the same time fail to know one another," especially in this century, whose "optic . . . has been conflagration and catastrophe." Tina Campt has urged us to listen to the frequencies beyond the visual (and the visible) that at once amplify and defy the photograph's studium. Teju Cole not only reminds us that photography is a synaesthetic experience in which seeing is always more than seeing, but "argue[s] for the urgency of using our senses—interpreted as capaciously as possible—to respond to experience, embrace epiphany, and intensify our ethical commitments." I am inspired by these thinkers and so many others who offer reading practices that "show us 'not seeing.'"[4]

Photography in pandemic—mine and others—felt like a desperate effort to see and to make meaning when meaning was premature and indeed when "there was nothing to see here." Instead of straining to see what we think might be missing from photographs, what if we embrace exactly what the photograph cannot tell us? Pivot (a favorite pandemic choreography) toward the unknowable, the illegible, the anxious repetition. What kind of reading practice emerges if photography's origin point is uncertainty and unknowing?

I end this book with Dawoud Bey's crepuscular, more black than white series *Night Coming Tenderly, Black* (2018) and Sadie Barnette's vividly technicolor assemblage *Family Tree* (2021) for two reasons. First, each artist pushes photography beyond its limits in their respective works, destabilizes the relationship between seeing and knowing, and forces viewers to see and situate themselves in new constellations of belonging. But, more subjectively, *Night Coming Tenderly, Black* was the last museum exhibition I saw before the pandemic lockdown. And *Family Tree* was the first I saw when the world made tentative steps toward opening again. As such, they bookend my thinking about home and photography. Had I seen them under different circumstances, I'm sure I would have asked different questions of them. They might have led me to different conclusions. I'm sure I would have needed them to solve different puzzles.

But alas here we are.

Looking Through

Freedom was a thing that shifted as you looked at it, the way a forest is dense with trees up close but from outside, from the empty meadow, you see its true limits.
—COLSON WHITEHEAD, *The Underground Railroad*

The photograph is dark, layers of black and gray and more black, its subject nearly indiscernible. In fact, you probably can't see much in the adjacent reproduction (figure 4.1), so you'll just have to trust my description. A tangle of thin tree trunks populates the entirety of the photograph. They root below the bottom edge of the frame and reach above its top edge, beyond our sight. The branches are mostly bare, having given up their leaves to form a blanket on the lower third of the photograph. Some leaves cling to branches: a blurry cluster appears in the left foreground, and at the top they appear as splattered watercolor droplets or tiny exploding black stars.

Dawoud Bey's *Untitled #17 (Forest)* is a photograph of a dense forest in late autumn. It is so redolent with darkness that it defies the very ontology of photography—writing with light, the index referent of what has been. Instead, a gelatin silver print patiently overexposed in the darkroom now ventures toward an abstractionist painting, a rendering of twisting black lines that form dark networks. It is not clear if those networks are there to impede or facilitate

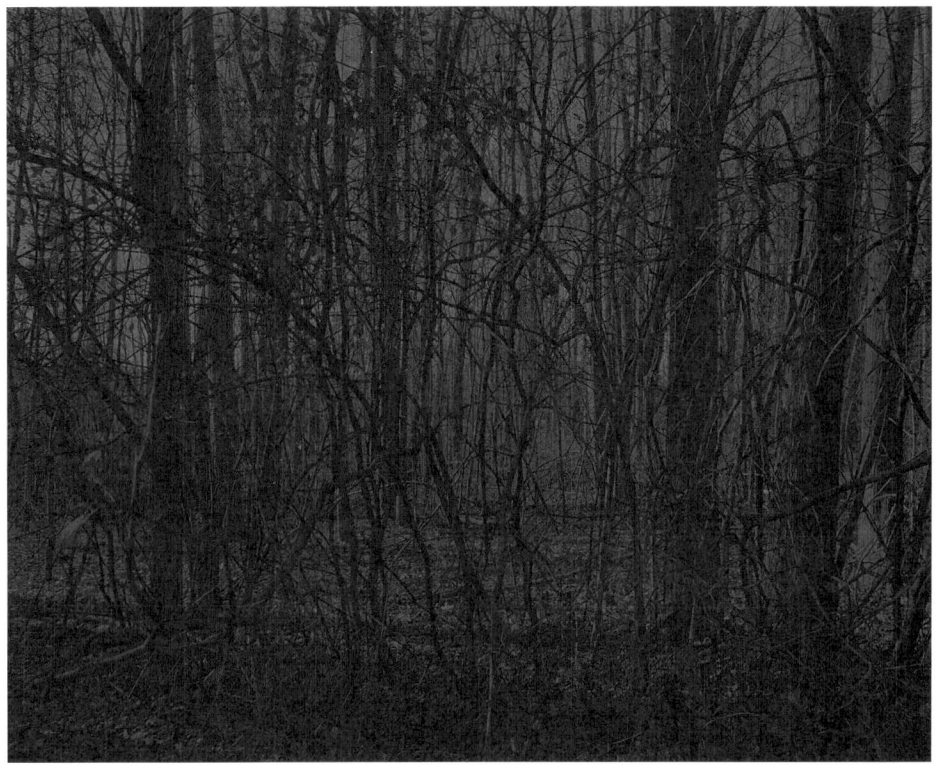

FIGURE 4.1. Dawoud Bey, *Untitled #17 (Forest)*, from the series *Night Coming Tenderly, Black*, 2017. Gelatin silver print, 44 × 55 in. Photograph © Dawoud Bey, Courtesy of Sean Kelly Gallery.

our movement. It is not clear that there is a path out, but when we move and sway in front of it, we find just enough light. It is dense but not impossible. I just have to trust that there is a way through.

Untitled #17 (Forest) is one of twenty-five images that compose Bey's *Night Coming Tenderly, Black*. This 2018 series of large (44 × 55 inches) black and gray photographs of the outdoors in and around Cleveland, Ohio, is Bey's rendering of "the sensory and spatial experience of fugitive slaves moving through the darkness of a pre–Civil War landscape—an enveloping darkness that was a passage to liberation."[5] Twelve of the series are featured in Bey's retrospective show *Dawoud Bey: An American Project*, which opened at the San Francisco Museum of Modern Art on February 15, 2020. But, like most everything else this spring, the show hasn't been seen in person since the Bay Area went to shelter-in-place orders on March 17.

It is strange and a bit disconcerting to think of these somnambulant images of a fulsome outdoors—photographs that demand a full-body engagement to be felt and reckoned with, that visualize the limits and possibilities of freedom, and that question the very notion of shelter—hanging unseen and unfelt in the silence of the museum.

To drop a pin, I write this in the midst of a global pandemic and a series of national uprisings. On my screens people have taken over the streets of Minneapolis, of Denver, of NYC. Oakland will join tonight. Most protesters wear masks. I wish they all would, both to mitigate the spread of the virus and to protect their identities. Right now, Black people are dying at higher rates of COVID than any other demographic, and right now Black people are risking their lives protesting the murder of Black people by police and other agents of the state. This writing comes in medias res; maybe when you read this you'll know if this was a short-lived explosion or the start of a long hot summer; if the state of emergency is soon to be forgotten or if this is the conjuncture, the portal, the honest-to-god revolution.

To drop a pin, I write from inside a moment so dense, so thick, so dark that it's hard to know where we are or what's ahead. All I know is that I need to keep moving, we cannot go back to the before, to the normal. Instead, I follow Cora, the protagonist of Colson Whitehead's novel *The Underground Railroad*, who "trusted the slave's choice to guide her—anywhere, anywhere but where you are escaping from."[6]

Ostensibly, *Night Coming Tenderly, Black* is about "the past," and Bey has reminded audiences that "the [photographic] language of history is black and white." Black and white is also the visual telegraph of archival document. *Night Coming* revisits and imagines stops on the Underground Railroad, the network of activists who aided fugitives' perilous journeys out of the South of their enslavement. Bey emphasizes the blackness of black and white to offer an imaginative act of visualizing history that doesn't feign verisimilitude. Indeed, the present announces itself immediately in the form of an air conditioning unit that appears, like a blinking eye, at practically the center of the very first photograph in the series, *Untitled #1 (Picket Fence and Farmhouse)* (figure 4.2). And the present repeats by way of telephone wires in *Untitled #3 (Cozad-Bates House)* and a satellite dish in *Untitled #18 (Creek and House)* (figures 4.3 and 4.4). Lest we imagine ourselves too far removed from the hold, the plantation, *Night Coming* reminds us that the time of slavery is also now. This part is not clever framing on Bey's part—the present and the past coexist all around us.

In its form, the series enacts the clandestine nature of the Underground Railroad,[7] enhancing the darkness that protects the runaway from capture back into

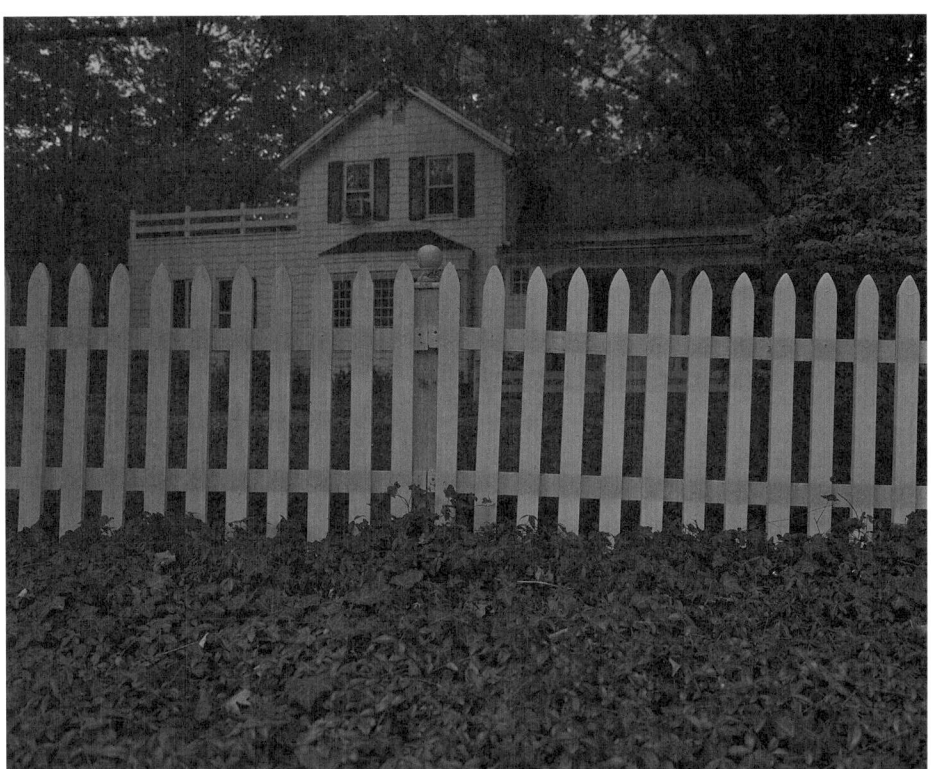

FIGURE 4.2. Dawoud Bey, *Untitled #1 (Picket Fence and Farmhouse)*, from the series *Night Coming Tenderly, Black*, 2017. Photograph © Dawoud Bey, Courtesy of Sean Kelly Gallery.

slavery; accentuating and reveling in the blackness that protects the would-be photographic subjects from overexposure and imprisonment in the camera's luminous glare. In so doing, Bey upends the movement from the shadow to the light as the teleology of representational progress.

Night Coming Tenderly, Black carves a path through so many of the visual conundra that have troubled the terrain of Black visuality. For Bey, long known and celebrated as a portraitist, *Night Coming* refuses "photographic capture" through its shift to landscape.[8] So too does *Night Coming* refuse the affirmation of the self that portraiture confers and confirms. There is no sitter in stasis, no subject made regnant by or subjected to the sovereignty of the photograph. It is the loving, enveloping blackness of Roy DeCarava, one of Bey's influences. It is the blackness of Édouard Glissant's opacity. It is the blackness that Cedric Robinson, Teju Cole, and Tavia Nyong'o have each reminded us we can't even yet imagine.[9]

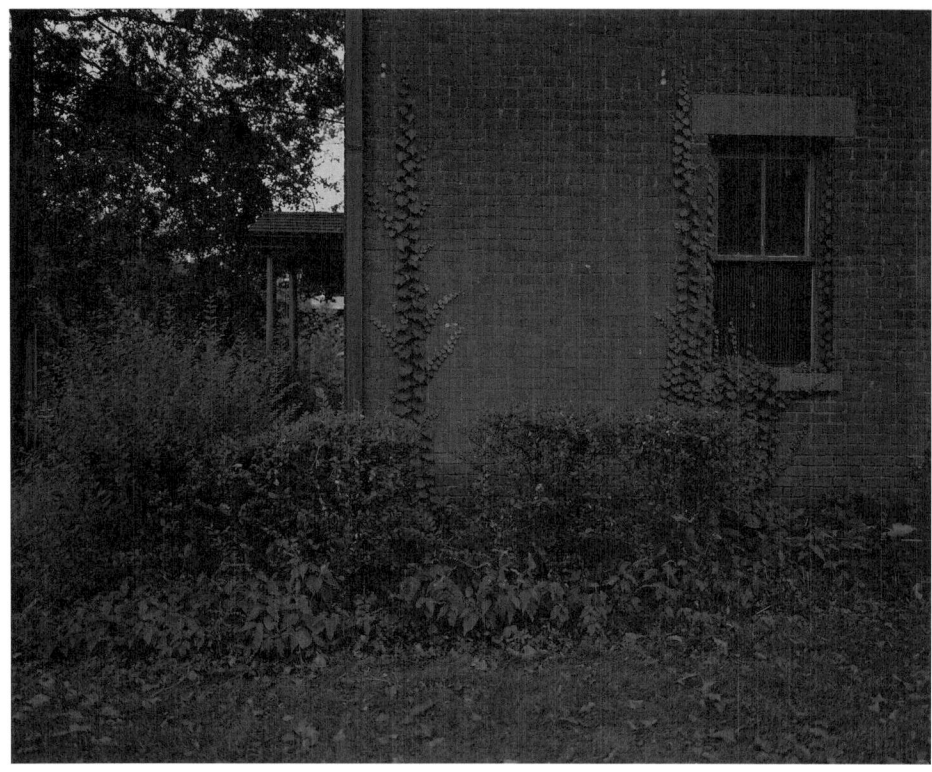

FIGURE 4.3. Dawoud Bey, *Untitled #3 (Cozad-Bates House)*, from the series *Night Coming Tenderly, Black*, 2017. Photograph © Dawoud Bey, Courtesy of Sean Kelly Gallery.

A landscape image practically too dark to reproduce, one that requires our "acute motion" to become legible (Dyson), that invites our slowed breath and listening ear to register their quiet (Campt), that references the terror of the hold and also the grace of being held (Sharpe), that enacts the tactics and strategies of "dark sousveillance" (Browne), that shifts our perspective from the seen to the seeing.[10] Is it possible that such a photograph utterly devoid of people is as true and as intimate as the portraits that have come to define Bey's work?

From his first series, *Harlem U.S.A.* (1978), to the *Birmingham Project* (2012), portraiture has been Bey's primary mode of expression. It was *Harlem Redux*, the 2015 series imaging the rapid gentrification of Black Harlem, that marked a move away from the centrality of the human figure to convey Bey's stories of people and place. Bey has acknowledged that *Harlem Redux* laid the groundwork for *Night Coming*. But where *Harlem Redux* depicts an urban landscape

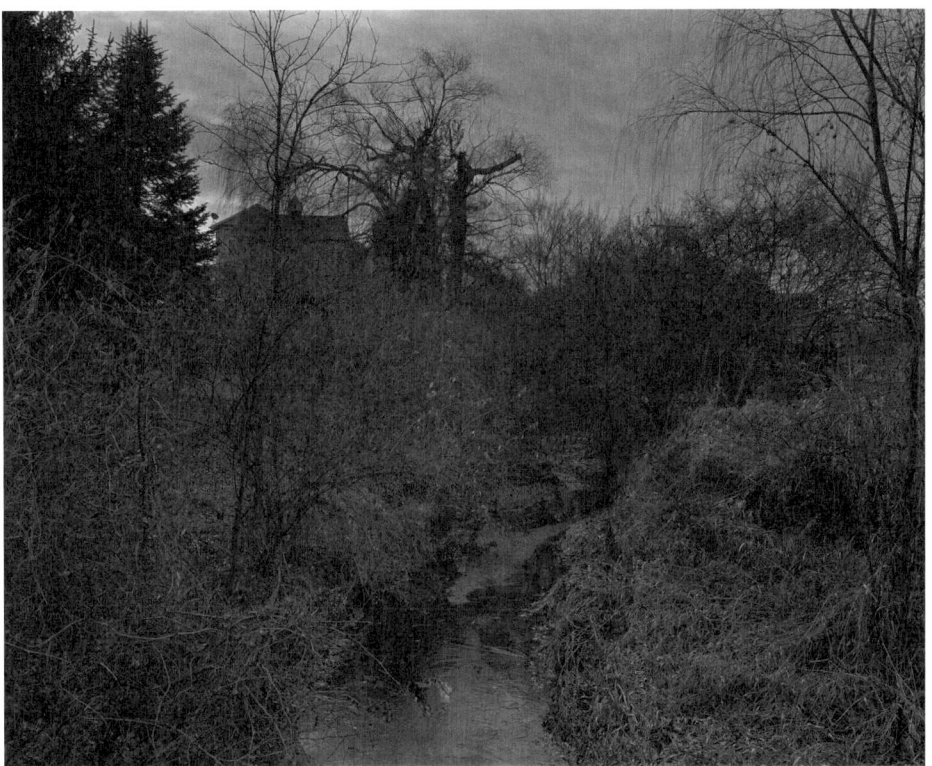

FIGURE 4.4. Dawoud Bey, *Untitled #18 (Creek and House)*, from the series *Night Coming Tenderly, Black*, 2017. Photograph © Dawoud Bey, Courtesy of Sean Kelly Gallery.

saturated in color and devoid of people to convey an electric erasure, *Night Coming* offers us fields, foliage, and waterways suffused in darkness and in subtle but constant motion. The move from *Harlem Redux* to *Night Coming Tenderly, Black* is a move from the enclosure to the outdoors; from confined and constrained spaces to air to breathe; from the ordered density of the city grid to "the uncleared and the overgrown."[11] It is a move from racial capitalism's neon dystopic future to the "potential history" of the runaway and the maroon.[12]

For me, the forest is a revelation, and also a cipher. In moving to landscape, Bey reminds us that Black folks both put their hands in the earth to build this nation's wealth and were hung from trees for daring to live as though we belonged.[13] So too does Bey assert the profound beauty and terror of the outdoors, and the uncertain pact that fugitives made with these places as gauntlets to freedom.

Neither past nor present, at once abstraction and figuration, both document and fiction: I can describe *Untitled #17 (Forest)* only as *crepuscular*, "of or relating to twilight." We often think of twilight as the passage between day and night. But "crepuscular" names its own time and its own sets of behaviors: frogs croak out a song in round, fireflies dance bioluminescent in shifting light. Mice come to nibble at left-behind scraps, and mosquitos search out blood to ensure their own survival. *Untitled #17 (Forest)* depicts the inexorable motion of the fugitive; it is a work of art that necessitates we take this time—so dense, so thick, so dark—on its own terms.

What if we choose, in the midst of flight (and fight), to linger here for a moment? To breathe together (which is the root meaning of "conspire")? To listen for one another and all other things living and once living and still living? What if we share this quiet and let the darkness hold us, our secrets, and our dreams? Is this freedom? Is this home?

> *On the bed of damp earth, her breathing slowed and that which separated herself from the swamp disappeared. She was free.*
> *This moment.*[14]

Looking Beyond

I need to talk about living room
where I can sit without grief without wailing aloud
for my loved ones
—June Jordan, from "Moving Towards Home"

It is COVID season 4 (January 2022). I am waiting for an announcement from campus about when, how, if the semester will start. I have purchased 150 K95 masks, and 20 rapid COVID tests in anticipation of full classrooms. I am steeling myself for my twenty-two-year-old kid's imminent departure back to New York City into the throes of Omicron and into a shoebox apartment. And also for another semester of my nineteen-year-old kid's ambivalence about a job (frontline) or school (online). The latter's malaise, wrapped in a vicious depression, is not wrong and echolocates them within the sea of my similarly enraged and despondent students. Before I spiral, I pronounce myself lucky, count benedictions, in order to squeeze my fear and disappointment back into their box. Instead, I've ridden a mostly empty BART to San Francisco to see Sadie Barnette's solo exhibition *Inheritance* at Jessica Silverman Gallery one last time before the show closes. Following June Jordan, I am in search of somewhere I can sit without heartbreak and distress, even for just a few minutes. This is not my first time

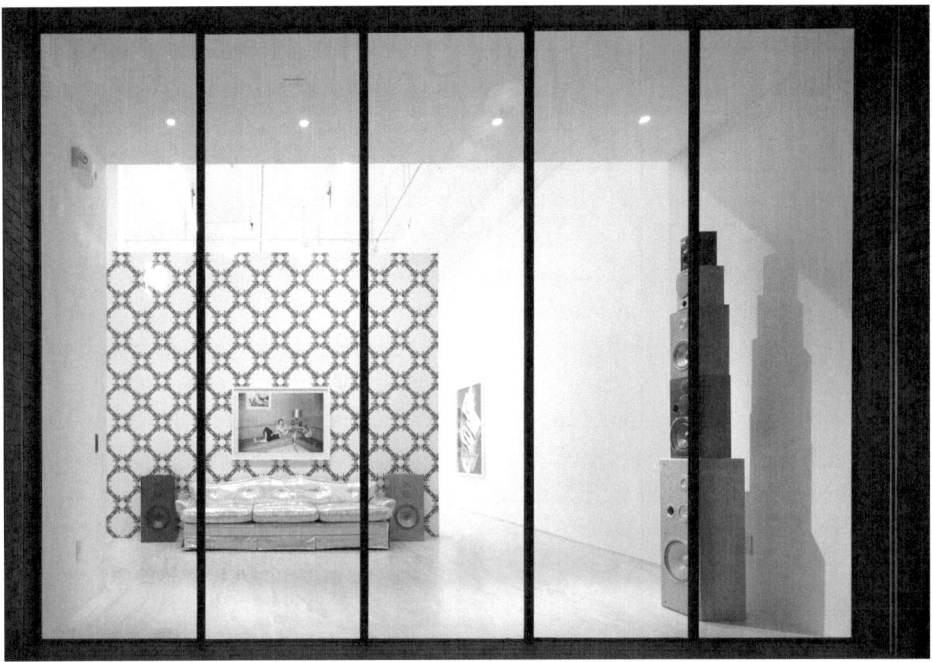

FIGURE 4.5. Installation view, Sadie Barnette, *Inheritance*, 2021, Jessica Silverman Gallery, San Francisco. Photograph by John White. © Sadie Barnette. Courtesy of the artist and Jessica Silverman, San Francisco.

back seeing art in public (I saw *Inheritance* when it opened two months earlier), but the Omicron variant has initiated a new wave of caution and closures. So I called the gallery beforehand to see if they're still open or if they're temporarily shuttered, as many public places have. There are no guarantees.

I know I've arrived at the right place, because a hot-pink glow radiates out onto Grant Street, generated by the white lights of the gallery streaming through the tinted front picture window (figure 4.5).

Inheritance is a show about family—as is Barnette's practice more broadly— about honoring the histories of the people we come from and, through flights of, and insistence on, otherworldly imagination, continuing our ancestors' ongoing work of carving spaces of belonging under the cruelest of conditions. *Inheritance* is the largest assemblage of Barnette's art to date, much of which revisits, reclaims, and reimagines Sadie's father Rodney Barnette's history specifically. One wall features a diptych of photographs of Rodney in uniform, both made by Rodney's then-teenage niece, Sharon. *Untitled (Dad, 1966 and 1968)* from

2016: a 1966 photograph of Rodney standing in his sister's living room wearing the uniform of the US Army during his service in the Vietnam War, and immediately to the right a tighter-focus portrait of Rodney two years later in the de facto uniform of the Black Panther (black beret and black leather jacket), when Rodney helped found the Compton chapter of the BPP and would later provide security detail for Angela Y. Davis following her years of incarceration.

Another gallery wall is devoted to five works (all 2020) in the *FBI Drawings* series, which continue Barnette's ongoing engagement with the five hundred–page surveillance file the FBI amassed on Rodney in the 1960s and 1970s. In previous iterations of this project, Sadie reproduced the documents at their original size and annotated them (per Christina Sharpe) with pink spray paint, glitter, rhinestones, and Hello Kitty stickers, endeavoring to undermine masculine authority and intervening in the state surveillance the original documents represent and reproduce. In the newer work on view in *Inheritance*, Barnette has reproduced the files as five-by-four-foot drawings, inverting the black on white to white on black by overlaying the images with graphite dust shavings applied freehand. Hello Kitty and flowers adorn these newer, larger drawings as they do in the *My Father's FBI File* projects, 2016–2018, not as store-bought appliqués but figures hand drawn in repetitive, meditative patterns. Look closely at the paper's corners and you can see an uneven edge or a stray graphite mark, subtle indications of Sadie's labor as draftsman, as researcher, as keeper and interpreter of family stories. Sadie redacts the FBI's redactions with accoutrements of a femme girlhood, performing "an impossible and tiny act of healing" and asserting a hot-pink rage.[15]

The wall opposite the *FBI Drawings* features three framed graphic drawings: the *Sister Sister* wallpaper reappears here as a framed five-by-four-foot, framed colored-pencil composition now in blue, purple, and two shades of pink, and alongside two others, "Together Together Together" and "Family Style," both white text on black backdrop, with pops of pink. Found speakers covered in pink and purple car paint and glitter stand in various locations on the gallery floor stacked in eight-foot towers. Though silent, they underscore the sociality of and between the art that surrounds them throughout the exhibition. The color pink punctuates all of these works, drawing attention to keywords in the graphic canvases, calling on viewers to listen closely and wait for the beat to drop.

Elements of the multimedia installation *The New Eagle Creek Saloon* are situated throughout *Inheritance*. An homage to Rodney's ownership of the first Black-owned gay bar in San Francisco (1990–93), *The New Eagle Creek Saloon* installation in Sadie's words "bend[s] space and time and reanimate[s] the bones" of the original bar "in an intergenerational revival."[16] Rodney Barnette established The New Eagle Creek as a refuge from the anti-Blackness of San Francisco's gay bar scene, where Black patrons were routinely asked for three forms of identification and excluded from white establishments. The New Eagle Creek, renovated by Rodney and his brothers, soon became a place for Black queer Bay Area communities to drink, dance, fundraise, celebrate, mourn, and just breathe. Sadie, with support from designer Steven Thompson, fabricated a full glittered bar replete with stools, live plants, photographs, books, and vinyl records, illuminated by a pink neon sign spelling out the bar's name. In its fullest iterations, *New Eagle Creek* was first commissioned in 2019 by The Lab, an experimental art and performance space in San Francisco. The closing of the installation featured *New Eagle Creek* as a float at the San Francisco Pride Parade and has since been activated multiple times by bartenders, DJs, dancers, poets, and partygoers at museums and experimental art spaces across the United States. *Inheritance*'s abridged version of *The New Eagle Creek Saloon* manifests as more altar than nightclub, featuring a small bar with glass display and an adorned photograph of New Eagle Creek patrons, all outlined in pink neon. Pink neon and glitter here is a party. And as it forms the background of the archival vitrines, pink is also potential history, not just the story of what was, but of what might have been and what could still be. A reminder of how we make the conditions of possibility for our collective survival.

 Inheritance explicitly visualizes the direct line from Black Power to Black queer liberation through Rodney's ongoing commitment to a Black sense of place. Sadie takes up her father's work here in this show and across the arc of her practice. Her inheritance is to remain attuned to living spaces and seek ways to find breathing room in the wake of oppressive histories and their shitty legacies. Pink—as portal, as rage, as party, as punctuation, as potential and possibility—here is a medium and a mantra, a frequency and a location. It is a through line to Barnette's practice. *Inheritance* is a family album of a show, inviting viewers into a family history that becomes richer and more magical with each retelling.

 Tucked into the back corner of the gallery farthest from the front entrance is *Family Tree*, a work of thirty-five framed images (figure 4.6). *Family Tree* opens with a graphic spray paint and pencil work in bold that reads "Cassandra's Great great Granddaughter" in varying fonts. Immediately to its right is a photograph of the artist herself as a toddler; wearing a red dress with a white pinafore, she holds a red crayon as she looks up at the photographer, as if she had answered to the call of her name in the midst of coloring. What follows are archival and new photographs, graphic drawings, collages of varying sizes in a rainbow spec-

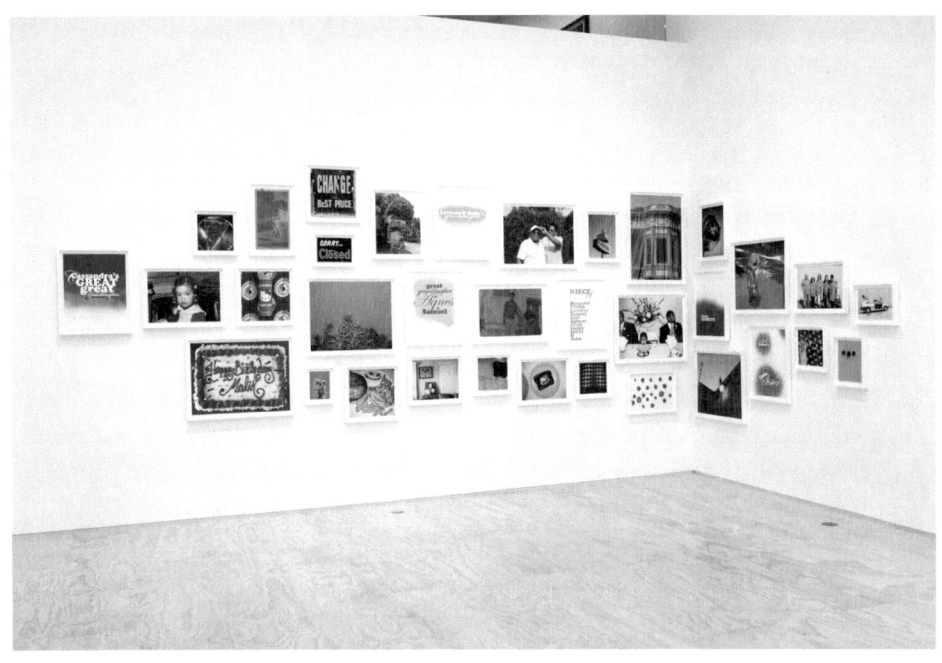

FIGURE 4.6. Sadie Barnette, *Family Tree*, 2021. Framed drawings on paper with spray paint, archival pigment-print photographs, and collages with overlaid rhinestones totaling 34 works; installed: 195 × 204 × 2 in. (495.3 × 518.2 × 5.1 cm). Edition of 1 (SB000901). Photograph by John White. © Sadie Barnette. Courtesy of the artist and Jessica Silverman, San Francisco.

trum of colors, framed in uniform white wood frames. *Family Tree* is hung salon style and bends around the corner of the wall.

It is a curious assemblage that first announces its queerness cheekily as a rainbow of faces, food, foliage, signs, stickers, and spray paint. Queer in the ways it highlights how we belong and don't belong, the way relations are claimed rather than assumed. The way family "members" are named and unnamed—blood, chosen family, and strangers alike. The way family manifests as people who, yes, may or may not bear resemblance, but also as places, plants, food, cars, and sparkling light. The way the family tree moves across mediums. The way images echo, the way the images together arc across two walls into a rainbow that works to unify, that holds difference without containing or muting it.

Calling this assemblage "family tree" strikes me as at once very sweet, somewhat kitschy, and also oddly traditional. As a form, the family tree dates back to medieval times as a means of visualizing lineage in order to document and sometimes mythologize male lines of descent and inheritance, to preserve and remember ancestors and "enhance the prestige of a lineage." The iconography of the tree emphasizes the verticality of filiation and of time—literally lines of descent—while also naturalizing heteronormative lineage as organic: "Like a tree, a family is born, flourishes, branches out and withers."[17] By the end of the twelfth century, according to medievalist Christiane Klapish-Zuber, attention to genealogy and lineage emerged "as the fundamental structural mechanism of power and social reproduction," that is, as the means to lay claim to past and future wealth and value. And the tree was genealogy's primary visual metaphor. The family tree has been a mainstay of apprehending and divining family ever since, whether "family" as private property or family as lost lineage, but always as family bound by blood.[18]

But what is family in the face of systems and structures that have denied Black peoples the opportunity to name and claim such a unit? What is family outside extractive capitalism and the passing down of wealth and prestige? Generations of Black and queer thinkers have necessarily questioned the articulation of "family" in the lived experience of Black peoples in the wake of the transatlantic slave trade. As Hortense Spillers writes:

> It seems clear . . . that "Family," as we practice it and understand it "in the West"—the *vertical* transfer of a bloodline, of a patronymic, of titles and entitlements, of real estate and the prerogatives of "cold cash," from *fathers* to *sons* and in the supposedly free exchange of affectional ties between a male and a female of *his* choice—becomes the mythically revered privilege of a free and freed community. In that sense, African peoples in the historic Diaspora had nothing to prove, *if* the point had been that they were not capable of "family" (read "civilization"), since it is stunningly evident . . . that Africans were not only capable of the concept and the practice of "family," including "slaves," but in modes of elaboration and naming that were at least as complex as those of the "nuclear family" "in the West."[19]

With nothing to prove, Barnette's *Family Tree* eschews the verticality of the traditional family tree. Instead, it moves horizontally left to right, appearing as a set of stories. In this way family unfolds. Inheritance is not passed down but accumulated, circulated. This family tree is rhizomatic, "flexible and improvisational," rather than fixed.[20] Édouard Glissant followed the rhizome's "enmeshed root system, a network spreading either in the ground or in the air, with no predatory rootstock taking over permanently," to imagine a nonhierarchical, nontotalitarian, impossible-to-know-everything-so-why-bother mode of being in the world.[21]

The rhizomatic form of the salon hang further suggests togetherness by way of individual containment. The display offers me a measure of comfort as we figure out how to be proximate again. The thought of any of us—our bodies, our breath, our three-dimensional living—rubbing too close produces anxiety. I find solace in a display in which elements are near but not touching. Curving as it does around the gallery corner, the elements of *Family Tree* feel in individual::collective motion, a murmuration.

What are these elements that make a family? In *Family Tree*, Barnette visualizes the "modes of elaboration and naming," the complexity of Black family to which Spillers alludes. Complexity and also uncertainty. Sadie's family isn't simply a compendium of people connected by blood but includes portraits of friends, and also a total stranger she photographed in a street encounter. Nor is this family simply people: it is equally an accumulation of places and colors, of food and machines, of signs and stickers and flashes of light. There is even a photograph of a verdant cannabis plant set against the orange sky of September 9, 2020, when wildfire smoke and fog cast an eerie, apocalyptic light over the Bay Area. This too is family? Sadie tells me that she was driven "to use as many things as possible so I could get closer to some truth or texture. To have all these little parts together was less about creating this definitive portrait.... Maybe we are a birthday cake, maybe we are a liquor store, maybe we are purple light.... The more we can layer up [the more we] don't give legitimacy to any one thing.... When you put them all together, it's about finding a texture of what it means to be alive."[22]

Close to the end of "Moving Towards Home," a poem about carving space for collective and communal care amid the onslaught of news about Israel's 1982 invasion of Lebanon in the Zionist state's decades-long project of Palestinian ethnic cleansing, the ever incisive June Jordan asserts that she remains perpetually transformed by the commitment to solidarity:

I was born a Black woman
and now
I am become a Palestinian
against the relentless laughter of evil
there is less and less living room
and where are my loved ones?[23]

"Moving Towards Home" intones the idea that we necessarily have to remap the contours of what we call home when the homes of oppressed peoples on the other side of the world can be reduced to rubble, when such destruction becomes so proximate and we are made to bear witness to such destruction in our daily lives. Whether the images arrive via a television set or a smartphone, the fact that we carry this violence and precarity with us in the intimacy of our own homes and daily lives reminds us that we are hailed to witness and bound in solidarity. Home for each of us is never guaranteed so long as home for any of us is under threat.

Jordan's comrade and friend Angela Davis might refer to Jordan's "becoming" in this poem as an "identity based on politics rather than a politics based on identity."[24] Stuart Hall might have noted it as a "politics of identification," one in which we recognize that identity is never fixed but always in process, not just being but also becoming.[25] Together with Jordan, Davis and Hall alert us and indeed invite us to form a sense of belonging through political solidarities, through what we owe one another and ourselves, through how we make and hold living room for all of us, especially those most vulnerable.

Family Tree, and Barnette's practice more broadly, foregrounds such political acts of kinship, not just (or even) with families of origin but with what and whom we chose to identify. Across *Inheritance*, here a father, a civil laborer, an ancestor, a color, a night sky, a nightclub might each reflect us back to ourselves. We might find certainty in claiming a flash of light, a portal into another dimension, a misunderstood plant against the backdrop of climate catastrophe, and might find belonging by, in turn, being claimed by each.

As I stand in front of *Family Tree* for the umpteenth time and prepare myself to go back out into the pandemic, I am reminded that the unknown is not a place or a time but a condition and an unfolding. That freedom shape-shifts as Whitehead would tell us, and home is only as strong, as just, as safe as we make it, according to Jordan. And I am reminded that it's time for me to do what we've always done: locate myself somewhere, let myself be claimed, make my own conditions of possibility for me and mine.

The pot of gold at the end of this rainbow is a white Honda hatchback, the one we saw earlier sitting small atop the "o" in Closed at the other end of the installation, trunk open, passenger door open, a rainbow sticker anchoring its back wheel. Ready. Waiting.

The end of *Family Tree* but clearly not the end. An intonation to keep moving. We out.

It is time to make our way home.[26]

Notes

INTRODUCTION. WHEN HOME IS A PHOTOGRAPH

1. Kathleen Neal Cleaver, "Memories of Love and War," unpublished memoir, Eldridge and Kathleen Cleaver Papers. Rose Library, Emory University, Atlanta, GA.

2. I wrote about this image in my essay "Restaging Revolution: Black Power, *Vibe* Magazine, and Photographic Memory"; and in chapter 3 of my first book, *Imprisoned in a Luminous Glare: Photography and the African American Freedom Struggle*. I first wrote about it in my senior thesis in college, on Black women and Blaxploitation films. When I say a long time, I mean a long time.

3. Davis, "Afro Images," 177.

4. Quashie, *Sovereignty of Quiet*.

5. Cleaver, "Memories of Love and War," n.p.

6. Deborah Willis, "Introduction: Picturing Us," in Willis, *Picturing Us*; hooks, "In Our Glory," 61.

7. Quashie, *Sovereignty of Quiet*, 3.

8. Campt, *Listening to Images*, 45.

9. Keeanga-Yamahtta Taylor coined the phrase "predatory inclusion" in her book *Race for Profit: How Banks and the Real Estate Industry Undermined Black Homeownership*.

10. Taylor, *Race for Profit*, 11.

11. See, for example, Sharpe, *Ordinary Notes*, 51.

12. Hooks, "Homeplace."

13. While 1619 is often cited as the year the first enslaved Africans were brought to the territory now known as the United States of America, as made popular by "The 1619 Project," this year merely marks the beginning of English slavery in the colonies. Spanish colonists brought enslaved Africans to the settlement in present-day St. Augustine, Florida, a half century earlier, reminding us that the history of African enslavement in North America, let alone the entire Western hemisphere, was a long, pan-European endeavor whose legacy cannot easily be undone (or erased, despite the best efforts of current authoritarian regimes). See Hannah-Jones, "1619 Project."

Orlando Patterson identifies natal alienation as a key aspect of the social death that marks the condition of the slave; that is, one's birth ties are not recognized, and familial structures are broken apart. Natal alienation, vulnerability to gratuitous violence, and the fungibility (expendability and interchangeability) of the Black/slave form the foundation of Afro-pessimist thought and fundamentally shape Western modernity. See Patterson, *Slavery and Social Death*; and Cunningham, "Argument of Afropessimism." See also Hayes, *Love for Liberation*, 4.

14. On belonging, see Glenn, *Unequal Freedom*, 52–54.

15. Azoulay, *Civil Imagination*, 26.

16. See Nash, *Black Body in Ecstasy*.

17. Hooks, "Oppositional Gaze."

18. Berger, *Ways of Seeing*, 8.

19. On "racial capitalism," see Levenson and Paret, "South African Tradition of Racial Capitalism"; Robinson, *Black Marxism*; Du Bois, *Black Reconstruction in America, 1860–1880*; Gilmore, "Abolition Geography and the Problem of Innocence"; and Huerta, *The Unintended*.

20. Azoulay, "Unlearning the Origins of Photography." See also Azoulay, *Potential History*; Lewis, *Unseen Truth*; and especially Kimberly Juanita Brown's powerful *Mortevivum: Photography and the Politics of the Visual*.

21. "Photography produces race as a visualizable fact." Fusco, "Racial Times, Racial Marks, Racial Metaphors," 60.

22. Pinney, *Photography and Anthropology*; Hirsch, *Family Frames*; Smith, *American Archives*; Krauss, "Photography's Discursive Spaces"; Berger, *Sight Unseen*; Mitchell, *Landscape and Power*; Berger, "Understanding a Photograph"; Berger "Changing View of Man in the Portrait." See also Sliwinski, *Human Rights in Camera*.

23. Sharpe's concept of the anagrammatical as developed in *In the Wake* builds on Hortense Spillers's "Mama's Baby, Papa's Maybe: An American Grammar Book."

24. Fanon, *Black Skin, White Masks*, 111.

25. Sharpe, *In the Wake*, 96; Hartman, *Wayward Lives, Beautiful Experiments*.

26. Katherine McKittrick writes, "A black sense of place is not a standpoint or a situated knowledge; it is a location of difficult encounter and relationality. A black sense of place is not individualized knowledge—it is collaborative praxis." McKittrick, *Dear Science and Other Stories*, 106.

27. On photography and the Great Migration of southern Black Americans to the US North and West in the first half of the twentieth century, see Morrison, "Quotidian Expenses." Alan Pelaez Lopez describes the arduous journeys of undocumented Afro-Mexican migrants to the United States in the early twenty-first century, in *Intergalactic Travels: Poems from a Fugitive Alien*. See also the compelling exhibition catalog *Home—So Different, So Appealing*, edited by Chon A. Noriega, Mari Carmen Ramírez, and Pilar Tompkins Rivera.

28. Brown, "Black Liverpool, Black America, and the Gendering of Diasporic Space"; Campt, *Image Matters*; Campt, *Listening to Images*; Griffin, *Who Set You Flowin'?*

29. Tate, *Domestic Allegories of Political Desire*, 7. See also Carby, *Reconstructing Womanhood*; duCille, *Coupling Convention*.

30. Alexander, *Black Interior*. See also Mitchell, *From Slave Cabins to the White House*.

31. Hartman, *Wayward Lives, Beautiful Experiments*.

32. Bailey, *Butch Queens Up in Pumps*; Allen, *There's a Disco Ball Between Us*; Shange, "Play Aunties and Dyke Bitches"; Green, "In the Life."

33. Du Bois, *Souls of Black Folk*, 8.

34. I am inspired here by Diné artist Will Wilson's description of his Critical Indigenous Photographic Exchange (CIPX) project, prompted by the question "What if Indians invented photography?" The project is, he says, "an intervention within the contentious and competing visual languages that form today's photographic canon," and a portal to imagining new practices. See Wilson, "About"; and Edwards, "'What If Indians Invented Photography?'"

35. Sealy, *Decolonising the Camera*.

CHAPTER 1. THE CYNOSURE OF THE EYES OF HARLEM: MARCUS GARVEY AND JAMES VAN DER ZEE IN STEREOGRAPH

1. Robert A. Hill, "Making Noise," 181.

2. Gilroy, *Against Race*, 155.

3. See Percy Hintzen, Jean Mutaba Rahier, and Felipe Smith, introduction to Hintzen, Rahier, and Smith, *Global Circuits of Blackness*.

4. Campt, *Image Matters*.

5. Throughout his career, Kobena Mercer has called on scholars to "wide[n] [the] horizon for understanding diaspora culture's complex histories and future possibilities" and to "show how artistic conceptions of modernity emerged from numerous directions across the globe." See Mercer, "Diaspora Culture and the Dialogic Imagination"; Mercer, *Exiles, Diasporas and Strangers*; and Mercer, *Travel and See*.

6. Jaji, *Africa in Stereo*, 11. On the stereograph and stereoscope, see Crary, *Techniques of the Observer*.

7. Holmes, "The Stereoscope and the Stereograph." For more on the stereograph, see Trachtenberg, *Reading American Photographs*; and Goldsby, *A Spectacular Secret*.

8. Mercer, "Art History and the Dialogics of Diaspora," 214.

9. Garvey, "The Negro's Greatest Enemy," 3.

10. Samuel A. Haynes, quoted in Grant, *Negro with a Hat*, 156.

11. Martin, *The Pan African Connection*.

12. *Negro World*, August 5, 1922.

13. The Black Star Line came to number four ships, one of which, the SS *Yarmouth* (renamed the *Booker T. Washington*), would be junked for scrap metal, before the company's financial dissolution in 1922.

14. The Bureau of Investigation, created in 1908, became the Division of Investigation in 1933 and two years later was renamed the Federal Bureau of Investigation (FBI). For more on the early Bureau's investigations of Garvey and others, see Theodor J. Kornweibel's *"Seeing Red": Federal Campaigns Against Black Militancy, 1919–1925*.

15. See Kornweibel, *"Seeing Red"*; and Mail Fraud Charges Against Marcus Garvey: Hearing Before the Subcommittee on Criminal Justice of the House Committee on the Judiciary, 100th Cong, 1st sess., July 28, 1987 (statement of Robert Hill). Garvey was

granted posthumous clemency by presidential pardon on January 19, 2025. See "Statement from President Joe Biden on Clemency Actions," White House, January 19, 2025, https://bidenwhitehouse.archives.gov/briefing-room/statements-releases/2025/01/19/statement-from-president-joe-biden-on-clemency-actions-3/.

16. See James, "Marcus Garvey."

17. Poupeye-Rammelaere, "Garveyism and Garvey Iconography in the Visual Arts of Jamaica."

18. *Negro World*, September 3, 1921, reprinted in Hill, *Marcus Garvey and Universal Negro Improvement Association Papers*, vol. 3, 698.

19. *Negro World*, September 3, 1921, 699.

20. Jennings, Doherty, and Levin, "Production, Reproduction, and Reception of the Work of Art," 12.

21. Benjamin, "The Work of Art in the Age of Its Technological Reproducibility: Second Version," 38.

22. Benjamin, "The Work of Art in the Age of Its Technological Reproducibility: Second Version," 54n36.

23. Marcus Garvey, interview with J. A. Rogers (1937), quoted in Gilroy, *Against Race*, 232.

24. Grant, *Negro with a Hat*, 13, 45.

25. Marcus Garvey, speech, January 20, 1924, in Hill, *Marcus Garvey and Universal Negro Improvement Association Papers*, vol. 5, 538.

26. Marcus Garvey, speech, Washington, DC, January 15, 1924, printed in *Negro World*, January 26, 1924; reprinted in Hill, *Marcus Garvey and Universal Negro Improvement Association Papers*, vol. 5, 522.

27. Stephens, *Black Empire*.

28. Boone, *Nimble Arc*, 106.

29. Edwards, *Practice of Diaspora*.

30. The Van Der Zees were lovers of art and believers in the power of culture as both an outlet for social expression and a mark of middle-class aspiration. James and his siblings—two brothers and two sisters—learned to play musical instruments and draw. One of Van Der Zee's earliest photographs is of his violin teacher. His sister Jennie and brother-in-law would later open the Toussaint Conservatory of Music on 135th Street in New York. See Rodger C. Birt's excellent and, to date, most comprehensive biographical essay in Birt and Willis-Braithwaite, *Van Der Zee: Photographer, 1886–1983*. See also Mercer, *James VanDerZee*; and Boone, *Nimble Arc*.

31. Browning, "Foreword," in *The Legacy of James Van Der Zee: A Portrait of Black Americans*, n.p.

32. Westerbeck, *James Van Der Zee Studio*, 15. See also Boone, *Nimble Arc*.

33. Westerbeck, *James Van Der Zee Studio*, 15.

34. Boone, *Nimble Arc*, 98.

35. Powell, *Cutting a Figure*, 62.

36. Claude McKay quoted in Edwards, *Practice of Diaspora*, 100.

37. This error on Van Der Zee's part might have followed from Garvey's own signature, in which he appears to drop the "e" in his last name.

38. James Van Der Zee, interview by James Haskins, quoted in Boone, *Nimble Arc*, 227n36.

39. Boone, *Nimble Arc*, 110–12.

40. For reproductions of these images, see Raiford, "Marcus Garvey in Stereograph."

41. Nyong'o, "Africa Never Looks Back from the Place Which We See It: Kehinde Wiley on the World Stage."

42. Mercer, "Diaspora Culture and the Dialogic Imagination"; Mercer, "Diaspora Aesthetics and Visual Culture"; and Mercer, "Art History and the Dialogics of Diaspora."

43. Min, "Aesthetics," 33.

44. Ralph, "Diaspora," 95.

45. Edwards, *Practice of Diaspora*, 14.

46. For more on the centrality of this photograph in Garvey's conviction, see Boone's chapter "The Newspaper and Ubiquity: 1924 Photographs as Moving Objects of the African Diaspora," in *Nimble Arc*.

47. Marcus Garvey, "First Message to the Negroes of the World from Atlanta Prison," February 10, 1925, in Garvey, *Philosophy and Opinions*, edited by Amy Jacques Garvey; reprinted in Garvey, *Selected Writings and Speeches*, 183. On Amy Jacques Garvey, see Taylor, *Veiled Garvey*.

CHAPTER 2. TO FEEL PERFECTLY AT HOME:
ESLANDA ROBESON'S ETHNOGRAPHIC LENS

The first epigraph is taken from a letter in the Robeson Correspondence, a collection within the Carl Van Vechten Papers Relating to African American Arts and Letters, James Weldon Johnson Memorial Collection in the Yale Collection of American Literature, Beinecke Rare Book and Manuscript Library, Yale University, New Haven, CT.

1. Robeson, *African Journey*, 121.

2. "The Headman knew at once that Pauli was very young, and was intrigued by his height and breadth. Paul in turn knew immediately that the Headman was 'old' (he was about forty) and was fascinated by his very small but perfect physique, which was sturdy and muscular, and in beautiful proportion." Robeson, *African Journey*, 121.

3. See, for example, the films and photography of Martin and Osa Johnson.

4. I draw "Here but not together" from Jasmine Elizabeth Johnson, *Rhythm Nation: West African Dance and the Politics of Diaspora* (Oxford University Press, forthcoming).

5. "What I'm suggesting is that we think of self-fashioning in these images as complex articulations of self that resist easy categorization and refuse binary notions of agency versus subjection." Campt, *Listening to Images*, 59. See also Diouf, introduction to Sall, *African Gaze*.

6. See Ransby, *Eslanda*.

7. *Literary Guild Review* (August 1945), 14–15, Eslanda G. Robeson Papers, Series B—Personal Papers, Box 11: *African Journey* Book Reviews, Paul and Eslanda Robeson Collection, Moorland-Spingarn Research Center, Howard University, Washington, DC (hereafter, Eslanda G. Robeson Papers).

8. Shaffer, "Out of the Shadows," 52.

9. Quoted in Shaffer, "Out of the Shadows," 52–53.

10. "That-has-been" is Roland Barthes's phrase to describe photography's relation to the past. See Barthes, *Camera Lucida*.

11. Pinney, *Photography and Anthropology*; Ewen and Ewen, *Typecasting*; Poole, *Vision, Race, and Modernity*; Mirzoeff, "The Right to Look"; Landau and Kaspin, *Images and Empires*.

12. Warren, "Appeals for (Mis)Recognition," 394. For more on the Harlem Renaissance ideas about Africa, see Alain Locke's *The New Negro: Voices of the Harlem Renaissance*.

13. Warren, "Appeals for (Mis)Recognition," 394.

14. Eslanda Goode Robeson, letter to Ma Goode (Eslanda Elbert Cardozo Goode), March 29, 1935, quoted in Duberman, *Paul Robeson*, 194.

15. Robeson, *African Journey*, 17.

16. Eslanda Goode Robeson, letter to Carl and Fania Van Vechten, September 9, 1945, Robeson Correspondence, Carl Van Vechten Papers Relating to African American Arts and Letters, James Weldon Johnson Memorial Collection in the Yale Collection of American Literature, Beinecke Rare Book and Manuscript Library, Yale University, New Haven, CT.

17. For more examples of Robeson's approach to writing about African peoples, see Robeson, *What Do the People of Africa Want?* See also Pearl S. Buck, with Eslanda Goode Robeson, *American Argument* (New York: John Day, 1949); and Eslanda Goode Robeson, "Unrest in Africa Due to Oppression," *Freedom* 3, no. 6 (June 1953), reprinted in Burden-Stelly and Dean, *Organize, Fight, Win*.

18. Robeson, *African Journey*, 20.

19. Ransby, *Eslanda*, 111. See also Umoren, *Race Women Internationalists*.

20. Robeson, *African Journey*, 89, 152.

21. Ransby, *Eslanda*, 121.

22. Robeson, *African Journey*, 18.

23. Robeson, *African Journey*, 119.

24. Baker, *From Savage to Negro*, 143. See also Freeman Marshall, *Ain't I An Anthropologist*; and Womack, *The Matter of Black Living*.

25. For more on Malinowski, see Clifford, *The Predicament of Culture*; Mahon, "Eslanda Goode Robeson's *African Journey*"; Kulick, *Savage Within*; and Asch, "Anthropology, Colonialism, and the Reflexive Turn." See also Malinowski's introduction to his student (and Eslanda's classmate) Jomo Kenyatta's important ethnographic work, *Facing Mount Kenya: The Tribal Life of the Gikuyu*.

26. Robeson, *What Do the People of Africa Want?*, 15.

27. Robeson, *African Journey*, 136–37.

28. "Handmaiden of colonialism" is a phrase taken up and popularized by Talal Asad to describe anthropology's role in validating colonial projects of Indigenous dispossession, forced labor, and conditions of abjection. See Asad, *Anthropology and the Colonial Encounter*. See also Clarke, "Toward a Critically Engaged Ethnographic Practice."

29. Scott, *Domination and the Arts of Resistance*.

30. Founded in London in 1925 by law students from West Africa, the West African Students Union (WASU) "became the most important pressure group devoted to African

issues and a center of black social and political activity in London," espousing both Black internationalist and Pan-Africanist politics. See Matera, *Black London*, 31.

31. Robeson, *African Journey*, 107.

32. Robeson, *African Journey*, 136.

33. Robeson, *African Journey*, 65. "Sofiatown" is Robeson's spelling for Sophiatown. Dr. Alfred Bitini Xuma would go on to be president of the African National Congress (ANC) from 1940 to 1949. See Ransby, *Eslanda*.

34. Robeson, *African Journey*, 128.

35. Robeson, *African Journey*, 108, 104, 109, 110.

36. Robeson, *African Journey*, 65, 73.

37. Clifford, *Routes*; Griffin and Fish, *A Stranger in the Village*. Indeed, *African Journey* is based on and hews closely to the handwritten diary that Robeson kept during the trip. "Eslanda African Diary 1936," Eslanda G. Robeson Papers, Box 17: Diaries (1934–63).

38. Hastrup, "The Ethnographic Present"; Sanjek, "The Ethnographic Present."

39. Robeson, *African Journey*, 48.

40. Ransby, *Eslanda*, 97–98.

41. "The Whites need to see everything in reverse for once," wrote Cameroonian activist Joseph Bilé in protest against *Africa Speaks!*, "to see what they do to us Blacks. What would the Whites say if we made a film in Germany and let a few lions loose that killed a white person? All Whites would be outraged. And rightfully so. But the Whites come to us, take a Massai [*sic*] and throw him to the beasts. The Whites come to take our land, which our forefathers have owned for millenia. Because the Whites are in power." Bilé in *Vorwärts* (Forward), magazine of the Social Democratic Party of Germany, Berlin, February 15, 1931, quoted in *Stand in Solidarity! Black Resistance and Global Anti-Colonialism in Berlin, 1919–1933* (exhibition), Charlottenburg-Wilmersdorf Museum in the Villa Oppenheim, September 25, 2023–March 17, 2024.

42. On the power of the caption in colonial African photography, see Sandrine Colard's "Introduction: African Writings and the Colonial Time's Pictures" in the stunning and field-shifting book edited by her, *Recaptioning Congo: African Stories and Colonial Pictures*. See also the important collection *Visualizing Empire: Africa, Europe, and the Politics of Representation*, edited by Rebecca Peabody, Steven Nelson, and Dominic Thomas, which focuses on visual material related to the French colonial enterprise in Africa.

43. Santu Mofokeng, Field Trip Report of December 4, 1992, quoted in "Arthur Walther and Tamar Garb: A Conversation," 15. Napandulwe Shiweda argues that colonial photographer Alfred Duggan-Cronin "does not necessarily employ a naïve or instrumental colonial gaze seeking to objectify colonized subjects but rather conforms to particular colonial stereotypes as the subjects themselves participated in new forms of self-fashioning." Shiweda, "Images of Ambivalence," 181–82.

44. As Tamar Garb writes: "The Manichean oppositions that post-colonial histories often produce of 'white versus black,' 'active versus passive,' 'powerful versus powerless,' and 'colonizer versus colonized' occlude the complexity of image-production that was possible even under colonial rule. Photographs that instrumentalize the bodies of colonial subjects are plentiful. But the archive also includes signs of fracture, anxiety, and

unease, instances when a more respectful or reciprocal encounter may be staged or the edifice of colonial confidence seems to falter. Fascination and curiosity, as well as power and profit, subtend the colonial archive." Garb, "Encountering the African Archive," 26. See also the enormously generative webinar "Decentering the Document," Museum of Modern Art (NYC) Forums on Contemporary Photography, April 19, 2023, convened by Roxana Marcoci and Oluremi C. Onabanjo, https://www.moma.org/calendar/events /8498.

45. Garb, "Encountering the African Archive," 26; Edwards, "Looking at Photographs," 54; Campt, *Listening to Images*, esp. ch. 2, "Striking Poses in a Tense Grammar: Stasis and the Frequency of Black Refusal"; Hayes and Minkley, "Introduction: Africa and the Ambivalence of Seeing," in *Ambivalent*; Colard, *Recaptioning Congo*; Azoulay, *Potential History*. See also Morton and Newbury, *African Photographic Archive*; Godby, "Alfred Martin Duggan-Cronin's Photographs for 'The Bantu Tribes of South Africa' (1928–1954)"; and Comaroff, Comaroff, and James, *Picturing a Colonial Past*.

46. Robeson, *African Journey*, 18.

47. The film reels from this trip are held in the Eslanda G. Robeson Papers but are currently unavailable for viewing. See also Musser, "Presenting 'A True Idea of the African To-day.'"

48. Moutoussamy-Ashe, "Eslanda Cardoza Goode Robeson," in *Viewfinders*, 92.

49. Michael Young, discussing Malinowski's photographic practice, quoted in Pinney, *Photography and Anthropology*, 55.

50. See Landau, "Empires of the Visual."

51. Robeson, *African Journey*, 96. Regarding the number of times she had to "register" her camera with colonial officials in Uganda, and on the advice Mukama, "an enthusiastic amateur photographer himself," offers her about hiding her cameras when they travel to the Belgian Congo ("'If the official sees it he will seal it.'"), see Robeson, *African Journey*, 111.

52. Robeson, *African Journey*, 134, 60–61. But she does wield the power of the camera with intention. As Azoulay avers, "Photography is one of the instruments which has enabled the modern citizen to establish her liberal rights, including freedom of movement and of information, as well as her right to take photographs and be photographed, to see what others see and would like to show through photographs." Azoulay, *Civil Contract of Photography*, 125.

53. Azoulay, *Civil Contract of Photography*.

54. Azoulay, *Civil Contract of Photography*, 25.

55. Azoulay, *Civil Contract of Photography*, 23. This "ontological-political understanding of photography" stands in opposition to colonial uses of photography. See Landau, "Empires of the Visual." See also Zoé Samudzi, "The Sovereignty and Poetry of African Photography," who writes, "The camera cannot be decolonized per se, but its utilization beyond the indexing and enclosing violence of whiteness presents a possibility for the technological sighting (to 'view,' rather than to 'capture' with all of its possessive connotations) of . . . the placemaking of African life beyond anthropological inquiry" (20).

56. Azoulay, *Civil Contract of Photography*, 117.

57. Marianne Hirsch, "Introduction: Familial Looking," xvi.

58. Robeson, *African Journey*, 14.

59. Robeson, *African Journey*, 133.

60. Samudzi, "The Sovereignty and Poetry of African Photography," 19.

61. Hutchinson and Nankivell, *Southern Africa*.

62. Hutchinson and Nankivell, "Preface," in *Southern Africa*, n.p.

CHAPTER 3. MAKING HOME IN EXILE:
KATHLEEN CLEAVER'S BLACK PANTHER FAMILY ALBUM

1. Kathleen Neal Cleaver quoted in Young, "Black Panther's Secret North Korean Fetish." See also Young, "North Korea's Unlikely History with Black Radicals"; Branigan, "How Black Panthers Turned to North Korea in Fight Against US Imperialism"; and Bloom and Martin, *Black Against Empire*. Regarding Joju's name, Kathleen stated in a 2017 interview, "Kim Sung Ae [wife of Kim Il-Sung] made it and meant 'Young Heroine born in Juche Korea.'"

2. See Kathleen Neal Cleaver, introduction to Eldridge Cleaver, *Target Zero: A Life in Writing*.

3. Kathleen Neal Cleaver, interview with author, Atlanta, GA, July 26, 2017.

4. Bentley, "Exclusive: Emory Acquires Papers of Former Black Panther Party Leader and Scholar."

5. See Cleaver, "Women, Power, and Revolution"; and Raiford, "Restaging Revolution."

6. Hooks, "In Our Glory."

7. The easy-to-use Brownie camera, invented by Kodak in 1900, made photography widely accessible for everyday amateur use. Cleaver, interview with author, July 26, 2017.

8. Hirsch, "Introduction: Familial Looking," xvi.

9. See, especially, Stoppard, "Everyone's a Curator Now."

10. Hooks, "Homeplace."

11. See, especially, Collins, *Black Feminist Thought*.

12. Kouoh, "Art, Knowledge, Action, Society." On the contemporary definitions of the curatorial, Hans Ulrich Obrist has written: "Today, curating as a profession means at least four things. It means to preserve, in the sense of safeguarding the heritage of art. It means to be the selector of new work. It means to connect to art history. And it means displaying or arranging the work. But it's more than that. Before 1800, few people went to exhibitions. Now hundreds of millions of people visit them every year. It's a mass medium and a ritual. The curator sets it up so that it becomes an extraordinary experience and not just illustrations or spatialised books." Hans Ulrich Obrist, "Art of Curation."

13. On homemaking, see Morrison, "Kitchenette Building"; and hooks, "Homeplace."

14. Raiford, *Imprisoned in a Luminous Glare*, 130. See also acierto, "Tracing the Peacock Chair's History from Manila to Nashville."

15. Cleaver, "Back to Africa," 242–43.

16. Brown, *Dropping Anchor, Setting Sail*. Jasmine Elizabeth Johnson's work on African dance suggests something similar about how African dance classes can provide a sense of travel and connection for those who are unable to cross national borders. See Johnson, *Rhythm Nation*.

17. Campt, *Listening to Images*, 4.

18. Campt, *Listening to Images*, 9.

19. Kathleen Neal Cleaver, interview with author, Atlanta, GA, January 18, 2018. See also Cleaver, "Back to Africa." In Henry Louis Gates Jr.'s *Leaving Cleaver: Henry Louis Gates Remembers Eldridge Cleaver* (PBS, 1999), Kathleen Cleaver states emphatically that her time in Algeria was "awful . . . just awful. . . . It was a very complex and obscure world. Especially for a person used to straight-ahead, you know, kick-ass Black Panther life."

20. In a letter to Eldridge Cleaver, his mother, Thelma Cleaver, writes how even at two years old Maceo worried about his father. While Joju was "more independent than he," Maceo was "not an ordinary boy." Thelma Cleaver, letter to Eldridge Cleaver, December 3, 1971, Eldridge Cleaver Papers, 1963–1988, Box 3 (correspondence), Folder 2 (Thelma Cleaver), Bancroft Library, University of California, Berkeley. Kathleen elsewhere describes Maceo as "always serious" and very devoted to his father's well-being. Cleaver, "Introduction," xi–xii.

21. Campt, "Reframing Family Photography."

22. Kathleen Cleaver, "The Evolution of the International Section of the Black Panther Party in Algiers 1969–1972," December 9, 1983, Yale Student Papers Collection, Manuscripts and Archives, Sterling Memorial Library, Yale University, New Haven, CT.

23. Finley, "Archiving Memory," 83. Finley's term "mnemonic aesthetics" is useful here to describe "a ritualized politics of remembering that uses image-making techniques, visual images, and image archiving practices to mediate the fragile association of memory and forgetting" (82).

24. On the International Section of the BPP, see Malloy, *Out of Oakland*. Besenia Rodriguez's unpublished dissertation is among the first scholarly works to address the subject of the International Section. Rodriguez, "Beyond Nation." See also Hayes, *Love for Liberation*.

25. Cleaver, "Back to Africa," 211.

26. Cleaver, "Back to Africa," 235.

27. Owen, "Ordinary Failures."

28. Tracye Matthews's excellent essay remains a standard bearer for calling the BPP to task on this issue. See Matthews, "'No One Ever Asks What a Man's Role in the Revolution Is.'" More recent histories have been less critical. See, for example, Spencer, *Revolution Has Come*; and Farmer, *Remaking Black Power*.

29. See Lockwood, *Conversation with Eldridge Cleaver—Algiers*; and Mokhtefi, *Algiers, Third World Capital*.

30. Brown's 1992 memoir, *A Taste of Power: A Black Woman's Story*, highlighted the brutal scene in the North Korean hospital room but omits the story of the murder of Rahim / Clinton Smith, save for Eldridge's contention that "the baby [Kathleen] was carrying was probably not his" (228). Elaine Mokhtefi, a friend and ally of the Panthers during their time in Algiers, recounts Smith's murder in her memoir, *Algiers, Third World Capital: Freedom Fighters, Revolutionaries, Black Panthers*.

31. Spencer, *Revolution Has Come*, 110.

32. Elaine Brown, "Free Kathleen Cleaver," *Black Panther* 6, no 6 (1971), supplement, p. 2. The leftist publication *The Berkeley Barb* published an article about Kathleen's situa-

tion, Brown's narrative, and the split in the Party that basically recounted and reproduced *The Black Panther* text and images across a two-page spread. See "'He Murdered Him and Buried His Body in Algiers,'" *Berkeley Barb*, March 5–11, 1971, 2–3. Thanks to scholar Paul Lee for bringing this article to my attention.

33. McGuire, *At the Dark End of the Street.*

34. Kathleen writes in her memoir that a year into her marriage—to both Eldridge and the BPP—"my personal confidence was expanding. My sense of accomplishment from learning how to be a revolutionary organizer and political candidate grew, but the same effort taught me other skills. I quickly figured out how to steel myself to Eldridge's brusqueness, to overlook the myriad times I felt ignored, and to block my anger at his prolonged absences. All these new-found abilities seemed to flow naturally from keeping pace with Eldridge as his life skated on the edge of death." Cleaver, "Memories of Love and War," unpublished manuscript, Eldridge and Kathleen Cleaver Papers, Stuart A. Rose Manuscript, Archives, and Rare Book Library, Emory University, Atlanta, GA.

35. Thompson, "Mrs. Eldridge Cleaver Returns to U.S. to Give State of Revolution Message," 25. See also Cleaver and Herve, "*Black Scholar* Interviews: Kathleen Cleaver."

36. Kathleen Neal Cleaver, conversation with author, Atlanta, GA, October 12, 2017.

37. As Ula Yvette Taylor reminds us, "The power of love is difficult to analyze," and for Black women in the Nation of Islam, the possibility of combining love of Black community and the strength of the nuclear Black family for the betterment of the Black race was a strong enticement to weather the diminishing confines of patriarchy. Taylor's masterful history provides a useful model for thinking about "how freedom and prosperity commingle around patriarchy." Taylor, *Promise of Patriarchy*, 141, 5.

38. See Gilroy, "'After the Love Has Gone'"; and Gilroy, "One Nation Under a Groove" and "It's a Family Affair: Black Culture and the Trope of Kinship," in Gilroy, *Small Acts.*

39. Cleaver, conversation with author, Atlanta, GA, July 25, 2017.

40. Love, *Feeling Backward*, 43.

41. Kathleen Neal Cleaver, conversation with author, Atlanta, GA, July 25, 2017.

42. Gordon Parks made multiple photographs during his visit with the Cleavers in Algiers, including a version of the image described above but with infant Maceo seated on his father's lap. The version with Maceo did not make it into the February 6, 1970, *Life* magazine article, Parks described the Cleavers's home as "the cluttered, temporary shelter of a black man in exile—where bags stay packed and all precious things are portable." Parks, "Eldridge Cleaver in Algiers, a Visit with Papa Rage," 20. See also Gordon Parks Foundation, "Tribute to Kathleen Cleaver," May 2016, https://www.gordonparks foundation.org/education/features/tribute-to-kathleen-cleaver.

43. Langford, *Suspended Conversations*, 21. See also Phu, "Diasporic Vietnamese Family Photographs, Orphan Images, and the Art of Recollection"; and Spence, *Family Snaps.*

44. Cleaver, "Women, Power, and Revolution," 124–25; Cleaver, conversation with the author, Atlanta, GA, July 25, 2017.

45. Cleaver, conversation with the author, Atlanta, GA, July 25, 2017.

46. Saidiya Hartman, *Wayward Lives, Beautiful Experiments*, xv.

47. Fuentes, *Dispossessed Lives*; Hartman, "Venus in Two Acts."

48. Hirsch, "Feminist Archives of Possibility."

49. Robinson, *Black Marxism*, 317.

CHAPTER 4. SHELTER IN PLACE: DAWOUD BEY, SADIE BARNETTE, AND THE PHOTOGRAPHY OF UNCERTAINTY

1. See most notably André Bazin's statement: "Photography completely satisfies our appetite for illusion by means of a process of mechanical reproduction in which there is no human agency at work." Bazin, "Ontology of the Photographic Image," originally published in *Film Quarterly* (1960).

2. "The only thing in the world worth beginning: The End of the world of course." Césaire, *Notebook of a Return to the Native Land*. "The concept of progress must be grounded in the idea of catastrophe. That things are 'status quo' is the catastrophe. It is not an ever-present possibility but what in each case is given. Thus . . . hell is not something that awaits us, but this life here and now." Benjamin, *Arcades Project*, 473 (N9a, 1).

3. Smith, *At the Edge of Sight*; Wynter, "'No Humans Involved,'" 44.

4. Wolukau-Wanambwa, *Dark Mirrors*, 13, 14; Campt, *Listening to Images*; Cole, *Black Paper*; Smith, *At the Edge of Sight*, 7 ("'not seeing'").

5. Dawoud Bey, "*Night Coming Tenderly, Black*: Artist Statement," Rena Bransten Gallery, San Francisco.

6. Whitehead, *Underground Railroad*, 311.

7. Nelson, "Dawoud Bey's Historical Turn," 20.

8. Smith, "Photography, Darkness, and the Underground Railroad," 30. See also Witkovsky, "This Story Shall Not Be Passed On."

9. "It does not disturb me to accept that there are places where my identity is obscure to me, and the fact that it amazes me does not mean I relinquish it. . . . We clamor for the right to opacity for everyone." Glissant, *Poetics of Relation*, 192, 194. "But the more authentic question was not whether the slaves (and the ex-slaves and their descendants) were human. It was, rather, just what *sort* of people they were . . . and could be." Robinson, *Black Marxism*, 125 (ellipsis in original). "But you have no idea how dark we yet may be, nor what that darkness may contain." Cole, "True Picture of Black Skin," 151. "The proposition here, against all liberal universalisms and scientific positivities, is to insist that we do not yet know what a human outside of an anti-black world could be, do, or look like." Nyong'o, *Afro-Fabulations*, 26.

10. Dyson, "Black Compositional Thought: Black Hauntology, Plantationocene, and Paradoxical Form," 78; Campt, *Listening to Images*; Campt, *Black Gaze*; Sharpe, *In the Wake*; Browne, *Dark Matters*.

11. Carter and Cervenak, "The Black Outdoors."

12. Azoulay, *Potential History*.

13. "The communion between scorned flesh and scorned earth offers another ecological ethos and view, one that moves beyond the degeneration enacted by existing maps." Carter and Cervenak, "The Black Outdoors."

14. Whitehead, *Underground Railroad*, 300 (italics added).

15. Sadie Barnette, "The FBI Project," in McGrew and Ennis, *Sadie Barnette*, 34.

16. Sadie Barnette, "The New Eagle Creek Saloon Forever," in McGrew and Ennis, *Sadie Barnette*, 37.

17. Klapisch-Zuber, "Genesis of the Family Tree," 107, 105.

18. See, for example, Nelson, *Social Life of DNA*.

19. Spillers, "Mama's Baby, Papa's Maybe," 74–75.

20. Hilson, "Reimagining the Family Tree," 199.

21. Glissant, *Poetics of Relation*, 11.

22. Sadie Barnette, conversation via Zoom with author, May 2, 2022. See also Barnette and Williams-Yackel, "Personal Library: Sadie's Books."

23. Jordan, "Moving Towards Home," 400. For a powerful analysis of what Erica R. Edwards calls Jordan's "insurgent grammars" and her literary and activist interventions against the United States' "long war on terror," see Edwards, *The Other Side of Terror*.

24. Angela Davis quoted in Lowe, "Angela Davis: Reflections on Race, Class, and Gender in the USA," 318.

25. See, especially, Hall, "New Ethnicities" (1983) and "Cultural Identity and Diaspora" (1990), in Gilroy and Gilmore, *Stuart Hall: Selected Writings on Race and Difference*.

26. Jordan, "Moving Towards Home," 400.

Bibliography

ARCHIVES AND MANUSCRIPT COLLECTIONS

Department of Photographs, The Metropolitan Museum of Art, New York.

Eldridge Cleaver Papers. BANC MSS 91/213 c. Bancroft Library, University of California, Berkeley.

Eldridge Cleaver Photograph Collection. Bancroft Library, University of California, Berkeley.

Eldridge and Kathleen Cleaver Papers. Stuart A. Rose Manuscript, Archives, and Rare Book Library, Emory University, Atlanta, GA.

Paul and Eslanda Robeson Collection. Moorland-Spingarn Research Center, Howard University, Washington, DC.

Schomburg Center for Research in Black Culture, Photographs and Prints Division, New York Public Library, New York.

Carl Van Vechten Papers Relating to African American Arts and Letters. James Weldon Johnson Memorial Collection in the Yale Collection of American Literature, Beinecke Rare Book and Manuscript Library, Yale University, New Haven, CT.

Yale Student Papers Collection. Manuscripts and Archives, Sterling Memorial Library, Yale University, New Haven, CT.

EXHIBITIONS

Sadie Barnette: Inheritance. Jessica Silverman Gallery, San Francisco, November 20, 2021–January 8, 2022.

Sadie Barnette: The New Eagle Creek Saloon. San Francisco Museum of Modern Art, San Francisco, April 22–May 11, 2023.

Dawoud Bey: An American Project. San Francisco Museum of Modern Art, San Francisco, February 15–May 25, 2020.

Inheritance. Whitney Museum of American Art, New York, June 28, 2023–February 4, 2024.

Stand in Solidarity! Black Resistance and Global Anti-Colonialism in Berlin, 1919–1933.

Charlottenburg-Wilmersdorf Museum in the Villa Oppenheim, Berlin, September 25, 2023–March 17, 2024.

INTERVIEWS

Barnette, Sadie. Conversation via Zoom with the author, May 2, 2022.
Bey, Dawoud, and Leigh Raiford. "Dawoud Bey in Conversation with Leigh Raiford." San Francisco Museum of Modern Art, February 13, 2020.
Cleaver, Kathleen Neal. Conversation with the author. Atlanta, GA, July 25, 2017.
Cleaver, Kathleen Neal. Interview with the author. Atlanta, GA, July 26, 2017.
Cleaver, Kathleen Neal. Conversation with the author, Atlanta, GA, October 12, 2017.
Cleaver, Kathleen Neal. Interview with the author. Atlanta, GA, January 18, 2018.
Robeson, Susan. Conversation via phone with the author, February 11, 2025.

ARTICLES, BOOKS, DISSERTATIONS, MANUSCRIPTS

acierto, alejandro t. "Tracing the Peacock Chair's History from Manila to Nashville." *Hyperallergic*, February 5, 2025. https://hyperallergic.com/987595/tracing-the-peacock-chair-history-from-manila-to-nashville/.
Alexander, Elizabeth. *The Black Interior: Essays*. Graywolf Press, 2004.
Allen, Jafari. *There's a Disco Ball Between Us: A Theory of Black Gay Life*. Duke University Press, 2022.
"Arthur Walther and Tamar Garb: A Conversation." In Garb, *Distance and Desire*.
Asad, Talal, ed. *Anthropology and the Colonial Encounter*. Ithaca Press, 1975.
Asch, Michael. "Anthropology, Colonialism, and the Reflexive Turn: Finding a Place to Stand." *Anthropologica* 57, no. 2 (2015): 481–89.
Azoulay, Ariella Aïsha. *The Civil Contract of Photography*. Zone Books, 2008.
Azoulay, Ariella Aïsha. *The Civil Imagination: A Political Ontology of Photography*. Verso Books, 2012.
Azoulay, Ariella Aïsha. *Potential History: Unlearning Imperialism*. Verso Books, 2019.
Azoulay, Ariella Aïsha. "Unlearning the Origins of Photography." *Verso Books* (blog), September 7, 2018. https://www.versobooks.com/blogs/news/4013-unlearning-the-origins-of-photography.
Azoulay, Ariella Aïsha, Wendy Ewald, Susan Meiselas, Leigh Raiford, and Laura Wexler. *Collaboration: A Potential History of Photography*. Thames and Hudson, 2023.
Bailey, Marlon. *Butch Queens Up in Pumps: Gender, Performance, and Ballroom Culture in Detroit*. University of Michigan Press, 2013.
Bajorek, Jennifer. *Unfixed: Photography and Decolonial Imagination in West Africa*. Duke University Press, 2020.
Baker, Lee D. *From Savage to Negro: Anthropology and the Construction of Race, 1896–1954*. University of California Press, 1998.
Barnette, Sadie, and Grant Williams-Yackel. "Personal Library: Sadie's Books; 20 Books Selected by Sadie Barnette and Grant Williams-Yackel." San Francisco Museum of Modern Art, September 2022. https://www.sfmoma.org/read/personal-library-sadies-books-20-books-selected-by-sadie-barnette-and-grant-williams-yackel/.

Barthes, Roland. *Camera Lucida: Reflections on Photography*. Hill and Wang, 1982.

Bazin, André. "The Ontology of the Photographic Image." In *What Is Cinema?* Vol. 1. Translated by Hugh Gray. University of California Press, 2005.

Benjamin, Walter. *The Arcades Project*. Translated by Howard Eiland and Kevin McLaughlin. Harvard University Press, 1999.

Benjamin, Walter. *The Work of Art in the Age of Its Technological Reproducibility and Other Writings on Media*. Edited by Michael W. Jennings, Brigid Doherty, and Thomas Y. Levin. Harvard University Press, 2008.

Benjamin, Walter. "The Work of Art in the Age of Its Technological Reproducibility: Second Version." In Benjamin, *The Work of Art in the Age of Its Technological Reproducibility and Other Writings on Media*.

Bentley, Rosalind. "Exclusive: Emory Acquires Papers of Former Black Panther Party Leader and Scholar." *Atlanta Journal-Constitution*, August 31, 2020.

Berger, John. *Selected Essays and Articles: The Look of Things*. Penguin, 1972.

Berger, John. *Ways of Seeing*. Penguin Books, 1977.

Berger, Martin A. *Sight Unseen: Whiteness and American Visual Culture*. University of California Press, 2014.

Berger, Maurice. *For All the World to See: Visual Culture and the Struggle for Civil Rights*. Yale University Press, 2010.

Bey, Dawoud. "*Night Coming Tenderly, Black* Artist Statement." Rena Bransten Gallery, San Francisco.

Bey, Dawoud. *Seeing Deeply*. University of Texas Press, 2018.

Birt, Rodger C., and Deborah Willis-Braithwaite. *Van Der Zee: Photographer, 1886–1983*. Harry N. Abrams, 1998.

Bloom, Joshua, and Waldo Martin. *Black Against Empire: The History and Politics of the Black Panther Party*. University of California Press, 2012.

Boone, Emilie. *A Nimble Arc: James Van Der Zee and Photography*. Duke University Press, 2023.

Branigan, Tania. "How Black Panthers Turned to North Korea in Fight Against US Imperialism." *The Guardian*, June 19, 2014. https://www.theguardian.com/world/2014/jun/19/black-panthers-north-korea-us-imperialism.

Brown, Elaine. *A Taste of Power*. Anchor Books, 1992.

Brown, Jacqueline Nassy. "Black Liverpool, Black America, and the Gendering of Diasporic Space." *Cultural Anthropology* 13, no. 3 (1998): 291–325.

Brown, Jacqueline Nassy. *Dropping Anchor, Setting Sail: Geographies of Race in Black Liverpool*. Princeton University Press, 2005.

Brown, Kimberly Juanita. *Mortevivum: Photography and the Politics of the Visual*. MIT Press, 2024.

Browne, Simone. *Dark Matters: On the Surveillance of Blackness*. Duke University Press, 2015.

Browning, Robert. "Foreword." In *The Legacy of James Van Der Zee: A Portrait of Black Americans*. Alternative Center for International Arts Inc., 1977.

Burden-Stelly, Charisse, and Jodi Dean, eds. *Organize, Fight, Win: Black Communist Women's Political Writing*. Verso Books, 2022.

Campt, Tina M. *A Black Gaze: Artists Changing How We See*. MIT Press, 2023.

Campt, Tina M. *Image Matters: Archive, Photography, and the African Diaspora in Europe*. Duke University Press, 2012.

Campt, Tina M. *Listening to Images*. Duke University Press, 2017.

Campt, Tina M. "Reframing Family Photography." Keynote address. Toronto, September 23, 2017.

Carby, Hazel V. *Reconstructing Womanhood: The Emergence of the Afro-American Woman Novelist*. Oxford University Press, 1987.

Carter, J. Kameron, and Sarah Jane Cervenak. "The Black Outdoors: Humanities Futures After Property and Possession." Humanities Futures (John Hope Franklin Humanities Institute, Duke University), 2016. https://humanitiesfutures.org/papers/.

Césaire, Aimé. *Notebook of a Return to the Native Land*. 1939. Translated by Clayton Eshleman and Annette Smith. Wesleyan University Press, 2001.

Clarke, Kamari M. "Toward a Critically Engaged Ethnographic Practice." *Current Anthropology* 51, no. S2 (2010): S301–12.

Cleaver, Kathleen Neal. "Back to Africa: The Evolution of the International Section of the Black Panther Party (1969–1972)." In Jones, *The Black Panther Party Reconsidered*.

Cleaver, Kathleen Neal. "Introduction." In *Target Zero: A Life in Writing*, by Eldridge Cleaver, edited by Kathleen Cleaver. Palgrave Macmillan, 2006.

Cleaver, Kathleen Neal. "Women, Power, and Revolution." In *Liberation, Imagination, and the Black Panther Party: A New Look at the Panthers and Their Legacy*, edited by Kathleen Neal Cleaver and George Katsiaficas. Routledge, 2001.

Cleaver, Kathleen Neal, and Julia Herve. "*Black Scholar* Interviews: Kathleen Cleaver." *Black Scholar* 3, no. 4 (1971): 54–59.

Clifford, James. *The Predicament of Culture: Twentieth-Century Ethnography, Literature, and Art*. Harvard University Press, 1988.

Clifford, James. *Routes: Travel and Translation in the Late Twentieth Century*. Harvard University Press, 1997.

Colard, Sandrine. "Introduction: African Writings and the Colonial Time's Pictures." In *Recaptioning Congo: African Stories and Colonial Pictures*. Lannoo, 2022.

Cole, Teju. *Black Paper: Writing in a Dark Time*. University of Chicago Press, 2023.

Cole, Teju. "A True Picture of Black Skin." In *Known and Strange Things*. Penguin, 2016.

Collins, Patricia Hill. *Black Feminist Thought: Knowledge, Consciousness and the Politics of Empowerment*. Routledge, 1989.

Comaroff, John L., Jean Comaroff, and Deborah James, eds. *Picturing a Colonial Past: The African Photographs of Isaac Schapera*. University of Chicago Press, 2007.

Crary, Jonathan. *Techniques of the Observer: On Vision and Modernity in the Nineteenth Century*. MIT Press, 1990.

Cunningham, Vinson. "The Argument of Afropessimism." *New Yorker*, July 13, 2020.

Davis, Angela Y. "Afro Images: Politics, Fashion, and Nostalgia." In Willis, *Picturing Us*.

Diouf, Mamadou. "Introduction." In Sall, *The African Gaze*.

Duberman, Martin. *Paul Robeson: A Biography*. The New Press, 1969.

Du Bois, W. E. B. *Black Reconstruction in America, 1860–1880*. 1935. Reprint, The Free Press, 1998.

Du Bois, W. E. B. *The Souls of Black Folk*. 1903. Reprint, Oxford University Press, 2007.

DuCille, Ann. *The Coupling Convention: Sex, Text, and Tradition in Black Women's Fiction*. Oxford University Press, 1993.

Dyson, Torkwase. "Black Compositional Thought: Black Hauntology, Plantationocene, and Paradoxical Form." In Kelley and Sherman, *Dawoud Bey: Two American Projects*.

Edwards, Brent Hayes. *The Practice of Diaspora: Literature, Translation, and the Rise of Black Internationalism*. Harvard University Press, 2003.

Edwards, Caitlyn. "'What If Indians Invented Photography?' An Exploration of Identity and Photographic Practices by Indigenous Photographer Will Wilson." *PhotoShelter*, [August 9, 2021]. https://go.photoshelter.com/photographers/blog/an-exploration -of-identity-and-photographic-practices-by-indigenous-photographer-will-wilson/.

Edwards, Elizabeth. "Looking at Photographs: Between Contemplation, Curiosity, and Gaze." In Garb, *Distance and Desire*.

Edwards, Erica R. *The Other Side of Terror: Black Women and the Culture of US Empire*. New York University Press, 2021.

Ewen, Stuart, and Elizabeth Ewen. *Typecasting: On the Arts and Sciences of Human Inequality*. Seven Stories Press, 2009.

Fanon, Frantz. *Black Skin, White Masks*. Translated by Charles Lam Markmann. Grove Weidenfeld, 1967.

Farmer, Ashley D. *Remaking Black Power: How Black Women Transformed an Era*. University of North Carolina Press, 2017.

Finley, Cheryl. "Archiving Memory." In Garb, *Distance and Desire*.

Freeman Marshall, Jennifer L. *Ain't I an Anthropologist: Zora Neale Hurston Beyond the Literary Canon*. University of Illinois Press, 2023.

Fusco, Coco. "Racial Times, Racial Marks, Racial Metaphors." In *Only Skin Deep: Changing Visions of the American Self*, edited by Coco Fusco and Brian Wallis. Harry N. Abrams, 2003.

Garb, Tamar, ed. *Distance and Desire: Encounters with the African Archive*. Steidl, 2013.

Garb, Tamar. "Encountering the African Archive: The Interwoven Temporalities of *Distance and Desire*." In Garb, *Distance and Desire*.

Garvey, Marcus. "The Negro's Greatest Enemy." *Current History Magazine*, September 1923. Reprinted in *Selected Speeches and Writings of Marcus Garvey*.

Garvey, Marcus. *Philosophy and Opinions*. 2 vols. Edited by Amy Jacques-Garvey. Universal Publishing House, 1923–26.

Garvey, Marcus. *Selected Writings and Speeches of Marcus Garvey*. Edited by Bob Blaisdell. Dover, 2004.

Gates, Henry Louis, Jr., dir. *Leaving Cleaver: Henry Louis Gates Remembers Eldridge Cleaver*. PBS, 1999.

Gilmore, Ruth Wilson. "Abolition Geography and the Problem of Innocence." In *Abolition Geography: Essays Towards Liberation*. Verso Books, 2022.

Gilroy, Paul. "'After the Love Has Gone': Bio-Politics and Etho-Poetics in the Black Public Sphere." *Public Culture* 7, no. 1 (1994): 49–76.

Gilroy, Paul. *Against Race: Imagining Political Culture Beyond the Color Line*. Harvard University Press, 2002.

Gilroy, Paul. *Small Acts: Thoughts on the Politics of Black Cultures.* Serpent's Tail, 1993.

Gilroy, Paul, and Ruth Wilson Gilmore, eds. *Stuart Hall: Selected Writings on Race and Difference.* Duke University Press, 2021.

Glenn, Evelyn Nakano. *Unequal Freedom: How Race and Gender Shaped American Citizenship and Labor.* Harvard University Press, 2004.

Glissant, Édouard. *Poetics of Relation.* Translated by Betsy Wing. University of Michigan Press, 1997.

Godby, Michael. "Alfred Martin Duggan-Cronin's Photographs for 'The Bantu Tribes of South Africa' (1928–1954): The Construction of an Ambiguous Idyll." *Kronos,* no. 36 (2010): 54–83.

Goldsby, Jacqueline. *A Spectacular Secret: Lynching in American Life and Literature.* University of Chicago Press, 2006.

Grant, Colin. *Negro with a Hat: The Rise and Fall of Marcus Garvey.* Oxford University Press, 2008.

Green, Kai M. "In the Life." *Women, Gender, and Families of Color* 7, no. 1 (2019): 98–101.

Griffin, Farah Jasmine. *Who Set You Flowin'? The African American Migration Narrative.* Oxford University Press, 1995.

Griffin, Farah Jasmine, and Cheryl J. Fish, eds. *A Stranger in the Village: Two Centuries of African-American Travel Writing.* Beacon Press, 1998.

Hannah-Jones, Nikole. "The 1619 Project." *New York Times Magazine,* August 18, 2019.

Hartman, Saidiya. *Wayward Lives, Beautiful Experiments: Intimate Histories of Social Upheaval.* W. W. Norton, 2019.

Hastrup, Kirsten. "The Ethnographic Present: A Reinvention." *Cultural Anthropology* 5, no. 1 (1990): 45–61.

Hayes, Patricia, and Gary Minkley, eds. *Ambivalent: Photography and Visibility in African History.* Ohio University Press, 2019

Hayes, Patricia, and Gary Minkley. "Introduction: African and the Ambivalence of Seeing." In Hayes and Minkley, *Ambivalent.*

Hayes, Robin J. *Love for Liberation: African Independence, Black Power, and a Diaspora Underground.* University of Washington Press, 2021.

Hill, Robert A. "Making Noise: Marcus Garvey Dada, August 1922." In Willis, *Picturing Us.*

Hill, Robert A., ed. *The Marcus Garvey and Universal Negro Improvement Association Papers,* Vol. 3, *September 1920–August 1921.* University of California Press, 1986.

Hill, Robert A., ed. *The Marcus Garvey and Universal Negro Improvement Association Papers,* Vol. 5, *September 1922–August 1924.* University of California Press, 1986.

Hilson, Mica. "Reimagining the Family Tree: Property, Biopolitics, and Queer Kinship in David Malouf's *Remembering Babylon* and Patrick White's *Riders in the Chariot.*" *Pacific Coast Philology* 53, no. 2 (2018): 198–216.

Hintzen, Percy, Jean Mutaba Rahier, and Felipe Smith, eds. *Global Circuits of Blackness.* University of Illinois Press, 2010.

Hirsch, Marianne. *Family Frames: Photography, Narrative, and Postmemory.* Harvard University Press, 2012.

Hirsch, Marianne. "Feminist Archives of Possibility." *differences* 29, no. 1 (2018): 173–88.

Hirsch, Marianne. "Introduction: Familial Looking." In *The Familial Gaze*, edited by Marianne Hirsch. University Press of New England, 1999.

Holmes, Oliver Wendell. "The Stereoscope and the Stereograph." *Atlantic Monthly*, June 1859. Reprinted in Trachtenberg, *Classic Essays on Photography*.

hooks, bell. "Homeplace: A Site of Resistance." In *Yearning: Race, Gender, and Cultural Politics*. South End Press, 1999.

hooks, bell. "In Our Glory: Photography and Black Life." In Willis, *Picturing Us*.

hooks, bell. "The Oppositional Gaze: Black Female Spectators." In *Black Looks: Race and Representation*. South End Press, 1992.

Huerta, Monica. *The Unintended: Photography, Property, and the Aesthetics of Racial Capitalism*. New York University Press, 2023.

Hutchinson, Herbert, and J. W. Nankivell. *Southern Africa: The Land and Its Peoples*. Maskew Miller, Limited, 1934.

Jaji, Tsitsi Ella. *Africa in Stereo: Modernism, Music, and Pan-African Solidarity*. Oxford University Press, 2014.

James, C. L. R. "Marcus Garvey." In *A History of Pan-African Revolt*. 1938. Expanded ed., 1969. Reprint, PM Press, 2012.

Jennings, Michael W., Brigid Doherty, and Thomas Y. Levin. "Production, Reproduction, and Reception of the Work of Art." In Benjamin, *The Work of Art in the Age of Its Technological Reproducibility and Other Writings on Media*.

Johnson, Jasmine Elizabeth. *Rhythm Nation: West African Dance and the Politics of Diaspora*. Oxford University Press, forthcoming.

Jones, Charles E., ed. *The Black Panther Party Reconsidered*. Black Classic Press, 1998.

Jordan, June. "Moving Towards Home." In *June Jordan Directed by Desire: The Collected Poems of June Jordan*, edited by Jan Heller Levi and Sara Joan Miles. Copper Canyon Press, 2005.

Joseph-Gabriel, Annette K. "Eslanda Robeson: Transnational Black Feminism in the Global South." In *Reimagining Liberation: How Black Women Transformed Citizenship in the French Empire*, edited by Annette K. Joseph-Gabriel. University of Illinois Press, 2020.

Kaur, Kinapreet. "African—Not African: Negotiating Textual Identities in Colonial-Era Travel Writing About Congo (1870–1950)." PhD diss., University of Birmingham, 2021.

Kelley, Corey, and Elizabeth Sherman, eds. *Dawoud Bey: Two American Projects*. San Francisco Museum of Modern Art, 2020.

Kenyatta, Jomo. *Facing Mount Kenya: The Tribal Life of the Gikuyu*. 1938. Reprint, Vintage, 1965.

Klapisch-Zuber, Christiane. "The Genesis of the Family Tree." *I Tatti: Studies in the Italian Renaissance* 4 (1991): 105–29.

Korda, Zoltan, dir. *Sanders of the River*. London Films/United Artists, 1935.

Kornweibel, Theodore J. *"Seeing Red": Federal Campaigns Against Black Militancy, 1919–1925*. University of Illinois Press, 1999.

Kouoh, Koyo. "Art, Knowledge, Action, Society: Curatorial Practices from the Global

South." Presented at the "Art as Critique Conference," University of California, Berkeley, March 1, 2019. https://www.youtube.com/watch?v=80YQhPb9YDI.

Krauss, Rosalind J. "Photography's Discursive Spaces: Landscape/View." In "The Crisis in the Discipline," special issue. *Art Journal* 42, no. 4 (1982): 311–19.

Kulick, Henrika. *The Savage Within: The Social History of British Anthropology, 1885–1945.* Cambridge University Press, 1991.

Landau, Paul S. "Empires of the Visual: Photography and Colonial Administration in Africa." In Landau and Kaspin, *Images and Empires.*

Landau, Paul S., and Deborah D. Kaspin, eds. *Images and Empires: Visuality in Colonial and Postcolonial Africa.* University of California Press, 2002.

Langford, Martha. *Suspended Conversations: The Afterlife of Memory in Photographic Albums.* McGill-Queen's University Press, 2008.

Lee, Anthony W., ed. *Photography and Diaspora* 5, no. 1 (2014).

Levenson, Zachary, and Marcel Paret. "The South African Tradition of Racial Capitalism." *Ethnic and Racial Studies* 46, no. 16 (2023): 3403–24.

Lewis, Sarah. *The Unseen Truth: When Race Changed Sight in America.* Harvard University Press, 2024.

Locke, Alain, ed. *The New Negro: Voices of the Harlem Renaissance.* Albert and Charles Boni, 1925.

Lockwood, Lee. *Conversation with Eldridge Cleaver—Algiers.* Dell, 1970.

Lopez, Alan Pelaez. *Intergalactic Travels: Poems from a Fugitive Alien.* The Operating System, 2020.

Love, Heather. *Feeling Backward: Loss and the Politics of Queer History.* Harvard University Press, 2007.

Lowe, Lisa. "Angela Davis: Reflections on Race, Class, and Gender in the USA." In *The Politics of Culture in the Shadow of Capital*, edited by Lisa Lowe and David Lloyd. Duke University Press, 1997.

Mahon, Maureen. "Eslanda Goode Robeson's *African Journey*: The Politics of Identification and Representation in the African Diaspora." *Souls: A Critical Journal of Black Politics, Culture, and Society* 8, no. 3 (2006): 101–18.

Malinowski, Bronisław. "Introduction." In Jomo Kenyatta, *Facing Mount Kenya: The Tribal Life of the Gikuyu.* 1938. Reprint, Vintage, 1965.

Malloy, Sean L. *Out of Oakland: Black Panther Party Internationalism During the Cold War.* Cornell University Press, 2017.

Martin, Tony. *The Pan-African Connection: From Slavery to Garvey and Beyond.* Majority Press, 1984.

Matera, Marc. *Black London: The Imperial Metropolis and Decolonization in the Twentieth Century.* University of California Press, 2015.

Matthews, Tracye A. "'No One Ever Asks What a Man's Role in the Revolution Is': Gender and the Politics of the Black Panther Party, 1966–1971." In Jones, *The Black Panther Party Reconsidered.*

McGrew, Rebecca, and Clara Ennis, eds. *Sadie Barnette: Legacy and Legend.* Benton Museum of Art, Pomona College, 2021.

McGuire, Danielle. *At the Dark End of the Street: Black Women, Rape, and Resistance—*

A New History of the Civil Rights Movement from Rosa Parks to the Rise of Black Power. Vintage, 2011.

McKittrick, Katherine. *Dear Science and Other Stories.* Duke University Press, 2021.

Mercer, Kobena. "Art History and the Dialogics of Diaspora." *Small Axe*, no. 38 (2012): 214.

Mercer, Kobena. "Diaspora Aesthetics and Visual Culture." In *Black Cultural Traffic: Crossroads in Global Performance and Popular Culture*, edited by Harry J. Elam Jr. and Kennell Jackson. University of Michigan Press, 2005.

Mercer, Kobena, ed. *Exiles, Diasporas, and Strangers: Annotating Art's Histories.* MIT Press, 2008.

Mercer, Kobena. *James VanDerZee.* Phaidon, 2003.

Mercer, Kobena. *Travel and See: Black Diaspora Art Practices Since the 1980s.* Duke University Press, 2016.

Mercer, Kobena. *Welcome to the Jungle: New Positions in Black Cultural Studies.* Routledge, 1994.

Min, Susette. "Aesthetics." *Social Text*, no. 100 (2009): 33–36.

Mirzoeff, Nicholas. "The Right to Look." In *The Visual Culture Reader*, 2nd ed., edited by Nicholas Mirzoeff. Routledge, 2002.

Mitchell, Koritha. *From Slave Cabins to the White House.* University of Illinois Press, 2021.

Mitchell, W. J. T., ed. *Landscape and Power.* 2nd ed. University of Chicago Press, 2002.

Mokhtefi, Elaine. *Algiers, Third World Capital: Freedom Fighters, Revolutionaries, Black Panthers.* Verso Books, 2018.

Morrison, Amani. "Kitchenette Building: A Cultural History." PhD diss., University of California, Berkeley, 2018.

Morrison, Amani. "Quotidian Expenses: Residential Repertoires and Domestic Pedagogies in Great Migration Chicago's Kitchenettes." *American Quarterly* 74, no. 1 (2022): 73–94.

Morton, Christopher, and Darren Newbury, eds. *The African Photographic Archive: Research and Curatorial Strategies.* Bloomsbury, 2015.

Moutoussamy-Ashe, Jeanne. *Viewfinders: Black Women Photographers.* Writers and Readers, 1993.

Museum of Modern Art. "Forums on Contemporary Photography: Decentering the Document." Convened by Roxana Marcoci and Oluremi C. Onabanjo, New York City, April 19, 2023. Video, YouTube. https://www.youtube.com/watch?v=Ko1aLolIYsU&t=54s.

Musser, Charles. "Presenting 'A True Idea of the African To-day': Two Documentary Forays by Paul and Eslanda Robeson." *Film History: An International Journal* 18, no. 4 (2006): 412–39.

Nash, Jennifer C. *The Black Body in Ecstasy: Reading Race, Reading Pornography.* Duke University Press, 2014.

Nelson, Alondra. *The Social Life of DNA: Race, Reparations, and Reconciliation After the Genome.* Beacon Press, 2016.

Nelson, Steven. "Dawoud Bey's Historical Turn." In Kelley and Sherman, *Dawoud Bey: Two American Projects.*

Noriega, Chon A., Mari Carmen Ramírez, and Pilar Tompkins Rivera, eds. *Home—So Different, So Appealing*. University of Washington Press, 2017.

Nyong'o, Tavia. "Africa Never Looks Back from the Place from Which We See It: Kehinde Wiley on the World Stage." In *Kehinde Wiley: The World Stage—Africa Lagos–Dakar*. Studio Museum in Harlem, 2008.

Nyong'o, Tavia. *Afro-Fabulations: The Queer Drama of Black Life*. New York University Press, 2019.

Obrist, Hans Ulrich. "The Art of Curation." *The Guardian*, March 23, 2014. https://www.theguardian.com/artanddesign/2014/mar/23/hans-ulrich-obrist-art-curator.

Owen, Ianna Hawkins. "Ordinary Failures: Toward a Diasporan Ethics." PhD diss., University of California, Berkeley, 2016.

Parks, Gordon. "Eldridge Cleaver in Algiers, a Visit with Papa Rage." *Life*, February 6, 1970, 20–27.

Patterson, Orlando. *Slavery and Social Death: A Comparative Study*. Harvard University Press, 1982.

Peabody, Rebecca, Steven Nelson, and Dominic Thomas, eds. *Visualizing Empire: Africa, Europe, and the Politics of Representation*. Getty Research Institute, 2021.

Phu, Thy. "Diasporic Vietnamese Family Photographs, Orphan Images, and the Art of Recollection." *Photography and Culture* 5, no. 1 (2014): 23–38.

Pinney, Christopher. *Photography and Anthropology*. Reaktion, 2011.

Poole, Deborah. *Vision, Race, and Modernity: A Visual Economy of the Andean World*. Princeton University Press, 1997.

Poupeye-Rammelaere, Veerle. "Garveyism and Garvey Iconography in the Visual Arts of Jamaica." *Jamaica Journal* 24, no. 1 (1991): 9–21.

Powell, Richard J. *Cutting a Figure: Fashioning Black Portraiture*. University of Chicago Press, 2009.

Quashie, Kevin. *The Sovereignty of Quiet: Beyond Resistance in Black Culture*. Rutgers University Press, 2012.

Raiford, Leigh. *Imprisoned in a Luminous Glare: Photography and the African American Freedom Struggle*. University of North Carolina Press, 2011.

Raiford, Leigh. "Marcus Garvey in Stereograph." *Small Axe*, no. 40 (2013): 263–80. https://doi.org/10.1215/07990537-1665479.

Raiford, Leigh. "Restaging Revolution: Black Power, Vibe Magazine, and Photographic Memory." In *The Civil Rights Movement in American Memory*, edited by Renee C. Romano and Leigh Raiford. University of Georgia Press, 2006.

Raiford, Leigh. "Soldiers and Black Beauty Queens: Making Home Abroad in the Miss Black America Album." In *Imagining Everyday Life: Engagements with Vernacular Photography*, edited by Tina Campt, Brian Wallis, Marianne Hirsch, and Gil Hochberg. Steidl/The Walther Collection, 2020.

Raiford, Leigh, and Heike Raphael-Hernandez, eds. *Migrating the Black Body: The African Diaspora and Visual Culture*. University of Washington Press, 2017.

Ralph, Michael. "Diaspora." *Social Text* 100 (2009): 51–72.

Ransby, Barbara. *Eslanda: The Large and Unconventional Life of Mrs. Paul Robeson*. Yale University Press, 2013.

Robeson, Eslanda Goode. *African Journey*. John Day, 1945.

Robeson, Eslanda Goode. *What Do the People of Africa Want?* Council on African Affairs, 1945.

Robinson, Cedric. *Black Marxism: The Making of the Black Radical Tradition*. 3rd ed. University of California Press, 2022.

Rodriguez, Besenia. "Beyond Nation: The Formation of a Tricontinental Discourse." PhD diss., Yale University, 2006.

Sall, Amy, ed. *The African Gaze: Photography, Cinema and Power*. Thames and Hudson, 2024.

Samudzi, Zoé. "The Sovereignty and Poetry of African Photography." In Sall, *The African Gaze*.

Sanjek, Roger. "The Ethnographic Present." *Man* 26, no. 4 (1991): 609–28.

Sealy, Mark. *Decolonising the Camera: Photography in Racial Time*. Lawrence and Wishart, 2019.

Scott, James C. *Domination and the Arts of Resistance: Hidden Transcripts*. Yale University Press, 1990.

Shaffer, Robert. "Out of the Shadows: The Political Writings of Eslanda Goode Robeson." *Pennsylvania History: A Journal of Mid-Atlantic Studies* 66, no. 1 (1999): 50–65.

Shange, Savannah. "Play Aunties and Dyke Bitches." *Black Scholar* 49, no. 1 (2019): 40–54.

Sharpe, Christina. *In the Wake: On Blackness and Being*. Duke University Press, 2016.

Sharpe, Christina. *Ordinary Notes*. Farrar, Straus and Giroux, 2023.

Shiweda, Napandulwe. "Images of Ambivalence: Photography in the Making of Omhedi, Northern Namibia." In Hayes and Minkley, *Ambivalent*.

Sliwinski, Sharon. *Human Rights in Camera*. University of Chicago Press, 2011.

Smith, Shawn Michelle. *American Archives: Gender, Race, and Class in Visual Culture*. Princeton University Press, 1999.

Smith, Shawn Michelle. *At the Edge of Sight: Photography and the Unseen*. Duke University Press, 2013.

Smith, Shawn Michelle. "Photography, Darkness, and the Underground Railroad: Dawoud Bey's *Night Coming Tenderly, Black*." *American Quarterly* 73, no. 1 (2021): 25–52.

Spence, Jo. *Family Snaps*. Virago, 1982.

Spencer, Robyn C. *The Revolution Has Come: Black Power, Gender, and the Black Panther Party in Oakland*. Duke University Press, 2016.

Spillers, Hortense J. "Mama's Baby, Papa's Maybe: An American Grammar Book." *Diacritics* 17, no. 2 (1987): 64–81.

Stephens, Michelle Ann. *Black Empire: The Masculine Global Imaginary of Caribbean Intellectuals in the United States, 1914–1962*. Duke University Press, 2006.

Stoppard, Lou. "Everyone's a Curator Now." *New York Times*, March 3, 2020.

Tate, Claudia. *Domestic Allegories of Political Desire: The Black Heroine's Text at the Turn of the Century*. Oxford University Press, 1993.

Taylor, Keeanga-Yamahtta. *Race for Profit: How Banks and the Real Estate Industry Undermined Black Homeownership*. University of North Carolina Press, 2019.

Taylor, Ula Yvette. *The Promise of Patriarchy: Women and the Nation of Islam*. University of North Carolina Press, 2017.

Taylor, Ula Yvette. *The Veiled Garvey: The Life and Times of Amy Jacques Garvey*. University of North Carolina Press, 2003.

Thompson, Cordell S. "Mrs. Eldridge Cleaver Returns to U.S. to Give State of Revolution Message." *Jet*, December 2, 1971.

Trachtenberg, Alan, ed. *Classic Essays on Photography*. Leetes Island Books, 1980.

Trachtenberg, Alan. *Reading American Photographs: Images as History, Mathew Brady to Walker Evans*. Hill and Wang, 1990.

Umoren, Imaobeng D. *Race Women Internationalists: Activist-Intellectuals and Global Freedom Struggles*. University of California Press, 2018.

Warren, Kenneth W. "Appeals for (Mis)Recognition: Theorizing the Diaspora." In *Cultures of United States Imperialism*, edited by Amy Kaplan and Donald E. Pease. Duke University Press, 1993.

Westerbeck, Colin. *The James Van Der Zee Studio*. Art Institute of Chicago, 2004.

Whitehead, Colson. *The Underground Railroad*. Anchor, 2016.

Willis, Deborah, ed. *Picturing Us: African-American Identity in Photography*. The New Press, 1994.

Wilson, Will. "About." Will Wilson. Accessed April 11, 2025. https://willwilson.photoshelter.com/about.

Witkovsky, Matthew S. "This Story Shall Not Be Passed On." *Art in America* (December 2019): 44–51.

Wolukau-Wanambwa, Stanley. *Dark Mirrors*. Mack, 2021.

Womack, Autumn. *The Matter of Black Living: The Aesthetic Experiment of Racial Data, 1880–1930*. University of Chicago Press, 2022.

Wynter, Sylvia. "'No Humans Involved': An Open Letter to My Colleagues." *Forum N.H.I.: Knowledge for the 21st Century* 1, no. 1 (1994): 42–71.

Young, Benjamin R. "The Black Panther's Secret North Korean Fetish." *NKNews.com*, December 20, 2012. https://www.nknews.org/2012/12/the-black-panther-north-korean-juche-fetish/.

Young, Benjamin. "North Korea's Unlikely History with Black Radicals." *Black Perspectives*, April 11, 2019. https://www.aaihs.org/north-koreas-unlikely-history-with-black-radicals/.

Index